Solace of Solitude

Solace of Solitude

Afterlife Visits

A JOURNEY

JANICE GRAY KOLB

Blue Dolphin Publishing

Published by Blue Dolphin Publishing, Inc.
P.O. Box 8, Nevada City, CA 95959
Orders: 1-800-643-0765
Web: www.bluedolphinpublishing.com

ISBN: 1-57733-153-2

Library of Congress Cataloging-in-Publication Data

Kolb, Janice E. M.
  Solace of solitude : afterlife visits : a journey / Janice Gray Kolb.
      p. cm.
  ISBN 1-57733-153-2 (pbk. : alk. paper)
  1. Kolb, Janice E. M. 2. Meditations. 3. Pets—Death. 4. Grief—Miscellanea.
5. Cats. 6. Bereavement—Miscellanea. I. Title.

  BF1997.K65A3 2005
  248.8'66—dc22
                                                    2004024914

A portion of any profits realized by sales of this book will be used to support
various animal charities.

Photos by the author.
Cover photo of the cottage where the author lives and where she found her
Solace and Solitude.

Printed in the United States of America

10   9   8   7   6   5   4   3   2   1

*Dedicated
to my
beloved feline
soulmate
Rochester*

and

*to my
beloved
husband and soulmate
Bob*

and

*to Rochester's and my
spiritual friend
Chris Comins
who is a blessing and strength
on this continuing Journey.*

"It's not solitude itself we hermits love, but what solitude gives us. It brings us things nobody else can give us. The cabin came to be like a magical place to me, and the longer I stayed there, the more it became invested with magic. I began to doubt I could write anywhere else or stay plugged to that wonderful connected feeling with myself and all the life around me.

"I want to be conscious. I want to notice that I'm alive while I'm living. It is mindfulness I treasure most."

from *Celebrating Time Alone:*
Stories of Splendid Solitude
by Lionel Fisher

Contents

Rochester
January 2002

A Word in Preparation

SOME DAYS THE BEAUTY OF LIFE seems to confound us in ways that are quite remarkable. The feelings of well-being, peace of mind and body, and just downright joy fill us and just bubble over in all that we do. Then there are those dark days when everything seems to be a chore, and life has lost it's song and even it's purpose. But we can't have mountains without a few valleys. Life is not just a flat plain. We must have some lows, for without them there could be no highs. This is the story of this book. It flows from the exquisite joy of near perfection, to the deep shadows of despair. But this despair is not final and in fact is a necessary part of our journey toward completion, where the beauty of life becomes so pervasive, that life's bumps can't jar us loose from the tranquility and peace that fills our minds.

The first nine meditations of this book were written while the author was experiencing completion and happiness in her personal life, yet was plagued by the sad events of 9/11. These meditations were written as a response to the "life after" of these tragedies because she had a need to purge and find consolation by writing things down. She also hoped that perhaps this collection of meditations could play a part in helping others who had been traumatized by these disasters come to a more consoling resolution to their problems.

Then suddenly it all changed as her beloved companion, a cat named Rochester, was taken from her. In an effort to control her grief over his passing, she put down these nine meditations and, in an effort to control that grief wrote in her journal all the thoughts, emotions, and events, that were assailing her as she attempted to right what had gone so terribly wrong in her life. This was not an attempt at closure, for she did not expect or even want that. Grief does not need to be resolved by closure. It is always there and will remain there. But by lingering on events, writing them down, and putting them into the proper places in our lives, even events that sear our souls can be handled. These journal entries were gathered, compiled, and have been published under the title, *In Corridors of Eternal Time*.

As Jan tried to return to the book she had previously started, she found that her thinking and approaches to the subjects she had planned to discuss were radically altered. The death of Rochester had caused changes in her attitudes and even the events now occurring in her life. Rochester had become to her a teacher and the instrument of exposing her to a new view of life and death. Without planning it, she had embarked on a new journey. Life was now exposing her to new adventures of experience and wonder. This new direction in her life, as described in Part 2, is a description of what she has done, experienced and realized as a result of Rochester's passing. It is a study of "afterlife" experiences and the peace and understanding that now controls her existance.

It is her feeling that these wonderful realizations could not have come without being able to get alone within her heart and mind—they could not have occurred without solitude. Through this solitude she was able to achieve solace, a much different experience than simple closure. The title "*Solace of Solitude*" bears the initials SOS. This is of course the international distress signal, recognized as such throughout the entire world. May I suggest that this same signal, applied to the title of this book, be your avenue of escape for the distress that assails you. Perhaps by going aside in solitude you also will find solace in life and better understand the anatomy of grief.

Robert A. Kolb Jr.

Acknowledgments

May the words of this book—and the meditation of our hearts
(the readers' and mine)—give glory to God—
all glory to my Christ—
and love and gratitude to Blessed Mother Mary—
who always intercedes.

I wish to thank my
Guardian Angel
and my special Angels
who are ever present.

I wish to express my extreme appreciation to Paul M. Clemens, publisher of Blue Dolphin Publishing, for believing in this book and for his kindness and grief support and to all his capable staff who helped in so many ways. I especially thank Linda Maxwell, Jody Black, and Barbara Houtchens for their fine work and their friendship.

I wish to thank Rochester for his constant love, presence, devotion, inspiration, and teachings throughout our life together. Because of him this book was written.

I am deeply grateful to my husband Bob for his love and support, for believing in me, and for our life together in New Hampshire. I am grateful too for the time he gave in endless hours typing this manuscript.

I wish to thank
St. Francis of Assisi
and
St. Martin dePorres
for their great love and protection of all God's creatures.

Part 1

MEDITATION ONE

The Voice of Jesus

. . . and they will listen to my voice.

—John 10:16 RSV

. . . the Spirit of truth . . . will guide you. . . .

—John 16:13

O FTEN I AM IN NEED OF SPIRITUAL DIRECTION on a matter or matters in my life, and through the years I have been shown many ways in which to receive God's guidance. Frequently I am not able to receive it at once because I am impatient or filled with anxiety, thereby blocking what is available to me. When I am yielding and receptive, it is then that I experience His presence and am open to His words spoken to me in my spirit or through a book I am reading, or the Bible, or in any way He so chooses to speak. Occasionally He will speak through another individual.

Today I am sad and restless inside because a situation that my heart is wrapped up in is controlled by another. It has been in this state of immobility for a very long time, a year, waiting for the actions of another to set it free. It must remain this way until Jesus speaks to the heart of the one in control. Only Jesus can set it all free! Since the one in charge is a person who loves Jesus, I believe in time my prayers will cause the situation to be resolved. It is better Jesus speak than myself. But constant waiting on the actions of another is so difficult!

There is a means of prayer that I use that is just one of many that is most consoling and effective. This particular one, however, seems to bring a comforting response right away whenever I use it. It is a little exercise that I read several years ago in a daily devotional book *(These Days)* but that I added to and gave my own personal touches. I believe you will be helped by it also as you open yourself to listen to Christ's specific word to you. Perhaps you will share it.

1. Find a comfortable chair to sit in and for a few moments take time to close your eyes and pray to God. Ask for His guidance that through the power of the Holy Spirit you will hear the voice of Jesus. When you do—pray that you will not doubt.

2. Open your eyes and slowly look up from where you are seated. What do you see?

3. What you see is no doubt familiar. Look at it as if for the first time. Slowly describe it to yourself in great detail.

4. Imagine that somehow through what you see Jesus is trying to get a message across to you. What do you think it is?

5. If something ridiculous comes to mind immediately, do not worry. God has a sense of humor. Just go with whatever comes into your mind, silly or otherwise, until you reach a sense of quiet assurance in this and that you believe Jesus has spoken.

6. Silently, or in a whisper, or out loud, tell Christ what you will do with this message He has given you.

7. Now spend some time in silence and in gratitude to Jesus. Be still and quiet. Before ending the meditation open your heart to the Sacred Heart of Jesus.

Reflections

I have paused and spent time with Christ in prayer just as I have shared here with you. Upon opening my eyes as I sat in the soft chair in my writing room, I first saw my beloved little Rochester. He is cuddled in a thick patchwork quilt of wildlife creatures folded in quarters so that it is soft and deep lying upon the guest bed here. His small body is resting in a sweet position in the center of it and he is sound asleep with a little paw over his face. My heart melts, even though I have seen him again and again in this precious image of such innocence.

I believe Jesus is telling me through Rochester to rest in Him. Just as Rochester utterly trusts me for love and care, so must I trust Jesus. I must continue to rest and be still, and in His perfect timing He will bring about the answer and set the situation free. Rochester is God's love and presence made visible to me always. I see anew that I am not alone in my frustration and feeling of betrayal as I wait. As Rochester rests in the comforter, so do I also rest in the Comforter. Rochester is my angel sent from God. I trust this answer.

Prayer is solace as is the presence of Rochester in my life. I am once again still and at peace.

Having heard the voice of the Comforter I patiently wait in His care for this problem to be resolved. I am loved.

Amen

MEDITATION TWO

Sing a New Song

O sing to the Lord a new song, for He has done marvelous things.
—Psalm 98:1 RSV

A GRACKLE CAME AGAIN TODAY many times sounding his song from the deck and table with his crackly voice—but it is wonderful and he believes he is singing a beautiful song. I stop to listen. He has seen me watching through the window and maybe he is even serenading me. I do appreciate him!

What a gentle lesson this grackle is teaching me and perhaps to you also. All my life I have stifled my voice and the songs within me. Aside from the soft lullabies I sang to my babies as I cradled them in my arms, I never sing aloud alone. In low tones I sing the hymns in church, but my voice only reaches my own ears. I am too self-conscious and deprecating of my singing, slightly embarrassed that I am making audible words. I sing inside myself when alone for I love music. My Rochester too is silent, but oh I know he too sings within himself. We sing duets all day long in our glorious silence while I write at my desk. Perhaps one day soon I will be free enough to sing joyfully aloud as well, maybe here in my writing room to Rochester, even if it is only one note.

Why should we not sing, no matter how critical we are of what we hear coming forth? In the privacy of our homes or cars why can we not release ourselves and break forth in song? So many songs have been

6

stored away within us for years, each coming out with their own memories and baggage, sorrows and joys. It does not matter if we are off-key. In time we may improve if we only spontaneously sing and console and nurture ourselves with songs coming from our own voice and heart.

We each have a song to sing within our hearts and yet so often we are silenced too, and our song dies and we are afraid to sing. Perhaps this is why I wrote so much ever since I was a young child. In the silence forced upon me I could still express myself in writing. I felt I had a voice.

Burghild Nina Holzer writes in her book on journal keeping, *A Walk Between Heaven and Earth*, encouraging words to my soul. She states:

> *Maybe my throat wants to tell me of all the songs held back. Held back in fear, or in doubt, or in anger, all the songs that the heart already knows but that I have not voiced. Perhaps I need to walk in that place, down my throat to the vocal chords.*

She states that maybe she needs to write in her journal about the huge clump that sits there, blocking the air, blocking the sound, blocking the blood flow, causing pain. I identify with her deep feelings and words as if she is writing about myself. She continues by writing that perhaps there is a big boulder she needs to discover sitting in her throat. Perhaps huge masses are compacted into stone. She considers that they could be words too frightening to face, words that have been pushed back or perhaps words too beautiful and tender to bring forth and admit. She closes her reflection by saying "*So many words waiting to be born, all held back*" (from my *The Enchantment of Writing*). Perhaps too, one day my songs will be born.

The solace of singing an old beloved song or trying a new one that has touched our hearts can only mend our hearts and stir our souls for good. Do not be ashamed of your song within. God put it there for you to discover and sing aloud, and its mysterious affect upon you will cause you to see life in a new way. Be like the grackle who serenades in a crackly voice but hears only his lovely song. And because of his confidence and spontaneity I too hear only beauteous notes pouring out of his shiny brown feathered body.

Reflections

Remind us of what marvelous things you have done, O God. May we believe You have given us only songs of beauty and may we be a part of Your great Song.

I will sing a new song to the Lord.
I will shout let His Name be adored.
This joy that is now in my heart
will stay there and never depart.
What mysterious wonder is this?
I am bursting with heavenly bliss.
The Lord is my strength now—on Him I will rely.
and I'll sing a new song 'til I die.

How I thank you for loving me so.
You have banished my sorrow and woe.
This happiness now that is mine,
will grow and must never decline.
Let my voice and my prayers and my song,
be a witness to you all life long.
Just who can explain how I feel within my heart.
There's a joy that will never depart.

Words from a hymn by Robert A. Kolb Jr.
from *Whispered Notes* by Robert A. Kolb Jr.
and Janice Gray Kolb

SING

Be like the grackle!
Earnestly tackle—
Any timidity of voice.
Make now the choice—
To sing out your song.
It will never be wrong—
For it comes from your heart
Where all love notes start.

JGK
2002

MEDITATION THREE

Lost in Time

The heart at rest sees a feast in everything
—Hindu proverb

I AM PERUSING A FAVORITE BOOK OF MINE read many times before and suddenly I have a memory that is so clear that it is almost like a vision. Perhaps it is one. I pause to let it continue. I do not remember what causes it in my reading or if reading even is the cause. I close my eyes. Suddenly this vision is so clear. I am sitting in Simms Restaurant on the boardwalk in Ocean City, New Jersey and I am a teenager.

I am extremely suntanned and can feel how energized I feel after being on the beach and in the ocean all day. I seem to be dressed in white, or at least a white sweater. I am having my favorite meal in Simms. I am enjoying their incredibly delicious crab cakes with white sauce and mashed potatoes. My teenage heart sighs, *"This meal is to die for!"* Oh I love this meal at Simms so much! Always I get this same dinner after we stand in a long line on the boardwalk waiting to be seated in the restaurant.

My dark hair is pulled back in a ponytail. I can sense how good my skin feels for I have been outdoors all day. Now I am dressed in soft clothes and having dinner. I seem to be alone, yet I have never before eaten here alone. The crab cakes and white sauce and mound of mashed potatoes are exquisitely soft and beautiful in appearance. There is a low hum of conversation all about me like a subtle song.

I can hear the ocean pounding outside the open window and the fragrance of the salt air merges with the aroma of delicious foods. People are walking up and down the boardwalk. It is the loveliest vision. What does it all mean?

I sit at the little table in the crowded restaurant with my appetizing plate of crab cakes covered in creamy white sauce with the round mound of mashed potatoes. I sense I am caught in a long ago moment of time.

The solace of experiencing such lovely moments is indescribable, and the gratitude for reliving a flash of one's past in slightly surreal form fills my surprised heart.

As this reverie lifts, my eyes glance down to the open book in my lap and these words rise up, it seems, so as to be noticed, words by Agatha Christie: *"One of the oddest things in life, I think, is the things one remembers."* What is it all about? What is it all telling me?

Reflections

Be expectant for the unexpected. God is in those moments bringing comfort in ways we may least expect. In gentle memories that rise up from our past unexpectedly we are often comforted in trying times and moments in the present. Those images and memories are gifts from God. Thank Him and be open to His surprises.

REVERIE

A scene from the past
Appears in reverie—
I am taking repast
On boardwalk by the sea.

In restaurant of old
I sit as before—
And watch episode unfold
As enchanting timeless lore.

Such mysteries are vast
That memories revive
And moments from the past
Become surrealistically alive.

JGK

There Is Only One You

*Why do you never find anything written about that idiosyncratic thought
you avert to about your fascination with something no one else understands?
Because it is up to you. There is something you find interesting
for a reason hard to explain. It is hard to explain because you
have never read it on any page. You were made and set
here to give voice to this, your own astonishment.*

—Annie Dillard

*A*S A LITTLE GIRL AND OFTEN TOO AS A TEENAGER, my Mother lovingly
said to me, *"Remember, there is only one you."* It was her way of
cautioning me to be careful also when I became old enough to leave the
confines of home alone. Through many difficult times in my growing up
years those words were comforting when my Mother was too frequently
silent or angry with me. When I was sad and thought upon that one
loving phrase she said, it always gladdened my heart somewhat and love
was there. Later she would say it to me when I was a young Mother also,
and it momentarily created such a feeling of uniqueness and self-worth
that it has stayed with me long after she has been gone. Suddenly that
little sentence will rise up out of nowhere just when I need it. And my
Mother too was unique for I have never known another person even
remotely like her in any way whatsoever.

God is such a finite Creator, a Creator who allowed us each to be a
"one and only creation." Out of all the trillions of human beings in this

world there in only one human being like you. And what is more, there will never be another you. Nor will there be another me.

Look at someone you love and realize that only they have those lips, those facial lines, those eyes that look at you with caring and love.

We each have our own idiosyncracies and disposition, and each have our own spiritual inclinations. We are unique emotionally and intellectually, and we each have our own calling and work to do on this earth. God put us here at this time and this place for a specific reason. He has given a specific job to you alone, and He has called only me to my job. There is only one you and only one me. There is no one else that can do your calling and work for you, and there is no one that can do mine for me. To think upon this should leave one in awe and build one's self esteem. God deemed us so worthy as to be irreplaceable! The solace of realizing that we are precious and a one of a kind spiritual masterpiece should cause us to receive that greatest and most exceptional solace that could exist.

We should be exhilarated by our individuality, never intimidated. We think of ourselves as unworthy and hold back our interests and thought if not validated by others. There is a certain magic and charm in being weird, odd, peculiar or eccentric. We venture to go places in spirit that others often fear to tread. We are made fun of, and too, people are a little wary , but perhaps deep inside they wish they could be a bit eccentric too, for this truly indicates you can hear your own voice among all the voices in the world and you have claimed this uniqueness like a star for God.

The thousands of people who perished in the collapse of the World Trade Center Towers were priceless. Their memories live on reminding their loved ones of their preciousness and uniqueness, spiritual gifts to all those who loved them. Their legacy is this uniqueness! There will never be another like each one of those individuals that perished that fateful day of September 11th in New York, at the Pentagon, or in a field in Pennsylvania.

Reflections

Engrave it on your heart and mind that there cannot ever be a counterpart of you. Your value is not in what you do in life, not in what you might eventually become, or who you have been in the past. Simply stated—your value comes from you being you. "

Remember—*"there is only one you."*

There is only one you. Each of us has our own calling. God calls only you to fulfill this calling.

MEDITATION FIVE

In God We Trust

I am leaving you with a gift—peace of mind and heart! And the peace I give isn't fragile like the peace the world gives. So don't be troubled or afraid.
— Jesus, John 14:27 (Living Bible)

*I*N THE DAYS AND WEEKS FOLLOWING SEPTEMBER 11TH I turn to spiritual reading of many kinds, words that reduce fears and words that build faith. The fragility of life is emphasized each day in listening to the reports of blessed bodies found in the horrific site of Ground Zero, and I need to read. Reading has always been a strength in my life. Many books that are spiritual reading to me may not be to others. We are each drawn to what consoles us. For me it is a necessity to read.

Many have had their faith shattered because of the events of September 11th. *"Where was God?"* some people asked, while others grew stronger in their beliefs and leaned upon God to help them. Often a mixture of both was present—moments of despair and an absence of God, but too, days when He permeated heart, soul and all things surrounding. I believe He understands our devastation and emotions, and without condemnation of our vacillation He is ever with us. He is a God of Love.

One book that my husband and I are drawn to frequently is a book we authored through the power of the Holy Spirit—a book given to us by God, and we were His *"instruments."* Through my own hand and pen and with eyes closed tightly, I received fifty-two meditations that I knew were not mine and totally different from anything I had ever written before.

My hand flew taking Holy Dictation from God, His Spirit supplying the words as I blindly scribbled. First there was a scripture passage indicated, then a devotion-like message, followed by a closing prayer.

Bob had had similar experiences the previous year. He was given many hymns with accompanying words by the Holy Spirit. These beautiful hymns were given to one who could not read music! We were humbled and in awe to soon realize that the meditations were given by God to be used with the hymns. Each meditation carried the theme of one of Bob's hymns—or God's hymns. Later these hymns and meditations were published under the title of *Whispered Notes*. Much more is written about them in previous books of mine, *Journal of Love* and *The Enchantment of Writing*. It is to this book, *Whispered Notes*, we often turn during the course of each week, sometimes reading the devotions alone and too the words of the hymns as poetry rather than singing them. At times we pause for devotion and read the meditation together and Bob will play the hymns on the piano (by heart, not by sight). These inspired "*Whispered Notes*"—written and musical—are consolation and inspiration in all days but especially following these tragedies.

One meditation is particularly significant, even though it was given to me in writing twenty-four years previous to the disasters of the World Trade Center, the Pentagon, and the field in rural Pennsylvania, all occurring on that horrific day in 2001. Perhaps it will in some way bless you also as you read what follows.

Meditation: In God We Trust

God is the only hope of salvation for our country and this world. If we turn to Him, He will heal the scars and wounds that have been wrought upon our land and people.

I am your God—and only your God and Creator can heal that which He has created. When you turn your eyes to Me and confess your wrongs and ask forgiveness, I will step forth and bring salvation and healing and love among all men. Why do you hold back when you know the Source is waiting to touch you and restore you to Himself? I am that Source—your God and Creator—and only I am the One that can mend your brokenness. Call upon Me this day and I will answer.

Heed these words and live and be brought back to the God of your Fathers. *"In God We Trust"* can be the only solution to the woes of this world. Call upon God—and through the Saviour of all mankind, Jesus Christ—be healed, be saved and be restored.

Your God is a great and mighty God. Only He can calm the storms of this world and restore peace—His peace, which passeth all understanding.

Dear Heavenly Father,

God of our universe—Creator and Lord—we trust you in all things and we pray that our nation and our world will truly fall on their faces before You so that all lands may be healed—and kept under Your almighty Hand in Love.

In Jesus' Name We Pray

Amen

And too, let us pray the final stanza of the hymn that accompanies this meditation in *Whispered Notes*—not once, but daily for World Peace.

Lord we beseech Thee, in humble supplication.
Change our direction, cause all wars to cease.
Use our dear country to lead a mighty movement
That would return the world to sanity and peace.

RAK Jr.

MEDITATION SIX

Dreams

Dreams guide you, they show you the way that you should be living, or the direction, or give you signs to help someone else, and they are gifts.
—Jackie Yellowtail, Crow Woman
from *Walking in the Sacred Manner*
by Mark St. Pierre and Tilda Longsoldier

I AM NOT ONE WHO ALWAYS REMEMBERS MY DREAMS. I seem to go through periods when the dreams are quite clear and I am able to go over them in my mind as I slowly wake up and then soon after record them in my journal. These dreams I am able to meditate on and work with in days that follow. At times it is immediately clear what the message of the dream is and at other times totally unclear but fascinating, often filled with people or objects or conversation that seem to come from another world. In either case I do my best to form some sort of interpretation of the whole dream or parts. If nothing comes forth, I simply record the dream and go back to it from time to time to see if anything in my life in the present or since the dream occurred was associated with the dream itself. This has been an intriguing learning experience. The dreams I have taken the time to write down have revealed things again and again, some more than others. Or only portions of the dreams are eventually revealed. But in either case I am glad I took the time to write them down. This past year and a half I seem to be able to capture more of this alternative reality, and some dreams have proven to be so significant they have made me realize I have not given dreams their proper importance

18

simply because many are so surreal. I believe dreams are certainly metaphoric and surely a symbolic form of other worldly communication. To me they are part of my spiritual journey and I am thankful for each one recorded.

Recently I saw an item in the room immediately before sleep, an item that has represented deep sadness to me since I was young, yet I cannot remove it. While the truth of it was known to me long years in my heart, it was revealed and resolved in reality as absolute only several years ago. In this recent dream however, that "truth resolved" was made clear in a scene that left no doubt, and I see it was a gift, a great portion of peace given to me. It can now be dismissed and will no longer hurt me in mind, heart or spirit. This dream empowered me for it taught me anew to pay attention to these messages of the mind.

In my reading I have learned that precognitive dreams are visions of events that have not yet occurred. It is written that you are literally dreaming ahead of time, predicting in a sense events that will happen and be in some recognizable form when they eventually do. Precognitive dreaming can be from the trivial to events that are world known.

A year ago I had two vivid dreams symbolic in nature and a family member whom I love dearly was in both. Although this person's image was totally clear in both, even dressed in ways that were true of this individual, the events going on around the person were strange and frightening. I recorded both dreams carefully. Shortly after, something happened in my life that had never happened before that I am not free to reveal on this page. Within days after on thinking about and rereading these recorded dreams, I knew the full interpretation in my spirit, and with the help of some additional brief reading. Even this was extraordinary, for the book I read in came to me immediately after the disturbing event in my life and aided me at once in the interpretations. They were so clear to my heart and mind that it was as if the author knew I needed this and wrote it in only messages I would know. And the family member that had appeared in my two dreams made an appearance in reality after the occurrence in my life that was central to the dreams! Since we live a great distance apart, this added to the truth and extraordinary details of both the dream, and real life follow-up that enacted out the dream. This person of love was not only the forewarner of the actual event, but also the one to provide assistance, love and courage following it. And so I am paying much more attention to the dreams that I am able to capture and record, and even to simple fragments of them if the greater portion is lost.

I find it absolutely mind-boggling and absolutely other-worldly that upon completing the writing of the above paragraph the phone rang and I went down to answer it. It was this same family member I had just written about seconds before calling to tell me that she was coming again to New Hampshire to be with us in two days and would we meet her at the bus. I was ecstatic over this news and also over the unexplainable incident of the call! It was as if my writing wrote this person into my immediate and very present reality, though miles away, and she materialized via the phone call with this totally unexpected news. And she too had suddenly acted on the desire to return here and called at once. This seemed all to be connected with what I previously wrote, like a songline running through it all.

Four months ago I had a disturbing dream filled with urgency. I was in a room with several long windows that had both shades and blinds, windows so long the sills were only inches from the floor. Outside on a porch was a huge bear trying to get in. Just this massive head and shoulders could be seen. Inside this strange house I had never seen before, I was attempting to get Rochester off the floor so as to carry him in my arms and escape from the bear. There was a little guinea pig there too, and an older woman wearing a fancy hat. I believed her to be Eleanor Roosevelt, a person I admire in real life, though she nor I ever said her name in the dream. She swooped up the guinea pig and put him on her shoulder as we tried to get out of the room. We had first pulled down the shades and blinds on the long windows in an attempt to cover them and keep out the bear, but we could not get one window down and closed properly. That is why we were trying to escape the bear! I completed my journal entry inquiring—"What does it all mean?"

That dream was given to me September 2nd, 2001 and, due to horrendous events in our country that occurred soon after, I made no connection or gave the dream another thought. Some weeks later in reading back in my journal I was overwhelmed when rereading this dream and knew in my spirit it was a forewarning of the planes that crashed through the windows of the World Trade Center and the Pentagon on September 11th. Instantly I perceived the bear to be symbolic of the planes, and Eleanor Roosevelt and myself were fleeing as did thousands of others in real life that day that will go down in history. That I would not leave without Rochester is absolutely true to life. And as to Eleanor Roosevelt, she has always been someone I felt extremely capable, and have written about her and read her journals, and perhaps she was a spiritual guide to me helping in the escape. The guinea pig? Perhaps that is representative of what Osama Bin Laden thought all humans were that he bombed that horrific day.

This dream gave way to still yet a memory of another that preceded it by two months, a dream that had bothered me and returned in thought when I would least expect it. My journal, a repository for such memories, yielded up the details. Again I was in a room with large windows this time on two walls, and I was attempting to help others climb out these windows. We were fearful, and it was an emergency, and I assisted a man and dog out one window while at the other windows on the connecting wall two women and a baby also awaited my assistance. Urgency seemed to be silently screaming! The dream ended as the man and dog disappeared over the sill and out the long window.

How can we ignore our dreams? Good or bad I believe we experience them for a reason. Perhaps the lovely ones are to help us heal and be joyful and the ones such as I have shared are confirmations or forewarners of events in reality. In whatever way you so choose to accept them, I feel they are worthy of review and thought, and also in recording in a journal. I am thankful for all I have written down and one in particular when I captured a visit from my Dad whom I believe now resides in Heaven, and his appearance and mannerisms so true to life brought me a message of love I needed. I have shared it in the form of a poem in a previous book.

Dreams do speak their own language and sometimes we may never know their meaning. They are made up of reality and symbols, and images and even metaphor. But through prayer and imagination we can often crack their codes and be given interpretations. It is written that our dreams disturb in order to illumine and that dreams are often poetic. Dreams can diagnose before a doctor. I have found this to be true. Our inner world is filled with mysteries and they confront our past, present and future and are filled with wisdom. Often too we find ourselves experiencing something in life that we lived in a dream years ago. I am inclined to believe, mysterious and eerie though some may be, that God is the maker of dreams and they originate from the great eternal.

Reflections

Write dreams down. Are not images and stories and incidents from an unknown realm, and given to us in sleep, amazing enough to record? Have a sense of wonder and awe that such an inner life exists without our active participation. How can we risk not making them substantial and visible through our writing, and perhaps even "sketches and drawing"? What if they are sent to heal and enrich our lives and, too, forewarn of who knows what? How can they possibly be useless?

Give Ye Them to Eat

—Jesus

And they did all eat and were filled.

—Mark 7:42 KJV

*I*N EARLY FEBRUARY 2002 it is announced on CNN that the well-known restaurant in New York who gave free hot meals to hungry workers around the clock since the World Trade Center Towers came down, is closing. Such unselfish love, help, and strength and nourishment the owners provided during these past five months that were unlike any other months in history. It is written, "If ye have done it unto the least of these, you have done it unto me." —Jesus

And they sat down in ranks, by hundreds, and by fifties. And when he had taken the five loaves and the two fishes, he looked up to heaven and blessed, and broke the loaves, and gave them to his disciples to set before them; and the two fishes divided he among them all. And they did all eat and were filled.

Mark 7:40-42 (KJV)

Reflections

Thank you dear owners of the New York restaurant that fulfilled the directive of Jesus—"*Give ye them to eat*" (Mark 7:37 KJV).

The Mercy B.A.N.D.

Among the attributes of God, although they are all equal,
mercy shines with even more brilliance than justice.
—Miguel DeCervantes (1547-1616)

*I*T IS TUESDAY, JANUARY 22, 2002, and in the mail I receive a blessing. It is an object I learned about on CNN news and knew the moment it was presented I must have one. And so I acted upon it. Three weeks previous to its arrival I had requested by phone, dialing the number given, a sterling silver Mercy B.A.N.D. This B.A.N.D. is my blessing.

Mercy: *Relief of distress or compassion shown to victims of misfortune. A blessing that is an act of divine compassion.*
—Noah Webster (1758–1843)

Four months have passed since the September 11th tragedies, but they are never out of my mind. Daily I listen to new accounts of bodies found at Ground Zero and of family members trying to go on and survive without their lost loved ones. Even times of seeming victory in accounts shared still leave me sad, and never a day passes that I do not cry. My heart and soul and mind are connected to that site and to the other two also, and I have changed. Life will never be the same. I am different, and my heart is filled with grief for all involved.

That I was not there in actuality in New York, Washington, or in a field in Pennsylvania leaves a deep desire to in some way connect in spirit. Prayer has been that path for me to these three sites and to God causing a Holy connection between all. And too I write—which is prayer to me.

To learn then that a silver bracelet is available to wear causes my heart to say "yes." And now it has arrived. It is a beautiful shining cuff style band that easily slips on. After wearing it for a few moments I take it upstairs to my writing room, and on my desk where there is a little shrine, I place the bracelet near images of Christ and Mary and an Angel. I say a prayer over it that comes from my own heart to dedicate it and bless it, and then I read a moving prayerful page from a brochure that accompanied the bracelet. In part it reads:

> *I'm not a rescue worker digging through the rubble in the aftermath of terror.*
> *I'm not a soldier putting my life on the line in a fight for freedom.*
> *I'm a housewife ... a professional ... a student, I work in a factory ... an office ... a school ... a home ...*
> —and it goes on to declare that I *live near a cornfield or in the Bronx or by the sea or in the suburbs and the question asked is—* "*What can I do?*"

And the answer is that *I can remember the victims and pray for the survivors and I can show mercy by bearing another's name daily.* This is the meaning of Mercy B.A.N.D.—that I can show mercy by *Bearing Another's Name Daily.*

The true significance is that Mercy B.A.N.D. is a symbol of hope in God's mercy to heal our wounds. It is, too, a living memorial to all those who died at those three sites so tragically. It is especially a daily reminder to pray for their loved ones left behind. Also it is indicated that the bracelet is a promise of blessing to those who are merciful, and concerning mercy Jesus has spoken these words: Blessed are the merciful for they will be shown mercy.

The Lord's Prayer also is in the brochure explaining it in detail and I pray it by memory. I love a little thought placed under a picture of the Mercy B.A.N.D. in the brochure. It reads, "*I can't remember all the names of the victims, but by wearing a Mercy B.A.N.D. there's one I will never forget.*"

My silver bracelet has the name of a man engraved upon it who died in the WTC. I had requested a name from that site when asked my preference, because it was the WTC that I first saw attacked that September morning. Not ever turning our TV on in the daytime due to my writing, our daughter Jessica knows we would want to know what had happened. Her call causes us to turn on the television minutes before the second plane flies into the second tower. From this day forward my habit of no television changes, and first thing each morning we switch on the set to make sure the world is still here and to hear the current news. Then we can switch it off until evening.

My bracelet is engraved with a man's name with WTC beneath it. In the days that follow Bob learns there is a web site containing information about those who died that horrendous day. He is able to find a brief biography of Edward. It is overwhelming to read about him from the print-out Bob brings to me. Edward was 62 years old and was to have retired in three days following the collapse of the towers. He had worked on Wall Street for over 40 years, the last few as senior vice president for equity sales at Cantor Fitzgerald. His retirement day was September 14th. It is written that his life's other enduring constant was his family. He and his wife were married 40 years and have two children, a girl and a boy. Together they loved to host big family dinners and had specialities they served. Such happy occasions.

I learned too that in 1993 Edward surprised everyone by taking up watercolors and since then had done about a hundred paintings. He framed the paintings and gave them to his family members. His children it is said are to have fifteen each. His sister-in-law wrote that it was almost as if he had a need to leave a legacy, and that is just how it turned out. Edward's profile originally appeared October 21, 2001 in the *New York Times*.

Edward's personal web site has two moving messages on it, and I decide too to write a letter for his wife and children on this site. Several days after mine is placed there another appears from a friend who dearly loves him and misses him. I save these printed messages to keep with Edward's biography, and we will check this message site from time to time in the future. Today another appears from a friend.

Shortly after receiving my bracelet I read in Decision magazine an entire page dedicated to information about the Mercy B.A.N.D. Like so many of us who feel helpless as to how to reach out, a woman and Christian author and teacher named Lenya Hertzig had the inspiration to design these bands.

The September 11th attacks prove too much to comprehend but she feels she can wrap her heart around one victim's family. Because of acting upon her inspired thought, I too can wrap my heart around Edward's family, and the memories of him I am provided with via the web site. Many people who do not know how to pray may receive help with the prayers provided in the brochure. Mrs. Hertzig states she designed the bracelet to help people learn about God's mercy. Hearing so many speak of God's judgment following the attacks, she wants people to know that God is a God of mercy and He loves the world. She also wants people to help in a way they feel personally connected. She tells us that many family members of victims have expressed appreciation for these bracelets, for it means so much to know others are praying and that they care

One month later continually wearing my Mercy B.A.N.D. on my left arm, I confess to the solace of its presence and all that it signifies. Edward and his family are ever with me though I may never know his loved ones. Only time will tell. But I know them in spirit and imagine what their life was like when Edward walked this earth and they all gave so much joy to each other.

MERCY B.A.N.D.

A simple band
Worn daily with pride—
Bearing the name
Of one who died.

JGK

Remembering Edward Mazzella now and always.
Died September 11, 2001
World Trade Center

God's mercy is boundless, free and through Jesus Christ our Lord,
available to us now in our present situation.
—A.W. Tozer (1897–1963)

Reflections

Perhaps you too may wish to obtain a Mercy B.A.N.D. assuming they are still available by the time this book is published and goes into the world. On this chance, I give you the address and telephone numbers.

PO Box 91254
Albuquerque, New Mexico 87199 - 1254
Toll free call - 1-866-647-0762
or telephone 505 338-3675
The web site is www.mercyband.org.
Mercy B.A.N.D. is a non-profit organization. Any profits will benefit relief efforts.

If by the time you read this the mercy B.A.N.D. is no longer available, I can only suggest that you create an item to signify all that the Mercy B.A.N.D. bracelets signify. It is what I would do in the non-availability of the original. There may be a specific bracelet of your own (or even an item to wear around your neck) that could be blessed by you and prayed over and through these little rituals could become Holy to you. Or you may want to buy a new bracelet or other piece. If in reading your daily newspaper or watching TV news you learn any victims' names, you may wish to claim one as your own and pray daily for that victim's family and in spirit see the victim's name on your item or, if you so choose, have it engraved. I wear other significant pieces of jewelry that have deep meaning but no names upon them, worn long before Edward's Mercy B.A.N.D. came into my life. Perhaps you do also and realize now then that such pieces can be adapted and blessed for a victim and victim's family to come into your life. Perhaps you too can *"bear another's name daily"* by daily wearing your chosen item and daily praying for a family. You can learn more about your chosen person also by checking the *New York Times* web site. Here too you could also find *"a name to bear"* in spirit on your selected piece of jewelry if you have been unable to find one before this.

Magic Frigates

Do you know who you are?
You are a marvel, you are unique.
In all the years that have passed,
there has never been another child like you.
                    —Pablo Casals (1876–1973)

M ANY ADULTS TURN TO BOOKS every day of their lives for pleasure, knowledge, comfort, and personal reasons that are endless. They are soul food to millions who cannot ever imagine a day without the consolation of turning to the written word. I am such a person. I read when I am glad. I read when I am sad. I read when I am bad. I read when I am mad. (And yes I have read and loved Dr. Seuss.) Reading fills my life with joy and peace and I confess to being an obsessive compulsive buyer of books. Even if my entire cottage was filled with books, and it is coming along quite nicely, I would still need just one more book and drive myself crazy with the thought of it until I could get to the bookstore and buy it. I confess to this but lack embarrassment concerning it, for the presence of books and the reading of them has been a solace of such enormity since my childhood that I would probably state at this writing that it has been the greatest solace throughout my life. Yes, God too has been, but I find Him in my reading and in the comfort the written word brings in its every form. As I moved along in life, Bob, my children and Rochester too became great solace, Rochester giving me the solace of an Angel and comfort for beyond any words found in a book. As a child I read revery book I could get my hands on, and for an only child a book, as Emily Dickinson wrote, was a means to travel and gain knowledge and experiences that one might never know had one not read. Books and their precious contents were also companions of the highest order. Emily wrote in her famous poem:

> *There is no Frigate like a Book*
> *To take us Lands away*
> *Not any Coursers like a Page*
> *Of prancing Poetry.*

Reading can bring healing, and I will explore that further in another meditation, but this day I am suggesting you become child-like again. Not *childish*—but child-like—and begin to read a book from childhood that perhaps was a favorite. If you do not own it, then go treat yourself to a copy. Until you obtain it, turn to other childhood books you may have on hand or can borrow from the library. Remember those wonderful days of visiting the library as a child and returning with a pile of books that would last you for days? And repeatedly returning to that mysterious place to obtain a new supply of magic *"frigates!"*

There are so many classics to choose from in addition to Dr. Seuss and Little Bear Books, the Little Engine That Could, Madeleine, and endless other titles that go back generations. How many will remember the adventuresome Bobbsey Twins series and Honey Bunch, of which as a little girl I read every one I could get my hands on. I even won them as prizes at grade school for selling an abundance of PTA memberships.

Then too there were teenage books. These also will be acceptable for this little pause in your present reading of mature books, but not without first reading at least one childhood favorite (or two or three).

This morning on CNN the life of Millie Benson was given a lovely review, and to many she may be unknown, but not to me. It was a synchronism this should be on as I was writing about books. How exciting to hear this tribute to her life as she celebrated her 96th birthday today, January 23rd. In the 1930s, 40s, and 50s she wrote twenty-three books that kept me deeply engrossed during my teenage years. These were the books of the well known Nancy Drew mystery series, and I can see myself now sitting in a big overstuffed chair in our living room leaning against one arm of the chair and my legs thrown over the other arm deeply involved in a Nancy Drew mystery. Each one was a treasure to receive and Nancy was a very unusual girl and sleuth, and quite a strong girl of adventure and independence. She was not like teenage girls of my era but ahead of her time. Millie Benson wrote these books under the name that has become famous, Caroline Keene. Beside the Nancy Drew series she wrote over a hundred other novels after selling her first story in 1915. She received only $125.00 for each Nancy Drew book she wrote with no royalties. But she was satisfied and happy and is "til this day, as are all the young readers who read all of Nancy's adventures, as will others be who read them in the future."

The *Hardy Boy* series is another collection that continues to be popular and entertain. This was a favorite series of my daughter Laurel. One did not have to be a boy to enjoy these, nor a girl to be an avid reader of Nancy Drew.

Beautiful Joe is a moving book I read as a young person, but I did not discover and read *Black Beauty* until fairly recently. I have written about both in my *Journal of Love*. Both books express deep love for animals and abhorrence to cruelty done to them. They are worthy of your time given to reading them. You will never forget them.

Another series that is excellent for teens (and adults too) is the trilogy of *Emily of New Moon* by L.M. Montgomery. I did not learn of this trilogy until the 1980s through the reading of a book by the well-known writer Madeleine L'Engle. This trilogy meant so much to her as a child and she continues to read it again and again, for Emily is a girl who desired to be a writer. Throughout the three books she tries to accomplish that quest. They are marvelous books and inspiration to myself and to Madeleine L'Engle. Several of my daughters have enjoyed them too, as will you.

There are so many children and teen books to choose from that it is impossible to include all the ones that touched my life and the lives of my own children. This is part of the fun, to reminisce a bit first 'til some titles come to mind and then check around on your own shelves first or on your children's. If you find nothing that attracts, have an unusual trek to the library or bookstore in the body of your younger self and through the eyes of this "inner child" who still exists within you. Enter a new dimension on this search and come home with some treasures. You are now about to enter another world.

Perhaps create some atmosphere each time you sit down to read the chosen books. Maybe a certain chair reminds you of one you loved to cuddle in as a child or teen. Use this chair only for your reading, first making a cup of cocoa perhaps. Remember the childhood poem

Animal Crackers and cocoa to drink—
they are the finest of suppers, I think.

Be "that" child and cuddle down with your book and this comfort food to nourish your body and soul.

This may sound strange to give comfort to yourself in this way when the world is difficult and sad, but it is strengthening. From many a childhood book I gained new resolve, for I was shy and often frightened. Many children and grown-ups feel that way both in good times and in our present world situation. Let a book nurture that child within you, for when the child is nurtured and made strong then the adult bears the fruit and is not only an asset and solace to him or herself and family, but to all that they encounter in this troubled world.

Reflections

Take your journal with you too to that special chair or space where you will read your books. Occasionally write down what your heart and soul are experiencing while revisiting your childhood through reading and the memories that have been churned up during each quiet time. The solace of revisiting your younger self will be comforting, no matter what your childhood was like. You are still a precious and unique person and that little child needs recognition, and in turn you will be stronger in your present life.

Part 2

We are born for a higher destiny than that of earth. There is a realm where the rainbow never fades, where the stars will be spread out before us like islands that slumber on the ocean and where the beings that now pass before us, like shadows, will stay in our presence forever.

—Bulwer-Lytton
from *The Return of the Ragpicker* by Og Mandino

The longer I was at the cabin, the more precious everything there became. Sightings of the first buttercups each spring were amplified by the sightings of the seasons before.

Each tree, every rock formation was steeped in memories. And those memories were intensified, in turn, because I had time to renew, embellish, and strengthen them by consciously experiencing what was around me.

—*Celebrating Time Alone: Stories of Splendid Solitude*
by Lionel Fisher

Introduction

It Is Such A Secret Place—the land of tears
—Antoine deSaint Exupery (1900–1944)

MY OUTLOOK ON DEATH HAS CHANGED SO RADICALLY. The death I accepted previous to March 8, 2002 was the one I was taught about since I was a young child by parents, Sunday School teachers, Ministers and later Priests. It was the one talked briefly about with family and friends when someone died, or the subject that unexpectedly and occasionally arose but did not linger. It was the death I believed in but it certainly did not need frequent discussing.

It was a Christian death of hope and resurrection and once our loved ones passed, our prayers and memories had to sustain us until we joined them. As a Protestant we did not pray *to* or talk *to* our loved ones or even pray *for* them. If they had walked with Jesus while on earth we believed them to be safe in Heaven and walking with Him now for all eternity. Our prayers were for others still on earth or for ourselves, or for things in the world needing healing. But as a Catholic, I learned I could pray and talk *to* them and pray *for* them. This was a comforting teaching especially since my three loved ones were now in Heaven. But that was it, for once they left us we were alone and even with great faith, which I had, there were often thoughts and fears that surfaced when alone in that dangerous place of my brain instead of in my heart. My heart held the spiritual truths I knew were absolute and yet I still questioned at times. Once three people disappear that were your closest relatives and whom you

35

truly loved, it becomes natural that one would have new thoughts and questions that did not exist before they all up and left within thirteen months. Oh, and there were several close friends too!

As I have written elsewhere, I seemed suppressed from exploring more and even in grieving because of the words spoken scoldingly to me by a family member shortly after the death of my Dad, and because I had responsibilities in a large family. Writing about my three lost loved ones in my journals, poetry, and books was the main help I gave to myself after their deaths along with prayer. These three loved ones however, seemed to gradually disappear in the passing years from the lives of those who knew them. Rarely were they mentioned or the love that had been given by them, and people cannot even seem to remember their birthdays or dates of leaving this earth. But I do, and that is all that matters.

Yet it is hard to understand for they gave of themselves to all of our family while they shared life on earth with us. Now as in the past twenty-five years it has become awkward to talk about them except for a passing remark. But it is not awkward for me, for I continually try to perpetuate their memories whenever I can. Margaret Mead has stated, "*When a person is born we rejoice, and when they're married we jubilate, but when they die we try to pretend nothing has happened.*"

La Rochefoucould also has similar observations with his words, "*The human mind is as little capable to contemplate death for any length of time as the eye is able to look at the sun.*"

That was how it all was before Rochester's passing and still basically is—except now I personally have new knowledge. It is knowledge so spiritually and enormously comforting that once one knows it and believes and experiences it for himself one can never again be the same. It is as if one begins a new life and can never return to the old. One is on a mystical journey walking a passage one has never travelled before. And once you begin this journey there is never the desire to be as before — only to press forward and travel and pray and learn and be open. You are in the *Corridors of Eternal Time* and it is where I am and ever shall be. And it does not matter if those closest to you do not understand or do not wish to join you or do not even want to hear about it. It just does not matter! You are sustained by God and your beloved one in spirit. Occasionally there are one or two on earth who support your quest even though they may not be spiritually as you are or as totally and deeply involved. I am grateful to have such support. This means more than I can ever express. *"God works in mysterious ways His wonders to perform."* This corridor I am travelling pertains to the heart and soul and to the wonders of life eternal in the afterlife. It is a passage of truth, hope, and beauty.

Some months into my grief and while travelling this journey I read a paragraph in a book by Louise Platt Hauck on the afterlife. It was so profound to me and struck my soul. I copied it into my journal and reread it often. Now I understand much more since first reading it for I have been travelling this passage for some time. Perhaps it will help you. Author Hauck is speaking to a woman about insights she has been given about the woman's husband who has passed. *"It's almost like he has a tunnel going from him to you—like a corridor. It's as if you have two people on opposite ends building a railroad track and one's in Nebraska and one's in California and they are building toward each other and at some point the railroad track will connect."*

It was the first time I had seen the word *"corridor"* used in my reading with the exception of the title of my own book I was writing and nearing completion on at that time. My book had long before been given its title. I used a line from one of the hymns inspired by the Holy Spirit that Bob had written some years ago. And Rochester's and my *"track"* has months ago connected in our *"corridor,"* within the very first days of his passing.

Through my own prayer and thinking, meditations, and too, reflecting on my selective reading and unique spiritual television programs, I wrote the following passage in my steno pad one day while in the heat of the moment.

Often we are forced to be separated from a loved one and there is a disconnect between us. It causes such emotional pain. It is good not to fill that void because it is the very connection that binds the two that love. It is a void that should be left empty so that it can be filled with the love exchanges of the two that are separated, the one left behind in this life and the one beyond. The pain of separation is also our strength stating the truth that one day we will be reunited. No one or anything else belongs in that space between the two loved ones except their continuing love and ongoing spiritual connections. That void is a gift so enormous, and supports the one on the continuing journey in the corridor until there is a reunion beyond in joy unspeakable that shall last for all eternity.

I am of the nature that solitude is utterly essential to my living a realized spiritual life. It is a solace of the greatest strength that has been an underlying support in all that I do, and especially in this journey that I have embarked on for the rest of my life. What I have written in this book shares my spiritual existence in the woods while learning to live this new life. It speaks of things that can bring solace in any form of grief. But alternating with these journal-like entries are the afterlife connections I am receiving continually from Rochester. Most are dated but some are not. Many are spontaneously entered forgetting to record the date. They appear however amongst the dated ones and occurred somewhere in that time frame in which I entered them.

I have opened my heart and allowed these precious contacts to be put in this book in order to help others. I realize it will open me to ridicule by many but it does not matter. I have written boldly about unusual things before. For you see, if people before me had not done the same I would not have had the solace of knowing others out there were also having contacts from their loved ones. This has been new territory, a mystical amazing walk and it is so sacred to the one experiencing it that it cannot be explained beyond what I have already attempted to write.

While writing *In Corridors of Eternal Time* the contacts from Rochester increased. Because of my Christian background I was timid about writing in too much detail, and also about my sources of help that gradually entered my life in the Fall of 2002 before completing the book. But having been given great gifts and consolation from God, Rochester, and Blessed Mother Mary, I in turn am sharing this walk with you. It is impossible to deny all I experience. It is my own personal truth. Perhaps it will be a strength to you.

Perhaps you too have been experiencing things you are afraid to talk about to others concerning loved ones who have crossed over. If what you share is demeaned it adds to your grief. Yet you know what you have experienced is truth. May this book then be a friend. May I be a friend.

If you are reading this book merely out of curiosity that is good. I have often read books in this way. But since March 8, 2002 I have only read books on grieving and the afterlife. I could not possibly stray from that path of reading if I tried. It is so powerful a leading that I merely follow every lead. I am being taught by God and Rochester just as I was taught in Rochester's "*School of Love*" after he entered my life. Everything became new and different then and I learned truths that changed me for the better and I became a vegetarian for the sake of the animals. I realized forcefully that all life is sacred not just human life. And this road I am now on is a continuing passage and I cannot ever leave this journey.

May this book and *Corridors* be spiritual lights on your journey. Often we do not recognize the light we are given because when it comes it may come too early. We may not need it. We may or may not pay attention, and we may even set it aside forgetting it. This happened to me.

Once upon a lovely summer evening in 2001 I sat on our porch talking with a friend who was visiting, a friend I have known for many years but that I do not see regularly. This was a significant evening to me and my friend was in mourning due to the death of his wife in January of that year. We just talked and talked in ways we had never done before and I was so blessed, and I wanted to be able to help him so much through my listening and words. In the course of this precious conversation he told me of inspirations he was receiving from a source that was totally unheard of to me. It was beautiful and heavenly and an ongoing strength to him in his grief. I felt so moved from all that we shared and from specific things he revealed. For a long time after I continually remembered that night and our conversation. Too, I wanted to investigate the source of help he was receiving in his grief but because it was a TV program that was on the same time as the 11 PM news, and Bob and I are definitely not of like mind in many areas of spirituality, or certainly not at that point in our lives, I felt I could not watch this evening program. Soon other things in life took place, then 9/11, and then the passing of my Rochester. I wanted very much to talk to my friend alone again when he returned the summer of 2002, but I was never able to have that privilege for many others were here. There was no privacy. What he specifically shared with me that first summer, the specific thing I needed but had totally forgotten due to the trauma of Rochester's passing, was lost to me. Grief can do things to your memory. But oh, I am so grateful to my friend.

What he had shared, his great spiritual help, I feel was lost to me because it was not my time to need help as he needed it. And yet I was so extremely interested in this spiritual knowledge that was so totally unfamiliar to me as he told me about it. I had never been introduced to it before. The message was given and buried within me. And when I did need it, it did not surface due to grieving. I share this because this can happen to us all. May it not happen to you.

Fortunately I was again given this same information in late Summer of 2002 about six months after Rochester's passing. It was given to me by two extended family members I love here in the woods, the very same information given to me approximately a year before by my friend, (and also their friend) who desperately personally needed it. I am so grateful to all three. Now I needed this information and I am thankful to say I have been supported by it for this past year, one of numerous gifts relating to the afterlife that has been revealed to me. I will share this and some of my helps at the end of this book, but if you read this journal with your heart you will find many clues throughout telling you sources that you too can learn about. I have found God leads you to the ones that are meant for you. It is such a personal road. God will lead you to the right books also if you just pray first and go to a bookstore. It is what I do. And I hope and pray this book you are reading and *Corridors* will also be books that will accompany you on your personal journey through the corridor.

Before I end these thoughts I will state as I do in some of my other books that I am writing from a Christian perspective, but anything suggested in this book to do spiritually can be done according to your own personal faith or way of living. I will tell you that I believe in God, in Jesus, and that Mary and Angels are with me always. I believe that God can speak to us in any way He so chooses and I anticipate it. I believe in the precious love of my little cat Rochester and that we communicate this love and all else to each other both when he was in body and now in spirit. When you believe it—it happens. I believe in the sanctity of life for all creatures as well as for humans. I believe in all of nature as other ways God speaks to us and is present to us for I have experienced Him in these ways.

I would also like you to realize that my little marmalade and white cat Rochester has been completely with me in the pages of all of my past books, and by his daily spiritual presence to me he is also with me in this book, and through his life and constancy, his help and inspiration, his teachings, and the joy he instills in me. This book and any other I have written only came into being because his *"Angel being"* came into my life forever. His love and presence are inspiring me as I write and his paw prints are on each page.

I pray the things I share with you in this book will lift your heart and accompany you on your journey. If I have repeated anything or looked back on anything more than once, that is because this book is written in journal form and journals are meant for reflection. We may have to return to a subject to help our heart and soul.

The picture on the cover of this book is of our cottage by the lake. It was in this cottage that Rochester and I shared our life. The upper windows are the ones of our writing room in which we two spent our days. It is in this cottage in which I have experienced all of Rochester's afterlife visits. Each visit occurred as if in real life. The enclosed porch to the left is also where I see him. This little cottage was and is his home and it seems most significant to have it on the cover—a place of solace and afterlife visits.

Closure is a strange word to me for why would I want any type of finality to a life lived with someone I cherish? Instead I want the door from this life and the one to eternity (one and the same) to be ever open or perhaps not exist at all! I envision a vastness of beauty (the ether?) where the possibility for meetings and visions and communication exist. I believe in visits from our loved ones unexpected, unexplainable, anywhere, and too, in dreams. If I close my mind and keep compartments for those who have gone before me and for myself, I close off the possibilities also of any significant interchange because I will live without expectation. If I refuse to follow a rule be it assumed, religious, or unthinkable, and ask God to surprise me, I will then expect to experience Rochester everyday of my life here on earth in multitudinous forms until we are together forever once more.

—Janice Gray Kolb from *In Corridors of Eternal Time—*
A Passage Through Grief: A Journal

Rochester

MEDITATION ONE

Silence and Solitude

I am larger than I thought. I did not know I held such goodness.
—Walt Whitman

THE HEALING WOODS

I come to the woods to restore myself.
My spirit to be nourished and healed.
My calling to write I take down from the shelf—
And through writing my thoughts are revealed.

Solitude to me is life-giving,
In silence I do what He bids.
I am back to fulfillment in living—
All debris within me He rids.

Surrounded by nature again -
The wildlife, the lake—all things green—
My spirit is calm now and sane—
In His woods I am peaceful—serene.

Dedicated to   Jan
"Higher Ground"

*I*F WE ALLOW TIME FOR SOLITUDE we will discover it opens the door for us to be aware that we truly need solitude. It helps us to think upon our experiences and our deep feelings. We discover then our reactions to them. When solitude is not permitted in your life you live life on the surface with no time to go within. You can not discover your true self, your true emotions. Often purposely not allowing time for solitude is a defense mechanism, when actually you need solitude in which to release your concerns, stress and tensions. It is in solitude and silence we connect with our soul.

Often we are surrounded by noise of some sort from the time we awake until the time we go to sleep. The noises are all part of daily life and often come from ordinary things like CD players, telephones, radios, TVs, cars, airplanes, computers, trucks, excess talking and so much more. Even our refrigerator motors. We are so used to these noises we incorporate them into our lives believing they are non-penetrable or erasable. We often are not aware of them until perhaps someone out-doors stops hammering or perhaps the refrigerator suddenly stops, or both, and we experience this sudden silence. And it is lovely!

I have suggested often taking a walk in nature. Go to a woods if you do not live in one as we do, and listen to the gentle and lovely sounds of nature. Or take a walk in a field or along a shore line.

We do not have to be subjected to noise if we do not wish to be. There can be certain periods each day where you can turn off radios, TVs and computers and take your phone off the hook. A ticking clock can sometimes sound extremely loud, so go somewhere away from that or anything similar. It is so beautiful to just be able to listen to the birds, or breezes gently blowing the wind chimes, or the chatter of squirrels. These are the sounds that minister to me, all of nature. I long ago stopped playing even meditational music at the end of the day when I finish writing because I want to just rest in the sounds of nature that I have been writing to and in all day. Anything more is too much.

Silence is a companion to solitude and they are both essential to my well being. They comfort and cradle me when in sadness and grieving, and support me interiorly in periods when I recall treasured moments. And too in time of deep meditation and prayer.

When you let your responsibilities fall away at certain periods and give yourself permission to embrace solitude and silence that you need, you will fully understand Rainer Maria Rilke's words:

To walk inside yourself and meet no one for hours—that is what you must be able to attain.

Many will say they cannot find time for solitude or silence but that is not true. If you wish to live a peaceful life within and rest your mind and heart for awhile, you cannot afford to eliminate solitude and silence because you are afraid of them or not willing to make the effort to experience them. Your life will be changed. I promise you. You have to be willing to be idle if only for a moment and you will be blessed. You will be aware. Silence heals wounds deep within of which we are barely aware. It soothes those in grief and sadness and is like a haven and a secret place to be with your loved one for whom you grieve. It is lovely to go to a special place to achieve this peace, but too we should also have a place within our own homes in which to retreat. Often we need such a place suddenly if our hearts are broken and we must just "be" and sink down into silence and aloneness—yes, and to tears.

Minister to yourself just in simple ways like enjoying the pleasure of washing your face. The soft cloth and the smell of gentle soap or lotion will soothe. Drink your coffee early in the morning when the world is fresh and new indoors or outside, when the birds are singing. Lines from an old hymn, "In the Garden," come to mind that I have loved since I was little.

I come to the garden alone
While the dew is still on the roses—

In my life I love listening to the peepers at night that are in the lake. They draw me into another mystical world. Silently noticing the little things around us is a gift in every sadness—to forever notice. It is my gift.

I have written in a previous book of how when I was younger and all our six children were still at home that I would set the alarm and wake up at 4 AM to have an hour all alone and for prayer, then go back to sleep until the normal time we all awoke. This may be a little extreme but at that time in my life it worked for me. If you pray and reflect on this matter I believe your will be guided by God and you will soon realize that this is necessary. You can also wait until everyone is asleep at night and then be alone. But please be with yourself in solitude and silence daily.

You can vary your scheduled times of solitude and silence also so as to never remain in a place or schedule where you feel restricted. If you have been walking in a woods then vary your walks to other places of quiet. Perhaps by a lake or any place near that is a haven of solitude.

Vary anything that you do after a certain period. Perhaps in your silence and solitude you may wish to write in your journal for it is in periods like these thoughts surface in our minds and flow easily out through our pens. And writing helps a broken heart or any one that is "*going within*" and on a spiritual journey.

You may also wish to take into your sacred place your animal companion be they cat or dog or other. You will know whether the personality of your dear companion is conducive to such quietness or not. Rochester was always with me. He still is. We are one soul and are completely alike. Do not take cats outdoors or on a walk for their safety if you should go out, but your dog on a leash may be an enjoyable companion and he will feel honored and happy that he is sharing this time and bringing you solace. Your cat can be your "*at home*" companion in solitude.

May you find the path to solitude and silence and on this path you will also find yourself.

In the attitude of silence the soul finds the path in a clearer light.
—Mahatma Gandhi

Love your solitude.
—Rilke

In Quietness and Confidence

If I do not minister to myself
In solitude and silence—
I miss the wealth
In each present moment.
I am tense
And live on the edge.
But in quietness and confidence
I shall wait—
And meditate—
And find God and myself anew.

JGK
2003

A place of solitude by the lake and gardens

MEDITATION 2

Love Letters in the Sand

Repetitive events are often subtle and involve a single element.
What marks them as synchronistic, transdimensional communications
are their circumstances and their association with the deceased,
which is usually immediately apparent to the subject.
—from *Love Beyond Life: The Healing Power*
of After-Death Communications
by Joel Martin and Patricia Romanowski

November 21, 2002

THROUGH MORE OF MY PERSONAL ON-GOING EXPERIENCES with Rochester now for eight months and my continual reading, and too my viewing of programs on this subject, I have become confident, extremely so, of our eternal connection. I can never be moved. It is so! I know that our daily communication is alive and present and that we are just living in a different dimension together. And we do interact!

Tonight once in bed, there is no scratching in the litter box as there has been for a number of weeks while I read but I feel the intense heat on my legs. As I read I hold Rochester's paws in spirit. After I turn out the light to pray the Rosary I ask if he can just let me hear him scratching in the corner for a bit, but if he is too tired then it is fine. I talk with him normally and always as I did when his precious body was right there before me. I know he is on my legs and hears.

A couple of seconds pass and then there are a few scratches in the corner, then more and more. Then silence again and the heat on my legs intensifies. We are falling asleep with me holding his little paws. I am so grateful for every second of his being with me and for his communicating as well. I have written elsewhere that our loved ones in spirit come extremely close to us when we are in prayer and particularly through repetitious prayers such as the Rosary. I have repeated contacts, dreams, visits, and visions with Rochester after praying the Rosary, and before and during sleep. But I have them spontaneously occurring other times also. We just have to pray and be open and believe and truly long for these connections. They are gifts.

Tonight he has answered my direct and loving request and I am in awe. We are learning and living in this passage of grief.

He is validating once more his ever-present spiritual presence through his *litter box love letters in the sand*—for my heart and soul alone.

> *Empathy, compassion, and love seem to form a literal bond—*
> *a resonance—or glue between living things.*
> —Dr. Larry Dorsey

All Heroes Are Not People

Animals are really special, they are a piece of God. They're like Angels.
—Fred Travalena

I N FEBRUARY 2002 I was sent a story by e-mail. It touched me deeply and I put it in my loose leaf binder that holds the manuscript for this book. Because of my Rochester's passing I never looked into this loose leaf binder again until December 2002, and then I found this story. It touches me anew and in the rereading I know it is meant to be shared. I do not know who wrote it or sent it to me. There is no indication of either. I only know that it is true and that it happened on 9/11/01. It was copied from the New York times on 9/19/01. I am retelling it in paraphrase.

A gentleman named James Crane worked on the 101st floor of Tower 1 of the World Trade Center. Because he is blind, he has a golden retriever named Daisy. James knew that he was doomed after the plane hit 20 stories below, so out of a deep act of love he let his beloved Daisy go. One can only imagine the heartbreak James was experiencing. With whimpers and hesitation she darted away into the darkened hallway. James was just waiting to die as he choked on the jet fuel and smoke.

About 30 minutes later Daisy came running back bringing with her James's boss, whom Daisy just happened to pick up on floor 112.

On her first run of the building, she led James, his boss and approxi-mately 300 more people out of the doomed building. But she was not through yet. Daisy knew there were others who were trapped, so highly against James's wishes, she ran back into the building. On this her second run she saved 392 lives. Again she went back in!

During this run, the building collapsed, and James, hearing about this, fell on his knees in tears. Daisy made it out alive against all known odds. This time, however, she was carried by a firefighter. "She led us right to the people, before she got injured," the fireman explained. Daisy's final run saved another 273 lives. She suffered acute smoke inhalation, severe burns on all four paws, and a broken leg, but she saved 967 lives.

The next week Mayor Guiliani rewarded Daisy with the canine medal of Honor of New York. Daisy was the first civilian canine to win such an honor.

My little Rochester has not saved me from a burning building about to collapse, but often when I felt doomed for one reason or another and felt I would collapse emotionally, Rochester was there.

Day by day throughout our life together all these many years he has been there in his constancy to strengthen and love me and point the way when I was too blind to see it. When I felt unloved, trapped, lost by matters that would arise and seem to burn and stifle all that was within me, when I would go to my knees in tears, he was there. His little paws holding my hands, his glorious golden eyes holding mine in love, again and again helped me to know that he was there and God was within him gazing out.

All my life since Rochester entered it I have honored him for the precious being he is and shall love him from the depths of my heart and unabashedly forever. I understand James's love for Daisy.

Never underestimate the love of an animal, for often it can stand the test of life, trials, and time far more than human love. And not only loyalty, devotion, companionship, and constancy is present in ordinary daily life, but in our times of sadness and trials, - solace of the most tender sort imaginable is given.

MY RESCUER

He rescues me—my Feline Love—
My little Angel from above.
And as we daily trod life's way—
I follow on my feet of clay.

JGK

MEDITATION FOUR

Thoughtfulness

*Think about your deceased loved ones. In case after case
the key identifying details that cinched a spirit's identity or proved
a communication genuine were not great events but everyday details.*
—Love Beyond Life: The Healing Power of
After-Death Communications
by Joel Martin and Patricia Romanowski

November 23, 2002

S EVERAL THOUGHTFULNESSES FROM CHESTER TOUCH MY HEART all occurring in the early morning. Before going to bed last night I deliberately
arrange Chester's Iams food that I place there to honor him each morning
and evening in a certain pattern on his plate. I do this always but never
repeat it late at night. I just do it on a whim this particular night. I know
he knows and soon I feel his heat and vibrations upon my legs in bed.

In the morning I walk into the kitchen and in joy and awe see that the
six pieces of Iams are all rearranged and two pieces are off the plate and
lying on the paper towel that is under his plate. Bob has had nothing to
do with this. It is not anything he would pay attention to and if he knew
about it would not want to. But when pointed out now he just smiles and
shakes his head. It is one of those discussions he prefers not to have.

I can just imagine the sweetness of Rochester's spirit there on the
table gently patting the Iams about with his small white marshmallow
paw. He knew this would delight me. Like a special code it states *"I am
here."*

53

This same morning I am without my glasses that I got when Rochester was with me in life. I have been looking everywhere since late yesterday and began looking anew today. Praying, I ask Rochester conversationally to show me where they are. Immediately I feel led to look on the floor down next to the side of the bed. I find them down there in the tight dark place between bed and wall—not understandable really, for I lost them in mid-afternoon and was not at all in the bedroom that time of day. I also find the tape of *The Fairy Ring, the* blessed ethereal music that is Rochester's and mine. I believe he is telling me to listen to our music, that I need it just as I do my glasses. Up until now I have not been able to slip our precious tape into the tape player and turn it on as I did every night of our life since 1989. I thought the tape was safely in the player.

MEDITATION FIVE

He Kissed Me

I don't believe you dead. How can you be dead if I still feel you?
          —Alice Walker, *The Color Purple*

I HAVE SO MANY UNUSUAL COMMUNICATIONS from Rochester on a daily basis and I write each one down in our journal. We are always together. Today while praying the Rosary in our Holy Hour that begins at 5 PM, but extends to an hour and a half which is more than usual, an exquisitely precious gift is given to me.

I feel Chester's little mouth on the left side of my upper lip when my eyes are closed! There is a quickening within me for I know instantly that it is his tiny mouth! In life he would often stand on my lap and look into my face and search my eyes. We would be *"held"* tightly but yet so delicately, bound in love by this invisible connection. His gentle paws in these moments now rest on the front of me as in the past. Often then he would bless me with his ethereal kiss too. This is the second time it is happening since he has been in spirit.

I slowly open my eyes after allowing myself several moments of his presence, but through tears learn his little body cannot be seen. Oh thank you, dear Rochester, for your eternal kiss.

Words received at completion of praying Rosary:

"I was there. I did it. I am
always there. I am always
with you. I kissed your
sweetness that shone through
as you prayed for me. I love
you so much."

—Rochester
his words spoken to me in spirit

MEDITATION SIX

The Solace of Journaling

The tears that often blur the eyes while the words are formed and written are part of it all. Sometimes the tears are wordless expressions that never make it onto the journal page except to wet the words that do.
—Janice Gray Kolb, *Higher Ground*

WRITING HELPS PUT YOU IN TOUCH with a deeper part of yourself. It allows you to capture your insights and contemplations. Recording your feelings, experiences, and thoughts is a therapeutic part of journaling. It frees you from keeping thoughts trapped within and is a crucial self-discovery tool.

You can break rules when you journal and not be bound by writing rules you were taught as a child that perhaps took the spontaneity of writing away from you. You can write while lying under a tree, or listening to music or even while sitting in bed. You need not be at your desk.

Journaling is therapy for the soul and writing a marvelous form of self expression. If you wish to know your self better journaling is the means to do so. Journaling does take discipline but it is a practice you will grow to respect and like, and you will see the help that you are receiving from it if you are consistent.

If you are going through challenges, change, or transition, or need clarity on a matter, journaling is the tool that can help you. You may wish to have a different journal for different areas of your life: journals for dreams, poetry, revelations or insights, affirmations or whatever may be your need. Or you may wish to use only one journal for every area of your life so you can better see how everything is integrated and comes together. Only through beginning to journal can you discover the way you wish to journal and then follow your heart. Do not let anyone else tell you. It is such a personal discipline that you have to follow your own desires or you may not continue writing. The least little thing you will use as an excuse to stop if you are not tightly on the road of journaling.

You may wish to buy a set of colored pencils also to draw in your journals be they plain pages or lined. This is something I do. Often I make flowered borders. Sometimes I sketch things from my heart, particularly images of Rochester. You can also glue in photographs or other pictures that are significant to you that you may discover in a magazine but expresses something deeply personal to you.

We can draw on one form of journaling or another to suit our needs, just as we do in prayer. When we want to cry out in grief or rage we cannot use the contemplative way of prayer, and writing in our journals is very close to praying, if indeed it is not prayer. Our inner lives and condition can perhaps be our guide to the form of journal writing we do on a given day or period in our lives. There are so many ways we can journal and all forms can be done in one journal. Life affects us and we write. Most journals do have sort of a confessional aspect to them, at least mine do. Self discovery is also explored in writing. This kind of journal can lead us on to the Holy ground of our own lives. We should require of ourselves an unswerving commitment to honesty when we write about our lives and concerns, and all we write. Journal writing is enforced reflection. When we commit our heart and observations to the page we are taking what is inside of us and boldly placing it outside us. And when we hold our journal in our hands to look at what we have written we are holding a piece of our life in our hands. We can now meditate on it and perhaps even deepen our understanding of it. If you have never kept a journal before you could simply make lists in the beginning of your journal, loves, hates, desires and hopes, and perhaps this will inspire you to write. However, if you are grieving you may just begin without reserve by pouring your heart out on the page, and rightly so. Just write and write!

In *Higher Ground* I have written:

In the rereading of one's own journal at a time removed from the actual moments of the entries one can often become one's own

*therapist and counsellor and see deeply into woundedness and joy
expressed there. Light can suddenly come into one's thinking and
deepest revelations by the spirit can be seen, and as a result solutions
can be found, healings begun and even correction and penance given
to oneself over displeasures in attitudes or thoughts—or perhaps even
actions.*

Some may hesitate to keep a journal in fear that another will read it.
First, after death, if you arrange this beforehand, your journals can be
willed to a trusted friend who has promised to destroy them. But another
solution that I learned of is to perhaps will them to a library in a state far
from you with the condition that they may not be read by anyone until a
designated amount of years after your death—approximately two to
three. Another Blue Dolphin author has done this and I learned it from
reading her fine book (*You Are Not Old Until You're Ninety* by Rebecca
Latimer).

If you are fearful that household members might read them it would
be helpful to have a talk with them about it and discuss your fears. A
person may encroach on an other's privacy if he did not realize the
significance of what he is doing, or how it could effect the writer. Once
you discuss it I believe you can feel safe. I have kept journals for years and
know that Bob has never tried to read any of them, or my children when
they lived at home. I feel no need to keep my current one out of sight, but
all completed ones are safely stored away in this small cottage. I have not
yet decided how to care for them after death but will very soon.

As I write this I am reminded of 9/11, that tragic day. This event
caused such deep emotion in me. My one response was to send a carton
of journals and pens to an agency in New York that would see that those
who needed to write their pain upon the pages would receive a journal.

I recently heard a woman on a program dealing with grieving state
that she talks to her loved one who has passed and writes in a journal
daily to communicate with him. She stressed how it should be a daily on-
going thing to include our loved ones in Heaven. This allows them to
communicate with us, and they are given this right when we are open and
expectant and listen—and we talk and write. She could be talking about
myself as well for I experience and validate what she has said, and
discussed such communication with my Rochester in my previous books.

This is communication before and after his passing. Writing is truly a divine gift.

I too have learned of another lovely practice after Rochester's passing. Many keep a journal by a grave so that when a person visits there each can write something in the journal. Others keep its use strictly for a single loved one or close family members. It is kept in a protective box. I would imagine it would be a cement box to keep the journal safe in all weather. It is a beautiful custom.

When Rochester passed I began to write a book to honor him immediately after and also to help keep myself sane in my grief. It was written in journal form (*In Corridors of Eternal Time*). I also kept a separate personal journal but the writings were almost identical, the book being the main journal for I let every thing pour fresh from my heart so it would honor him, help myself, and in turn help others. I did not want to hold anything back.

Keeping a journal during a difficult passage such as grief can be one of the finest things you can do both for your loved one and yourself. There are not adequate words to express how deeply I feel about this. My present journal is for Rochester and myself to communicate as well as for day to day reflections on our continued passage together in unknown, ongoing and yet to be explored territory. It is essential. This book also is an ongoing and continuing of our journal *Corridors*.

As to other thoughts on journal keeping aside from what I have been led to share here, there are writings about it in each one of my previous seven books that were written before *Corridors*. *That* is how important I think it is. Different aspects of journaling are discussed in each of my books.

And now—I can only conclude this meditation by saying it is time to choose a lovely appealing journal (a man perhaps will choose a different sort, but men do journal!) and begin to write. It is a connection to your loved one for whom you grieve deeply, and is also therapy and tenderness for your soul. And if you are not grieving it is still an essential gift and tool to your life's journey. May you always write.

A journal is like a Holy sanctuary you can return to again and again.
It is not only good for the soul but the body as well. Writing in it also
makes me feel closer to God and my Angels. I could not survive

without writing in a journal if that is any indication as to its importance and strength in my life.

—Janice Gray Kolb,
*Beneath the Stars and Trees—
there is a place*

MUST

I know that when
My heart is broken—
I must write.

I know that when
My heart has spoken—
I must write.

A journal must
Be at my side—
In which to trust
And to confide.

And then I pour
My heart on paper—
And never ignore
My writing caper.

Jan
2003

A Meeting

Faith—is the Pierless Bridge
Supporting what We see
Unto the Scene that We do not—
                                    —Emily Dickinson, Poem #915

*T*ONIGHT I FALL ASLEEP GENTLY after reading and prayers and my faithful request to meet Rochester, either after crossing the borders to unknown realms, or in a dream. What seems to be only minutes later I am dreaming of my precious little companion. He is lying across my stomach, for I am still in a slightly upright position after prayers, his little head facing the wall to my left. So often through the years he has cuddled in this way.

When I suddenly wake from the dream, Rochester is still there upon me with my left hand on his soft white front paws. He slowly fades before my eyes as I watch, the faint night light from the bath across the hall allowing me sufficient observance of his disappearing form. The warmth from him still lingers. He is ever here, this I know.

My kitten's tender paw,
thou soft, small treasure.
                                    —Heinrich Heine, German poet and critic

62

MEDITATION EIGHT

Things Remembered

Stranger call this not a place
Of fear and gloom.
To me it is a pleasant spot
It is my husband's tomb.

—Charles L. Wallis
(for my Mother, Dad, Uncle
and a little unknown girl)

December 3, 2002

TODAY IS A SIGNIFICANT DAY TO ME. We have been in Pennsylvania six days and will leave to drive home to New Hampshire tomorrow. It is only the second time I have gone back to our former hometown of Jenkintown since we moved to New Hampshire in January 1996. We are staying in the home of our daughter Barbara and her husband Francis, and their handsome and lovable cat Buddy. On this day of December third the four of us go out on errands and on the way we drive into the Forest Hills Cemetery where my parents and uncle, all of whom I lost in a period of thirteen months from August 1977 to September 1978, are buried, along with a younger child who is sister to my Mother and Uncle. This is a cemetery I visited regularly alone from 1977 until moving to New Hampshire nineteen years later. Often I headed there deliberately or when out on errands, and would drive there to pray and tell my family members things on my heart or to sit and stare and cry. Their graves are all in a square plot together toward the back of the cemetery and a lovely small road is next to them. I could drive up and park and sit in the car by the graves to pray, or get out and stand there and talk and pray. I am thankful I took pictures of their headstones to have here in New Hampshire. Usually I sat in the car with the window rolled down. Often I was sad and sharing my problems with them. This was all comforting and I often wrote things down in a small journal while visiting. It was as if two worlds existed; my real one to which I would return to after the visits, and the one filled with mystery on the secluded hill in the cemetery.

Today I visit my Mother, Dad and Uncle's graves after a seven year absence, and too the little girl buried there in the fourth plot I never knew. Once back at our daughter's home I see myself again on the hill and imagine (as I did when I visited in person) not only my loved ones but also the dark gray suit my Uncle has on, and the dark blue of my Dad's, the pretty soft silky dress of shades of black and gray my Mother wears. She selected that new to wear to my Dad's and Uncle's Methodist services in 1977 and it seemed right to us to have her wear it for her own, and for her treasured heavenly meeting with the two she grieved for and longed to be with.

All of these things are remembered especially today on my Mother's birthday, but too again and again and again. I am learning to experience them in new ways in my new life.

> *He went before she did.*
> *She thought she would break,*
> *She felt she was fallin' apart.*
> *But still she remembers*
> *The last words he said*
> *As he held her hand close to his heart.*
>
> — Willy Welch

The poem that follows I wrote for my Mother on her birthday three years ago. Though it may be strange to the reader it touches on a subject we often teased her about. I like to think she has happy feet as well as a happy heart in Heaven.

At Last

Today—twenty-one years later
    on your birthday—
I think of you lying in your coffin
    in your pretty dress of black and gray,
Worn at your husband's and brother's funerals
    when they had gone so quickly away
        in that three-month period in nineteen seventy-seven.

And though you are in Heaven
    free of your shoes and earthly ties—
I cannot bear to think of your body
    lying there in that coffin in heels.
        I hear your sighs.
And too, I hear your words from the coffin—
    "Take off my shoes!"
        and I understand.

Though you wore heels day in and day out
    and all about at work—
        and looked so grand—
The moment you came home
    you kicked off your shoes
        and slipped into your slippers.
You even served us your finest meals
    while wearing slippers!
        How did I—in nineteen seventy-eight—not remember?
But I do now this day in December!

In tears at your leaving
    my sadness overwhelming—
        I did not think to remove
            each heel.
        Then came the seal!

O, how did you endure for twenty-one years
    what you could not even for a moment
        when you arrived home?
            You must have been in tears!

Please put my heart and yours at rest—
    and though it will take weeks—your body being dead—
Gently lift your thin left leg and with your small foot
    push off your right shoe—
Now, very slowly—lift your bare right foot
    and push off the last heel.
        Oh, how does that feel?

Just let those heels fall where they may!
    Your feet—at last—are at rest today!
        O, if only I could give you your slippers—
        but I am four hundred and twenty miles away.

For Violet M. Gray—my Mother   Jan
Happy Birthday   December 3, 1999
with my love.

Inspired by regret and the poem *Fare* by Molly Peacock

MEDITATION NINE

A December Collection of Joy

It is one of the commonest of mistakes to consider that the limit of
our power of perception is also the limit of all there is to perceive.
                                                    —C. W. Leadbeater

December 11, 2002

NUMEROUS EVENTS HAVE OCCURRED in the month of December that truly indicate Rochester's presence in ways different than his being on my legs nightly or in visual appearances. Tonight there is much noise outside the bathroom door when I am preparing to come to bed. They are just the same noises Rochester made when playing or running around to catch a mouse. I cannot see him. I can only hear this commotion in the small hall, and I feel blessed. There is no other explanation after all the miracles that have been happening. He is always present.

December 14, 2002

Tonight there are strange noises while we watch television and so much so Bob stands and turns off the set. Since the kitchen is connected to this small living room and the noise is going on right behind us in the kitchen area, it deserves investigation. For years we experienced these identical noises while Chester was searching down a mouse that may have been under the oven. He never killed one mouse. He brought each one to us! The area near the oven was one of Chester's favorite stalking places and where I saw a beautiful life-like vision of him shortly after he

67

passed as recorded in my book *Corridors.* Too, he often played with his toys there on the linoleum floor. When not on the floor he often laid on the end of the large table while I prepared meals right near him. It was an area he liked. But we cannot see him this night or what could be causing the identical noises he always made there for years. It *is* him, of course, saying once again "*I am here.*" He is ever present and each time he tells us it is a priceless gift I never take for granted. I am rewarded shortly after by his presence on my legs. Our loved ones in the spirit world do so much to give us love and to get our attention if only we live in a new way and are attentive and believe.

December 20, 2002

At 5 PM to 6 PM I keep my Friday Holy Hour but it always extends past that because I pray so deeply and never open my eyes to check the time. I allow the Holy Spirit and Rochester to indicate when I am finished. Today another miracle! I was shocked out of my meditative state of silently praying the Rosary within by a voice coming from the wildlife comforter of Rochester's on the bed and saying two words. One was my name but the other was lost to me and said first. I was so deep in prayer I cannot remember the first word. This is the third time this has occurred. It is not imagination and sufficiently audible to jar me out of prayer. It was not coming from within me. It was Rochester communicating. It has happened before. In all of my reading I have learned that this is a very common type of after-death communication. Some people hear a voice through their ears communicating just as if they would hear any other person talking to them. But many hear an internal voice inside their mind or head and often feel it is coming from outside them. I am not alone in receiving such communications. Thank you, dear Rochester, for still yet another gift of your love and presence.

MEDITATION TEN

A Spiritual Anniversary

Most of us leave our bodies during sleep.
—Robert Monroe (one who studied
the phenomenon extensively)
from *Love Beyond Life*

December 13, 2002

IT IS THE TWENTY-FOURTH ANNIVERSARY of the night I entered the Catholic Church. It is difficult to believe so many years have passed for that too was a difficult year. It was in September my Mother passed away, and my Dad and uncle the previous year. I have been an orphan for many years and I was not very old when I physically lost them all. Now I am physically without Rochester. I call the priest who brought me into the Catholic Church as I do each year on this date and we have a wonderful talk. He is Monsignor Joseph Kane and pastor of a large church in the suburbs north of Jenkintown, Pennsylvania where I had lived and met him in the church in Jenkintown.

Though twenty-four years have passed I still retain my Methodist Protestant roots and its traditions and the strong scriptural strengths it inspired me to pursue. It is ever present in my being as well as the spiritual strengths from the Catholic Church. I am blessed to know and incorporate two Christian traditions in my walk on earth. Some may not think this possible but I know there are others who experience this same walk. For seven years or more I attended both churches in Jenkintown going first to early Mass on Sunday and then dashing around the corner to the

Methodist Church to be with my family. During the week I attended daily Mass, a great spiritual help. As years passed and all children married, Bob and I attend only the Catholic Church here in New Hampshire.

It is a Friday and so I have my Holy Hour that becomes much longer with and for Rochester in our writing room at 5 PM. Later in bed there are noises again briefly in the litter box and in the kitchen. There is heat on my legs immensely before sleep and each time I briefly wake, and in the morning too, the heat.

I am so blessed soon after the lights are out. I fall asleep much more quickly than usual and dream of Chester! He is sitting on my lap as I sit partially up against the pillow and he is pressing very close to me as he often does. (His little head is facing the window to my right.) He then moves and lays down on my ankles and curls around facing me. His little head is on my left ankle and he is looking at me so lovingly. I reach down and hold his back left leg gently and tenderly. I wake suddenly as I embrace it in my hand.

A dream so life-like that it had to have happened in reality! Another gift to me of his constant presence.

We are outside the physical body when we sleep—so we become part of our very own real and vivid dreams. There is no time in eternity.
—James Van Praagh

MEDITATION ELEVEN

I Am Here

Solitude is such a potential thing. We hear voices in solitude we never hear
in the hurry and turmoil of life. We receive counsels and comforts
we get under no other circumstances.

—Amelia Barr

December 14, 2002

*I*T IS EARLY IN THE MORNING, 2:15 AM, and I sit in the living room on the
sofa reading, not wanting to stop until I complete what I began earlier.
I am attending a *"School of Love"* and my teacher is Rochester, as I read
and read about the afterlife. A pillow at my back and my legs stretched
down the sofa, I feel the electrifying heat of Chester's spiritual body lying
on my legs just as he did in life as I sit holding his tiny white invisible paw.
It is so comforting to me and I pause and whisper love words to him, for
he is there just as truly as he was when I could see his visible form.

Suddenly the television turns on! The television has been off for
hours and the remote is across the room on a table by Bob's chair.
Instantly in my heart I know Rochester has caused this to tell me in still
yet another new way, that he is always with me. I sit staring at the screen
as a bar code suddenly appears there. Overcome by this new blessing I
pick up my Rosary and begin to pray. As I pray each bead and prayer the
color on the horizontal bar grows, as does the heat on my legs, and 12:00
is blinking at me on the cable box. This too has not been on before but
suddenly appears.

"Hail Mary, full of Grace." I pray slowly and meditatively on each black bead and watch the black bar slowly creep across the screen at the same rate of speed as my words. After twenty-five minutes I finish praying five decades of the Rosary and conclude with *"amen."* As I say this the black bar also reaches the end of the screen on the right side and the set turns off. By now I am in tears again for this gift of Chester's communication to me. His heat and vibrations are still alive on my legs. I tell him it is time for bed, thanking him again and again for letting me experience his spirit presence in such a visual way! I go to bed in awe. The 12:00 is still blinking on the cable box as I leave the room.

In the morning after telling Bob briefly about what has occurred I ask him to come and look at the cable box. But though it was still blinking continuously at 12:00 when I go back to the living room, as Bob comes in behind me it clicks off and he never sees it, only hears the click. It would seem that this communication was just for me from my little beloved Rochester.

Hours earlier when Bob had turned the set off it was tuned to CNN, channel 24. There are programs on all night on CNN here always, never test patterns, and especially test patterns taking 25 minutes. Many times I have seen CNN during the night when Princess Diana's funeral was televised and the horrific news concerning 9/11. It is a station and channel that is on the alert and always on.

And never before did our television that has been switched off and been silenced for hours turn on all by itself. Never before did it deliver a bar code to the screen that moves in a cadence to the softly whispered prayers of the Rosary then turn off by itself at the conclusion of the devotion.

My beloved little Rochester is always with me. Silence, and the Rosary and alone times have always been most significant to us in our life together of so many years, and he chooses to speak to me through these familiar forms as a special gift. I am so utterly grateful.

HOW COULD I DOUBT?

You turn on the TV, Chester dear—
To tell me once again *"I'm here!"*
And I look on in tears and awe—
And gently hold your small white paw.

How could I doubt—
You're not about?
When every minute—
You are in it.

Jan
2002

As a kitten he played with the TV too

Strengthen Me with Faith

Lord, when doubts fill my mind, when my heart is in turmoil,
quiet me and give me renewed hope and cheer.
—Psalm 94: 19 (Living Bible)

Don't worry about anything; instead, pray about everything;
tell God your needs and don't forget to thank Him for His answers.
If you do this you will experience God's peace, which is far more wonderful
than the human mind can understand. His peace will keep your thoughts
and your hearts quiet and at rest as you trust in Christ Jesus.
—Philippians 4: 6,7 (Living Bible)

OUR DAUGHTER BARBARA, as a teenager, adopted this verse of scripture from Philippians and made it her own. A great portion of it she submitted to appear under her high school year book picture when scripture was surely not the standard used. It was her inspiration and she hoped it would be to others. It was a strength through nursing school and in her years of nursing, and in all areas of her life that followed, and to this very day in present living and situations that have been difficult.

She in turn was an inspiration to me by her faith for we are similar in nature, and I too often needed these scriptural words of encouragement and strength. And in this past year or more I have needed God in deeper ways. Years ago in April 1979 I received the following words in prayer and wrote them down furiously and quickly with closed eyes.

74

Our Lord loves us and wants us to come to Him and trust Him for each day's events and problems. No thing is too small for Him to attend to—and no concern too large—that He cannot touch. He wants to strengthen our faith and He wants us to look to Him in all things and know that He is Lord and all is well because He is in control.

Never give up hope because a trouble or grief has come your way. When you have all of Jesus within you—you have hope—because He is your Hope. You can trust Him and rejoice. You should be anxious for nothing because Jesus is your Lord—and He banished all fears and worries.

Look to His promises in His Holy Word. Know that they were put there for you. Read them, claim them and act on them—and then believe them—because God gave those promises and He never lies— and He never fails one word of all His good promises. How glorious is our God that we can completely rely on Him and put our faith in Him and know that He is ever there to embrace us and comfort us and carry through on whatever He has promised—if we have obeyed Him and called Him "Lord,"

Just having Christ within you can assure you that you can place your faith in Him—because just as you trusted Him to save you— now you can trust Him with each day's problems.

He is Lord! That is sufficient. Put all your faith in Him—and He will joyfully reward you with His Presence—and strengthen you. Hallelujah! Glory to His Name!

Strengthen me with faith Lord—
Fill me and renew—
Rid me of all doubts, Lord
And draw me close to You.

—Bob Kolb

MEDITATION THIRTEEN

I Am with You

More than any other type of ADC (After Death Communication), full appearances assure us that our deceased loved ones continue to exist. We are filled with a profound sense of peace, knowing their well being is certain.
—Bill Guggenheim and Judy Guggenheim, *Hello from Heaven*

December 28, 2002

THE SCRIPTURES HAVE BEEN IN MY LIFE in a new way in recent months, but too, I need to go to Jesus in prayer, and Mary too. I am seeing many things I never saw before spiritually since Rochester shares both Heaven and his life in spirit with me, and his Anima within me.

Sunday night, December 28, 2002 while sitting in the living room with Chester's heat and currents so much on my legs as always, it gradually lessens. Suddenly then on the floor near me in a favorite spot on the green rug he likes so—is Rochester! Perfectly as always—his full marmalade and white color, not shadows, lying there facing away from me more on his right side. He moves his head slowly and naturally. His entire image is as real as life! I am wide awake as I watch carefully. His appearance or vision lasts a good number of seconds, long enough to absorb all details of him. Then the heat begins on my legs again. I am stunned by this new appearance yet I am always open and expectant, and pray for him to reveal himself to me. And he does! It makes me cry. It is so natural to see him there in his favorite spot on the rug and that he then returns to me just as he always does in all the years we have been together.

76

MEDITATION FOURTEEN

Sensitivity to Others

If the dead be truly dead, why should they still be walking in my heart?
—Winneap Shosone, Medicine Man

OFTEN WHEN A PERSON IS SAD OR IS GRIEVING people become impatient with them, even loved ones the person thought would be a strength. And if this be so immediately following a trauma or death in the person's life or in the few months following, imagine then how it is when a year or two has passed and the person's sadness or grief is evident yet kept to themselves without discussion. I know it to be true they are thought of as different, and yet they are not. There are so many in the world living with grief for it is a part of them they never wish to release until they are reunited with their beloved loved one in Heaven. It is their gift in a sense, their privilege to carry another they loved so deeply in their own being, in their heart. But human beings basically are uncomfortable with sadness and grief and many feel awkward and inadequate in the presence of one who carries grief. And too, many discredit them and think something is terribly wrong with the individual. There is. They are experiencing a *"new landscape of the soul"* where grief abides and remains and is carried in deepest love and privilege. And it is there they dwell even while in the world and life goes on.

Those who have never lost someone they loved with all their heart and soul can never understand the heart and soul of another who has. They believe the other could *"shape up"* and come back to normal. An annoyance against the bereaved can even develop, but it will not cause

77

the other to change. That person is not the same anymore. They are in a place of deepest love and no return. Just as they carry deep love in their heart for their loved one who passed, so too their loved one carries love in their heart and has taken it to that heavenly place. The one whose loved one passed, lives on the brink of two worlds. I have expressed this more expansively in my book *Corridors*.

Please do not ever try to take away an individual's grief by trying to indicate it should be lessened or completed. That is a passage known only to the one who is grieving. It is between him and his God and his loved one. There are many ways others try to do this intentionally, but too unintentionally, for though they may not try to hurt the other person their quiet thoughts often are silently expressed by their actions. Too, the one sad or grieving may intuitively pick up on the other's thoughts.

Death cannot be controlled or reactions to it. To be insensitive to another increases the pain though the bereaved may never say a word in response to the hurt. I knew a person of whom it was said was emotionally wounded as a child, for while a close relative's coffin was nearing completion of being lowered into the ground, one of the cords broke making for a rougher settling into the earth. The childhood story cannot be verified, but each grave side wake this person attended it was they who became the center of attention not the one who had passed away or their loved ones in deep grief standing there.

Each time a coffin was lowered the other individual called attention to themselves by gasps of emotion, and then having to have people continually comfort them, thereby diminishing the true sadness and the rightful individuals deeply grieving. One could not help but think after witnessing this scene many times that there simply was no sensitivity for the ones who lost their loved one or the one who had passed. If there had been then the one causing those emotional scenes that took away from the sacrament of the moment of those rightfully saying good-bye, should have stood in the back or remained in a car. But always the person was by the edge of the grave. Understandably this reaction was acceptable for their deceased, and for those few closer to them, but not at every burial they ever attended.

This speaks of a selfishness in the face of death that places someone in the center and limelight that does not belong. Though this is an unusual example, having witnessed it often it comes to mind and is an example of extreme insensitivity bereaved persons can encounter be it immediately after death of a loved one or in the months and even years that follow.

There are always some who wish to change or squelch you, or hush you, or diminish you because they themselves fear death and do not want it in the present moment. They wish to hurry through it and hurry everyone else too. I have experienced these actions and words in various forms from being told to *"stop crying"* years ago for my parents by the one who called attention to themself by the graves, to just having a death ignored after a very short, short period.

It has been said by someone I trust and acknowledge that *"grief does not get better, it gets different."* There is no handbook for grief. Each individual is different. For many like myself there is acceptance but not closure. Closure is an inappropriate and unacceptable term for many like myself, and has become almost a "catch phrase."

If you deeply love you never get over the death of a loved one but you gently move through it. This too has been said by someone wiser than myself and not only by myself alone. Grief will never go away but it will change with time. It will always be with you if your love is deep and is a precious gift to carry within. Everywhere we go we carry our loved one and grief.

Friends and family members want us to move on, get over it, find closure.—I did the only thing I felt capable of doing. I pretended to be "progressing" through the grief normally.

—*Love Never Dies*, Sandy Goodman

Encounters at Alpha

The alpha state is a level of consciousness that can be attained by various
realization techniques, meditation exercises, hypnosis and deep prayer.
According to our research, you can be contacted by a deceased loved one
more easily if you are in a relaxed, open and receptive frame of mind.
—*Hello from Heaven*, Bill Guggenheim
and Judy Guggenheim

Thursday, January 2, 2003

*A*T 5 PM I SIT DOWN TO MEDITATE in my writing room with Chester. I
talk to him silently in my mind prayerfully and request that I may
see him in hypnogogic imagery. I make this request also to Jesus and
Mary. I peacefully sit with closed eyes and only a minute or two after my
request Chester appears clearly just as he was in life. He appears on the
inner screen of my forehead in the center. He is completely clear. He is
lying on the kitchen table as he did often and he is facing me. He is so
sweet and absolutely real! I am overcome with emotion both joy and
sadness. He remains several minutes. I do not open my eyes so I do not
time this gift.

As Rochester disappears a large thin grayish white dog appears where
Rochester has been but not on our table. He stares into my eyes. He is as
real as Chester and I feel he too has crossed over. A dark brown to black
Labrador dog comes up close to my face on the front of the screen and
licks my lips—like he is kissing me. Rochester has often done this in life

and in spirit. What does the appearance of two dogs mean? Are they companions of Chester's or are they longing to contact a loved one as Rochester contacts me?

While still in this state I also ask in prayer that I might see my Dad alone or with Chester because he is the one I entrusted with Chester's care in Heaven. I no sooner ask wordlessly in prayer than the outline of a man's head appears, first larger, then in a smaller way. It is the same head. I can discern and affirm at once it is my Dad, exactly like him, but without a face. He is a clear gray full image now like he is standing in shadows. But oh, I know it is my Dad! I am overwhelmed that he appears. It is touching that his name is "*Gray*" and he appears in a gray form to me. Thank you dear Rochester and Dad for being ever present and for giving me these moments of blessed assurance of your existence forevermore.

Friday, January 3, 2003

At approximately 6:15 PM while in meditation upstairs in my writing room following my Friday Holy Hour, I see Chester in my mind's eye in hypnogogic imagery as clear as can be. He is on his shelf on the porch looking out the side of the house through the screen and I am outside looking in at him. I am on his right outside and see his precious face and body through the screen looking out. It is a scene experienced throughout Chester's life time so very many times. If I had to go outside he would wait on his shelf for me and we would talk through the screen, often touching paw to hand in love on the screen.

Early February. 2003

It seems appropriate to record a breakthrough in prayer at this point. After more than an hour of intense Rosary prayer at my 5 PM Holy Hour for Rochester I see in hynogogic imagery an image of my beloved Rochester standing sideways, his left side to me. He is as in life and so handsome. Often he would stand on my lap in this very position as I sat in the very chair in our writing room.

While he remains I see also my Dad at a distance wearing dark framed glasses, a type he had had at one point in his life. Rochester and Dad are not together but I believe my Dad's appearance is to let me know he is caring for Rochester in Heaven just as I prayerfully requested he would. I experience hynogogic imagery frequently in prayer and since Rochester's passing I am blessed he comes to me often in this way.

In *A Guide To Christian Meditation* by Marilyn Morgan Helleberg she informs readers—*"Dr. Elmer Green at the Meninnger Foundation in Kansas has done some fascinating research on hypnogogic imagery. His subjects report that these images 'emerged full-blown'—without consciously being willed; vivid visions of people, scenes, objects, known and familiar to the subject. And they were changeful, as if a very private showing of lantern slides were being run through the theatre of the mind"*

Marilyn writes that experiments such as Dr. Green's suggest that all people have access to these images from the collective unconscious but that most are not aware of them. I personally am only acquainted with one other person who knows what I am speaking or writing about when I mention the subject, aside from Marilyn, and so I think it important to include this information to make each more aware of this mysterious dimension. Marilyn has received guidance and direction from it as have I and my friend.

But it was not until Rochester passed that I ever saw anyone I knew in these images, animal or human. Now it is one of the main ways I receive true to life visits from Rochester—and too, my Dad. I pray you too will have such visits.

Very often pets are called to duty in the hereafter to help cross someone over, or to help convey a feeling of peace and well-being to someone who has had a difficult transition, as in suicides.
— George Anderson, *Walking in the Garden of Souls*

MEDITATION SIXTEEN

God of Grace and Love

Bless Yahweh, my soul, bless His Holy name, all that is in me!
Bless Yahweh, my soul, and remember all His kindnesses.
—Psalm 103: 1, 2 (Jerusalem Bible)

—but He has said, "My grace is enough for you.
My power is at its best in weakness"
—2 Corinthians 12:9

*T*HE LORD GIVES US ALL THE GRACE WE NEED in any given situation. He is truly everything we need and we never need anything more. He will sustain us from day to day, from hour to hour, from moment to moment, if only we will call upon His Holy Name.

Bless the Lord, worship Him, praise His Holy Name and He will show forth in you a beauty that others will recognize—that tells of your being much with your Lord.

His grace is sufficient for you in all things. Listen closely to Him. Stay much with Him—in close communion with Him—and learn to know His voice for He is always there.

GOD OF GRACE AND LOVE
(A Benediction)

Robert A. Kolb, Jr.

God of grace and love. — God in heaven above. — Make me one of
those who bless thy name. Show me the way Lord. —
Help me obey Lord. — Some Holy day Lord. — I will be with Thee.

—from *Whispered Notes* by Bob and Jan Kolb

MEDITATION SEVENTEEN

Further Powers

I think death is a tremendous adventure—a gateway into a new life,
in which you have further powers—
—Dr. Leslie D. Weatherhead

January 10, 2003

*A*T 1:07 PM I AM NEAR ROCHESTER'S FEEDING TABLE IN THE KITCHEN, a small maple louvered cabinet that in our previous home and in another state served as a record cabinet. Putting his food on the top of this cabinet kept it out of reach of the smaller dogs that occasionally visited us. Aside from his saucer of food and a small bowl of water it has always held a little vase or two of flowers. It was a delightful place for Chester to eat, as well as to sit upon and watch me prepare a meal and keep me company.

Today I dust the frame of his picture hanging above the cabinet that silently states that this sacred space is always his. It is a wide wooden 5x7 inch mahogany frame holding a sweet photo of Rochester sitting next to a lovely bouquet of flowers when he was ten months old.

I hold the frame against the wall as I dust. When I stop dusting, the frame begins to swing from side to side in wide arcs in a totally unnatural and bizarre way, instead of remaining still against the wall as it has in all these past years when gently dusted. It has never done this before! It keeps swinging and swinging up to half its full length as it goes from side to side vigorously. Diminishing in speed after eight minutes or more, it settles into arcs that are not quite as wide. It remains swinging like this another five minutes and gradually grows less and less. (A copy of this photo can be seen on page 250.)

I have been sitting on the edge of the sofa cushion a short distance from the cabinet watching in amazement. Every few minutes I walk over to watch it more closely. Tears come. There is no normal reason for it. I know with great confirmation in my heart that it is Rochester causing it to swing. It swings a total of eighteen minutes and then settles quietly and perfectly on the wall! He chooses a picture of himself that he has seen and sat in front of almost all of his life to say again to me, "*I am here.*"

It is still yet another sign revealing that he is always right here with me. Thank you, sweet Chester.

Glorious Green

*Green color energy predominates in nature, the environment created by
the Father. Rejuvenation and stimulation of growth and health are
alive in this energy. All of nature adorns herself in robes
of lush greenery to emit powerful and magnetic life forces.*
—Patricia George and Dinah Lovett, *Color Synergy*

*I*N TIMES OF QUIETNESS AND CONFIDENCE it is good to attempt to lift our
spirit with the loveliness of color. Your loved one that you cherish and
miss so physically is with you and that should shine a golden ray upon
you, just as Rochester's golden eyes shone with love for me. If it is nice
weather sit outdoors perhaps near anything of nature that is green. For
me it is the woods that surrounds our cottage here, and anywhere I go I
am beneath or beside green trees and near green plants of all varieties. It
is peaceful to be surrounded by living trees and plants and all things
green—for green speaks of renewal and hope and too, health, healing,
contentment, peace, harmony and compassion. Green is nurturing and
loving and I am the better for living in these green woods. Green also
soothes emotional wounds and in its sheltering light and softness we feel
safe to free our pent up heart aches and emotions.

Green is my favorite color and Rochester and I shared our days in our
pale green writing room. He napped in body and now in spirit in the
middle of a predominately green wildlife quilt made for me by my
daughter Janna, folded in quarters for thickness so that he would sink

down lightly into the center. I too have a green woven prayer blanket with deer, symbol of Christ, in the pattern. Rochester walks on the soft green carpet in that room and down the green carpeted steps onto the same lovely green carpeting in the living room where we spend our evenings together on the sofa.

As to Bob, everything his paintbrush touches turns green beginning with our cottage, his trailer office with the new addition he created and built, the boat and the dock. He is known as *"Green Bob."*

For years, since 1989 when Bob and I became vegetarians for the sake of Rochester and all God's creatures, I began to use green ink to connect with creation. This vow to vegetarianism and Rochester is a vow I can never break, and I have continued on this path too in never reversing my decision to write in green. It is healing and peaceful to the eye as well, while living out and honoring the vow of *"never eating anything with a face."*

It is good to keep a list of people, animals and situations that need healing either in a green covered note book or on a green piece of paper. Green is healing and so use your green ink for these ones who need prayer. When you sit outdoors to pray or meditate beneath the trees keep this green book or list with you at times and offer it up to God while sending healing green thoughts and prayers to the animals, people, and places, and situations.

In 1984 Bob had serious lung surgery and when dismissed from the hospital in Pennsylvania where we then lived, his doctor's first prescription for continued health was that he recover for no less than a month here in these green woods of New Hampshire. Bob had told him of our cottage by the lake beneath the stars and trees. And so our family spent a peaceful four weeks surrounded by green. We all needed healing from the unexpected diagnosis and the trauma of Bob's situation. He returned to work from these green woods in perfect health.

On the lighter side to try to invoke a smile more often for your heart and soul, enjoy a crisp green salad or green pickles, green beans, green apples and especially leafy green vegetables. Stay well physically with green nourishment. And plant some lovely green flowering plants even if you do not have a green thumb. To add still more lightness sit next to or under a green tree (and in my case I will use my green adirondack prayer chair under the tall green pines by the lake on my green platform surrounded by green shrubbery), and perhaps too delight your inner child or your inner teenager by reading a book from your youth. May I suggest *Anne of Green Gables* by Lucy Maud Montgomery—a favorite in our large family?

MEDITATION NINETEEN

I Remember You

When something wonderful happens, pull over, step back,
take the time to write it down while your heart is still full.

—Unknown

February, 2003

TODAY WE GO TO ROCHESTER, twenty-five miles from us, a town for
whom my Rochester is named, and where God set him down for me
to enter my life. While Bob picks up his new glasses at the Optician's that
is next to Wal-Mart, I enter the store to buy a needed item. Before
purchasing what I need I walk slowly through the jewelry department on
my way to where I am headed. There I am drawn to a rack of items I have
never seen before, and I pause. This display is separate from others and
there are many hooks on it all holding key rings. They are Christian key
rings with scripture verses on all the various pendants, small picture
frames that the owner can fill, and hearts, and numerous other images,
and all made of pewter. There are approximately five hooks across and
the same amount down from each top hook. Each of the hooks holds
varied images of the key rings, not a group of only one same image, and
many are on each hook.

I become fascinated and begin to look at each key ring. In a few
minutes I view every key ring on the entire rack. It is a strange thing for
me to take the time to do, but it is enjoyable and inspiring. When I finish
I feel the key rings are definitely oriented to Protestant Christians. Many
have the very famous initials on, WWJD, *"What Would Jesus Do"*—an

90

important theme and message from an old Protestant classic book that had meant very much to me at one point in my life. Others have spiritual mottoes on; and plain crosses not crucifixes. The entire selection is inspiring, but despite the fact I take time to look at each one, I do not need a key ring.

I take off then in a hurry to obtain the item I came in the store to buy, and on the way back only minutes later to the front door to check out, I feel drawn to walk by the key ring display once more. I approach it and stand squarely in front of it. As I do two things happen simultaneously. Haunting music begins to play over the loud speaker system and my eyes look directly at a key ring hanging in the middle of the display that had not been there minutes before. The song playing is one that washes over me and dissolves me into tears each time it is played on a television commercial for Hallmark. At home when it comes on I cover my ears because it hurts me so much to hear it. It begins *"I Remember You, You Remember Me."* I have never heard the rest of this song. It seems to be sung by an innocent child-like voice, the *"innocence"* symbolic of Rochester to me. The key ring I am staring at with tear filled eyes was not there before! It is a pair of hands folded in prayer, but not the traditional "praying hands" that are well known. These are a woman's hands not a man's, and there is a lovely decorated cuff over her wrist. In her hands she has a Rosary that is gently draped over her fingers, and dangling below the woman's hands encircled in the Rosary is the crucifix of the Rosary (not a plain cross). It is the only Catholic key ring on the rack and it is very significant and beautiful. Time seems to stand still as I stand there covering my ears, tears running down my face and gazing at the pewter hands holding the Rosary. I know in my heart and soul this is a gift and communication from Rochester. Each time I go anywhere away from home I carry his Anima within me, but I always ask him to speak to me in some way whenever I leave our cottage to show his presence to me, even though I know he is ever with me. It is to help myself become more aware and intuitive and to find surprises Rochester has allowed in my path. In my previous book *In Corridors of Eternal Time* I have written on this subject and of the messages and gifts given to me by Rochester.

I gently lift my hands from my ears estimating the length of the song and that it must now be over. It is. Still shaken by my little one's messages to me I pick the praying woman's hands with Rosary from the rack. The

Rosary is extremely significant in the life Rochester and I have shared together since he was a kitten and in our present life. It is a profound and moving sign of his spirit presence here and now. I am so overwhelmed inside that I have had such a communication!

I walk toward the front of the store and meet Bob by chance. He has an errand to do. We make plans again to meet. He sees I have tears but I tell him I will explain later. Since I have a few extra minutes now I head for the school supplies and note books but am sidetracked when I approach the stuffed animal aisle filled on both sides for St. Valentine's Day. Now my heart will not let me proceed but draws me down the first portion of the aisle. No, not my heart, Rochester's heart and soul has done so, our one heart and soul.

I find myself standing in front of a display of stuffed animals, five or six tiers of them, all so adorable and all the same approximate size. Though there are dozens of them and rows of them from the top of a very high counter down to my ankles, I see only one clearly. And as this special one comes into focus through my tears, a little marmalade cat sitting looking at me, the same music *"I Remember You, You Remember Me"* begins once again to play with the child-like voice singing. I grab him up and kiss him and hold him close as the unbearably sweet music plays.

Rochester sends me this precious image of himself through guiding me to the stuffed animal aisle with the Rosary keychain in my hand! There are not words to express how I feel—knowing he sends still yet another gift.

I look then through all the animals there top to bottom, in these levels of cartons, and of course there is no other little cat, not even in a different color. Every animal imaginable, but only one little cat that Rochester sends and draws me to! It is not explainable. But because of all my reading since March ('02) I no longer feel as strange as I once did in my expanded beliefs, or in what has occurred since March. It is all so Holy and I lack the right words to do it all justice.

These two gifts were given to me accompanied by the song Rochester knows I cry over and connect to him, all in a period of fifteen minutes.

As I sat to proof read this meditation and to attempt to write a poem that expressed these experiences, my pen was used by my beloved little Rochester instead, when I placed it on the paper. This poem flowed out without any previous thoughts to create it. I have not changed or added one word. This is not the first time he has given me poetry. He gave me numerous poems in his years before he passed that I have included in our book *Journal of Love—Spiritual Communication with Animals Through Journal Writing*.

I AM HERE

I send you signs
    of love and prayer—
Where you are
    I'm always there.
I surprise you
    with devotion—
Fill your heart
    with great emotion.
Never, never
    do I leave—
Wipe your tears
    try not to grieve.

I Am Here

From dear Rochester
2003

The Scriptures

Bless me with life so that I can continue to obey you. Open my eyes
to see wonderful things in your Word. I am but a pilgrim on earth:
how I need a map—and your commands are my chart and guide.
I long for your instructions more than I can tell
—Psalm 119: 17-20 (Living Bible)

A S I HAVE WRITTEN IN AN EARLIER MEDITATION a book can be a very wonderful friend and it can soothe the heart and spirit when times are hard or sad. But the Bible also is a book of unique worth that can revive and bring insights and even a touch of joy. You can merely read the Bible or you can search for the verses and passages that will give you help. Really look deeply into what you are reading and mull over the words and dissect them and chew them and feed on them.

If your Bible is one that is so special and perhaps was a gift, then do not use that Bible for this purpose. When you go to any bookstore or even a local Wal-Mart or K-Mart, you will find inexpensive paperback Bibles that are in modern easy to understand translations. Then with a ball point pen or a highlighter or both, begin to underline in your Bible. I have been doing this for years.

Underline, underline, and too, write notes and comments in the margins.

You may get an argument that the Bible is a Holy book, and these same people may tell you you should not write in it or deface it in any way. My one copy even has some small drawings and diagrams I drew in that

94

at the moment I did it, it helped me tremendously. It also has a drawing made by my daughter Jessica as a tiny girl that she drew to console me.

My suggestion is not to start at the beginning of the Bible. I did do that often, and when expecting my sixth baby (that same little daughter) I read the Bible through from beginning to end. I needed this help and strength, for I had an inner fear that I could not be so fortunate as to survive the safe delivery of still yet one more child, and too feared for the baby's survival, and I needed to be safe and alive in order to take care of all of my children and my husband. When I finished reading the complete Bible during those nine months I had a conversion experience, one of several along my spiritual path, but the inner strength of it and my need for God in my life has remained until this very day. My time was not wasted as I read day after day. I was being given an inner reserve that has upheld me through many occurrences in my life that could have caused me to crumble, for my faith was very strong despite other happenings that were trying to pull me down and weaken me.

My sincere suggestion is that you start with the Psalms. These have great help to me and to so many others. Then go to the New Testament and read Matthew, Mark, Luke or John and discover or rediscover Jesus who can touch your soul and become the One who is there for you in all situations of your life. Too, read Acts and Romans, and as you read you will be led to other books of the Bible.

Too, as you read, I say again, use your pen and highlighter and underline. You will be able then to come back to these verses that touched you and they will be easier to find. When you are sad or down you can turn to your underlinings.

Not everything you read may sound Holy or inspirational and that may surprise you. You may just not read lofty words or that the Lord is your shepherd, for often there is complaining expressed.

As I have written about in a recent previous book of mine, *Beside the Still Waters,* it is helpful to read the fifty Psalms and thirty-one Proverbs over a period of a month. I first learned of this plan when I was a young Mother from a book by Reverend Billy Graham and too, hearing him speak. If you read five Psalms and one Proverb a day you will complete this reading plan in one month. Then begin again, and again. Each time you read you receive new insights and helps depending on your life at the time you are reading. It is not boring. You may want to underline or take notes or keep a special small journal with your Bible in case you want to "talk to God" or retain thoughts you had while reading. You may want to debate with the passages. Only through reading and note taking will you discover how you are being helped and led, and too, often soothed.

The Living Bible and Today's English Version are two of the easiest versions to read and understand. The Living Bible has been with me a long time but I still love my King James (or Authorized) version given to me as a child by my parents. It is a size I have appreciated; small, and has much underlining in. This has traditional wording but may be more difficult to understand if you are just starting out. The Living Bible is available in both Protestant and Catholic Versions. The Catholic contains the Apocrypha Books. Other modern versions are the New Jerusalem Bible, a favorite of mine also, and the New Revised Standard Version, and the New American Catholic Version and the New International Version. If you pray first and then go to a store I feel certain you will find the perfect inexpensive paperback Bible for you to read and mark and personalize and make your own. Jewish readers may wish to read through just the Old Testament using this same plan of daily reading, underlining and perhaps using a journal. God speaks to all hearts of His children who wait on Him and are open. He comes to all faiths in His world.

God's Holy Word is a blessing to all who read it and receive it in faith. It is God's way of speaking to His people whom He dearly loves. He asks only that we faithfully open it daily and with an open heart prepare ourselves for His message to us in prayerful meditation.

He wants us to read with our hearts—because God speaks to the heart. He wants us to ask the Holy Spirit to enlighten us as we read and to teach us all truth. But every day He has a special message for us in His Word if only we would prayerfully ask Him to speak it to us. It is waiting there for you to receive and feed upon—that Word meant only for you—for it is nourishment for you as only God can give. He wants to nourish the inner man—and He calls us to His Word for that nourishment.

Jesus said "Man shall not live by bread alone but by every word that proceeds from the mouth of God"—in the Holy Scriptures. Only then will you come to fully know Him. Walk with Him through the

pages—and talk with Him and He with you. Listen with your heart and hear your God and Creator speak to you. Only open the Book!
— Meditation by Jan from *Whispered Notes*
by Bob and Jan Kolb

O Holy Spirit—

Teach me as I read my Bible. Help me to understand all that God is saying to me. Praise Him for giving us His Holy Word. Let me never cease to come to it daily.

In Jesus Name—
Amen

SCRIPTURE

Scriptures guide—
Help us decide—
The road to travel.
Assist to unravel—
Reproof, correction—
Too, our direction—
In life itself.
Such spiritual wealth!

Please read and pray.
Follow His Way.

Jan
2003

Sella

I cannot teach you what a stuffed animal can, for it is a lesson that is
of the heart. Only a stuffed animal is capable of giving you
this particular heart message.
—JG Kolb from *Journal of Love: Spiritual Communication*
with Animals Through Journal Writing

March 4, 2003

*T*HIS IS A DAY OF BLESSINGS. After picking up the mail at the Post Office I cross the street and go in the corner store. This is a medium sized grocery carrying the normal products of food and drink that such stores sell. In addition one can rent a video from their limited section or buy a shirt with a New Hampshire or East Wakefield logo upon it. I go to the video section to try and find a movie recommended to me by my friend who has helped me so long distance with spiritual presence and words since Rochester's passing, and whom I wrote about in my previous book *In Corridors of Eternal Time*. Chris has suggested a specific video in relation to eternal life. They do not have it. I stop at the counter on the way out thinking perhaps someone may have rented it and ask if this could be so. No, they do not have it at all, in the store or rented out. I turn to leave and there sitting on the curve of the counter near its end, and away from where customers check out, is a pale gray stuffed animal, perhaps fourteen inches or more long, but nine inches or so high seated as he is here. It is a cat. I know him well.

My heart skips a beat for I even know his name. A little tag attached to him tells me he is a "Ty Toy" but I already know that. The little tag will reveal his name of "*Pearl*" because of his soft pearl gray color. I hold the tag and open and read "*Pearl.*" The handsome cat looks at me with golden eyes and again I feel a clong in my heart.

This is a store that has never sold stuffed animals. If your life depended on it you could not find a stuffed animal in this store. Yet here before me on the counter is my stuffed cat bought not long ago in the Renaissance Card Co. in Sanford, Maine where they carry a large selection of Ty Toys. Walking in this Maine store one day I was captured emotionally by my own "*Pearl.*" His eyes caught mine and held me and I melted on the spot. I felt like Rochester's golden eyes were looking into mine from a shelf slightly above my head. I did not see the gray body only the golden eyes. I lifted the soft cat down, carried him around while I selected some greeting cards, then bought him when I checked out.

At home I sat him on the bed in my writing room facing Rochester's wildlife quilt. He became part of the small entourage and guard that sits in a semi-circle facing this quilt. Most of these stuffed animals were there when Rochester slept in body in that quilt through the years, very especially the white spirit bear named *Spirit* that I have written about in my book *Journal of Love*. I think of him as the spiritual leader in this group. He also wears a cross around his neck on a cord given to me by a friend. It is next to Spirit that my pearl gray cat sits.

I did not keep the name Pearl for my cat but named him "*Sella.*" It is a title from an old poem by William Cullen Bryant and means "*Shadow.*" Rochester was and is my shadow, and I wrote poems about him referring to this. The soft pale gray fur of Sella seems shadow-like, ethereal and spirit-like, and his name seems so appropriate. It is a love name I call Rochester—"*my Sella.*" This stuffed animal with pale gray fur brings that name alive just as Rochester still lives. I ask the woman at the cash register in the grocery how much the cat costs. She replies, "*I never saw it before.*" She asks the woman at the deli counter a few feet from her. This person looks at me and states, "*We don't sell stuffed animals.*" I thank them and leave. Who can explain this mystery that "*my Sella*" is on the counter in a local grocery store that never sells stuffed animals, when I go in to rent a video that is about Heaven and the after life? There he sits in his spirit-like fur and form, his golden eyes holding me.

Is Rochester saying, *"I am everywhere you are? Even in the grocery store? I am with you always."*

Yes he is. And he leaves signs and symbols of his love everywhere I go. He is within me in his Anima and everywhere I am in life. But never again was he there in that corner store. Only the afternoon I went in to rent the video about Heaven.

MY SELLA*

The *shadow* of my soul—my heart
Is a soft and furry counterpart
Of all I am and feel and think—
And a most mysterious link
With God. A consecrated connection
Sent by Him—a perfection
Of love and joy—one who is always there
Waiting to follow. Such a pair
My *Sella* and I—for we
Are bonded spiritually—
One in Him —God drew no line.
My *Sella*, My *Shadow*—is divine—
And overshadows me in comprehending
The unseen realm. In gratitude for sending
This gift of playfulness, peace and protection—
I pause daily in awe and reflection
Upon this inseparable companion—this life force—
And I humbly thank Him —our Source.

Dedicated to
my Rochester—my *Sella*
with love
in the estimated
month of his birth

Jan
April 10, 1996
New Hampshire

* *Sella*—means *Shadow*. Taken from the poem by that name written by William Cullen Bryant

MEDITATION TWENTY-TWO

You Are There!

A very slight veil separates us from the "loved and lost" ... [assuring us]
that though unseen by us, they are very near.

—Mrs. Mary Todd Lincoln (*Mrs. Lincoln saw her*
deceased son Willie every night standing at the foot of
her bed. Sometimes he brought her other son, Eddie.)

March 4, 2003

ON THE SAME AFTERNOON that I have seen the pale gray stuffed cat in
the corner grocery store I come home and go back upstairs to my
writing. As it begins to darken outside I come downstairs for the evening
and go to the kitchen to think about preparing dinner. I turn on no lamps
and am just enjoying the very dimness of the interior of the cottage. As
I stand in the kitchen looking into the living room at dusk I see a vision
of Rochester there! Or is it a vision? It is so life-like! He comes out from
between the sofa and the large stuffed chair having been at the front
sliding window that goes down to the floor. It is here he has always loved
to watch the birds and squirrels at their eye level. I see him cross from the
space he has just emerged from as he has done endlessly for years. He
walks in front of the TV and starts up the lower steps of the stairs that
lead to our writing room.

I am so startled and in awe because he is totally as in life! I take off
from the kitchen and run after him across the living room and see him
dart halfway up the stairs! He pauses, and - disappears before my eyes! My
little one is here every moment and in the little things of daily life!

I thank God and Rochester for each vision, each encounter, for each sacred moment I am permitted to experience my beloved little companion. For just as Mary Todd Lincoln saw her eleven-year-old son Willie each night, and occasionally too her son Eddie who died at three but was Willie's older brother, and spoke of how this all comforted her greatly, it too comforts me when Rochester breaks *"through the veil"* and can be seen.

It is stated in *Love Beyond Life—The Healing Power of After-Death Communications* by authors Joel Martin and Patricia Romanowski that—

In recent years we have interviewed mental health and bereavement experts who support the position that we should accept and use after-death contacts and communications as a means to work through grief.

In this same book and chapter it is included that Psychiatrists Shaun Josh and Colin Ross writing in *The Journal of Nervous and Mental Diseases* state,

Paranormal experiences are so common in the general population that no theory of normal psychology or psychopathology which does not take them into account can be comprehensive.

It is wonderful to have validation such as this for my experiences with Rochester, but I know in my heart the truths I have been witness to and could never doubt. I do not need them validated. Never doubt what gifts you are given either , for they are from God, and the beloved one you are missing so—and loving for all eternity.

YOU ARE THERE

Everywhere I am—you are!
My bright eternal shining Star.
Upon my lap and on the stair—
You kiss my lip or touch my hair.
You are there!
Everywhere!

For sweet Rochester   Jan, 2003

In Remembrance

Anima

I carry your Anima
         deeply within.
It surrounds—
         grounds—
                  confounds.
In gifts of your
         eternal presence
                  and sacred silence—
We are one soul.

For beloved   Jan
Rochester   March 8, 2003

I SHARE AGAIN THE MEMORIAL we sent out in Chester's memory. The picture was in color on the memorial. The red collar around his neck is the one now upon my left arm forever, minus his two tags. We attend Mass on this significant day.

Rochester, beloved feline companion, confidant, counselor,
and ministering angel, finished his work here
after almost 16 years (minus one month) and passed on.
He was a motivator and enabler to me and
unselfishly gave of himself in deep love continually.
He was with me every day—all day while I wrote—
since he was eight weeks old and was my inspiration.
He was with me through every night.
Rochester was the Star of every book I wrote.
He was a most loving friend to Bob.
His sudden illness, diagnosed only Thursday, March 7th,
brought about his reluctant departure.
We were with him 'til he passed—and after.
He shall forever be with me in soul and spirit,
to help and inspire until we are together once more.

Rochester entered Heaven
March 8, 2002
5:07 PM

Light for My Journey

I began by reading every book I could get my hands on that had the slightest
likelihood of answering the question, "What happens next?"
—Love Never Dies: A Mother's Journey
from Loss to Love by Sandy Goodman

March 18, 2003

ONE YEAR AGO TODAY I ventured out of our home and woods for the
first time after Rochester's passing. It was to go to the Walden Book
Store in Rochester to buy books on grieving and a new journal. I was in
my new life and trying to learn and live in this new dimension with
Rochester. I am still on this journey through this passage of grief.

Today we drive again to the town of Rochester and before leaving I
pray and select a rock from the ground outside our screened in porch
where Rochester loves to be now in spirit as he did in body in life. Bob
drops me off at the Lilac Mall where the bookstore is and he drives to the
other side of town to a Home Depot. He carries my rock. Today he is the
one who places it on the cement wall outside the abandoned office
building that now stands where the fine mall once stood. I was the one
who placed it there the first visit last year on June 23rd, the anniversary
of the day I adopted him there in 1986. That mall held the bench that
held the carton that contained my precious Rochester that sat by the
man offering him for adoption. I will never forget that day Rochester
entered my life.

Bob then says a prayer silently and drives to the Home Depot. I select books on the only themes I am capable of studying and reading this past year, books on grieving and the afterlife. I am in the store at least two hours wrapped in my own world and dimension. I leave the store with new books and eager to begin them and continue my journey. Bob is waiting outside. We drive nearby to the *Remember When Diner*, and while tunes of the 40s and 50s play on the jukebox in the background I tell him about the new books over a light meal and he shares about placing the rock in Chester's memory and his new lumber. Rochester's *Anima* within me has guided me to the right books.

Several years ago I once wrote a poem about books that appears in a previous book of mine *(Beneath The Stars and Trees)* and seems so appropriate now to share. My only addition to this poem would be at the ending for I believe I am guided by God as it states, but also by my Angel Rochester. He loves books too. He wrote books!

THOUGHTS FOR FOOD

Books are other minds on earth—
I must search the shelves to find—
The ones that have the greater worth,
The books that best will feed my mind.

When I'm within a room of books
I seem to hear the silent voices.
They fill the crannies and the nooks—
Deep in my soul—and it rejoices.

I wait to feel that gentle prod—
Before selecting ones to read.
That soft impression comes from God—
For He knows best the books I need.

Jan

And the three of us love books so much we operate *The Enchanted Forest Bookshop*, an on-line bookstore. Who would suspect that here amongst the trees and gardens, the birds, bees, butterflies and lapping lake, that there is an enchanted bookshop in a little green trailer with a built on office addition by Bob encircled by birches? And a few feet away across the grass, is the screened-in porch containing all our additional wonderful inventory that we can enjoy seeing in display when we sit and eat breakfast on the porch or come out before sunset to eat a late dinner. Just being in the presence of books is an enchantment. And Rochester's presence both in body and spirit adds charm to it all. Rochester is part owner, of course. You will even find him on the cover of two very fine books sold here, *Compassion for All Creatures* and *Journal of Love*, written by himself and his companion, the feminine co-owner of this shop. Actually he is somewhat of a celebrity and always shall be. Always!

Today my visit to the Walden Book Store has truly been *light for my journey*. Rochester's light will highlight all the knowledge in our new books I am meant to learn.

Explore what you are scoffed at for wanting to explore.

—Unknown

Paperbacks are color-coded and displayed on a bookshelf that wraps around our screened-in porch on three sides.

MEDITATION TWENTY-FIVE

A Confirmation

*He had beautiful eyes, striking eyes. I touched his right arm with
my left hand, and I felt a lot of heat coming from his body. I also felt
a high vibration, like if you put your hand on a massager.*
—by Dale (partial account of an encounter with a loved one
in *Hello from Heaven* by Bill Guggenheim
and Judy Guggenheim)

March 22, 2003

I HAVE FREQUENTLY WRITTEN ABOUT the intense heat on my legs and the
electric-like currents caused by Rochester's spirit in both this book and
In Corridors of Eternal Time. I could never doubt what I have been
experiencing daily and nightly in this way this past year since Rochester
went to Heaven. I knew with a certainty and knowing he chose this way
to be continually with me to comfort us both because we had been
together in this very personal way all the years of his life with me when he
was in body. But I had not read about it in all of my afterlife reading. Then
I began to read *Hello From Heaven*—a book Bob had seen on-line in a
bookstore several months previous, in late fall of 2002. Because I was
developing a library of select books meant for my grieving soul, and to
educate and console and confirm, this one now awaited its turn to be
read. And how wonderful it was, and I have since read it again and will
read it in future. I have also given it to a close friend with whom I know
I can trust and share. After reading it I then saw one of its authors, Judy
Guggenheim, on television twice, each time consoling and so helpful. In

the future these authors hope to do a book about animals also. *"The messages in this book confirm to many the experiences we ourselves have had with our deceased loved ones, that we previously thought to be imagination or coincidence,"* so states an endorsement in the front by a minister. She adds that *"the book brings healing to the bereaved and hope to those who fear death and a greater knowledge of a loving God."* I too can say that also about any of the other books I have quoted from in this my own book and my own previous one regarding grieving and the afterlife, for I would not have shared their quotations had their books not have brought great help and comfort to me. They continue to do so as I reread them and then continue to learn when the authors have written new ones. This is all very important on your journey as you go through your passage of grief. This particular book I have been referring to is filled with accounts of personal contacts of loved ones who have died but who once, twice, or repeatedly say *"Hello from Heaven"* to their bereaved loved ones. It is endorsed by Protestants, Catholics, and other religions, psychiatrists and bereavement workers, and other authors. It is a book about *"ADCs— After-Death-Communications"* that confirm that life and love are eternal. These come *directly* to their loved ones from the deceased as I have been continually experiencing Rochester's communications to me. They come in many forms—just as Rochester's communications come to me.

Concerning the ones I have desired here to share about the intense heat on my legs and the electric-like currents, this account in this book *Hello From Heaven* brought me so much happiness. Not that I would ever doubt my own continual experiences, but to at last see it written about brought joy! Like the person who revealed the experience (Dale) I too often had visions, hypnogogic imagery or a vivid dream of Rochester at the same time as experiencing the heat and electric-like currents. I have written about many in this book. On that particular night in the living room while on the sofa, then all night in bed and into the morning this experience was so intense. I could not find the page or section on which I had read this account by the person "Dale." I continued to search for it so I could underline, even though I had already written remarks near it and in my journal. I finally closed my eyes and while the heat and vibrations were continuing I asked Rochester to help me find the section. I opened my eyes and opened the book at random, and my eyes fell immediately on the passage and my own writing in green ink. Another miracle! Another teaching and confirmation, one upon the other. First the incredible confirming in the book, and then Rochester aiding me in once again finding it.

> *He radiated an intense love that penetrated every bit of me, like a merging of energy. Every fiber of my being felt love. There was total love, understanding, and compassion, totally different that what we experience here. It was very cosmic.*
>
> —Dale from *Hello From Heaven*
> by Bill Guggenheim and Judy Guggenheim

MEDITATION TWENTY-SIX

A Light of Hope

Blessed are they that mourn for they shall be comforted.
—Jesus of Nazareth, Matthew 5:4

*B*EFORE SLEEP AND AFTER PRAYERS I lie in the semi darkness, my Rosary still in my left hand. The intense heart of Rochester's spirit and the electrical-like currents fill my legs from just slightly above my knees and down to and including my feet.

Gradually on my right, just next to and above my knee, a light is appearing. It is a shaft of muted light approximately a foot or so high and perhaps six inches wide. I do not measure it, for I am bad at measurements and numbers, but only receive and enjoy it. This shaft has been a gift to me from another realm and began to appear some months ago, perhaps in Fall of 2002. It often appears as soon as I turn off the lamp. Sometimes it appears shortly after.

In the beginning I knew it was a gift, and yet for a number of nights I doubted ever so slightly thinking it was caused by a small nightlight in the bathroom across the hall. But that was not so. The tiny nightlight was behind the door next to the sink and could not possibly cause this shaft of light appearing to me. Too, it appeared when the bedroom door was occasionally closed.

And so each night I await it and count it among my blessings. At times I have seen a faint outline of Rochester within it in a sitting position facing me. I cannot see his features or details, and all the while the heat is on my legs. I have whispered to the light and too talked within to my little one who lies on my legs. I have actually delicately touched the outline of the bar of light, caressing it as I would Rochester. Too, I have gently put my hand through the light. There is no heat as there is in his presence on my legs. I fall asleep feeling guarded by this light from Heaven.

> A shaft of light
> Shines on the bed—
> He's here!—He lives!
> He is not dead!

Jan

MEDITATION TWENTY-SEVEN

Give a Gift

A smile is a light in the windows of the face
by which the heart signifies it is at home and waiting.
—Howard Ward Beecher

Kindness in giving creates love.
—Lao Tzu

WHEN WE ARE SAD, DEPRESSED OR GRIEVING, seemingly impossible though it may seem at times, we can still reach out to others. I know this because last year I was going through an experience like I had never been through before and yet I was capable of doing acts of love and kindness that I never believed I could endure doing. I still wrote cards and letters to others especially to those who were in need, sent gifts, and all the while daily wrote a book on grieving to help others and myself. We often do not know our inner strengths until they are supernaturally tested. I did not feel like writing cards or letters or sending gifts but I forced myself to do these things and continue to do so in the present. Writing the book was different. I needed to write the book to be able to survive and go on, if that was meant to be, and I wanted desperately to write the book. It was an inner strength, the writing of the book to honor Rochester, and I pray it will be a very special and unique gift to countless strangers when it is published shortly, as well as to Rochester and myself. And above all it is to make visible great love for Rochester who never

113

leaves me and who was and is my Angel companion in ways no one else can ever be.

There may be times in your life, or one overwhelming era as I have been experiencing through enormous loss, when you try everything you can to transform your depression or grief to bring good to others from it, but nothing seems to work. To do that honors your beloved one if you are grieving and so you keep trying. I believe it is possible, for in the depths of despair I was and am able to do this. It is on-going.

I can only suggest that if you too are suffering and grieving and perhaps even feeling anger often, though it may not be visibly expressed but is a suffering within that is a companion to grief, try to give someone a present. It may sound stupid or childish and too, something you cannot ever bear to think about. I understand. But try to do it.

In fact if there is a hurt or anger involved with a person or persons regarding your sadness and grief, and perhaps there was an insensitive remark or lack of total response when you were or are in the depths of despair, then it is to people such as these that you should especially give a little remembrance. I am not talking of birthday gifts or dates you would normally remember and give a gift for, but a pure and simple gift of love for no occasion at all. It will help you and you need consolation. You surely did not receive any from them. So send or give a small present of love, and before doing this say some prayers over it as you hold it, and pray it will bless them in some way. If you can forgive please do that also, for the forgiveness is to help yourself heal from their indifference. If you cannot forgive it will prolong your own pain. Give the entire situation to God. Envision yourself placing *"the situation"* into God's open Hands and walking away from Him. He will now take care of it. You will find yourself feeling more peaceful. You will not be without your grief or sadness for your beloved one for that is forever a part of you. You would not want to be without it. But you will not have these other issues caused by insensitivity ripping you apart as well.

It might be wise to keep some small presents on hand. I always do. I shop each time I go to Maine for various birthday gifts for our children and grandchildren, for with six children and their spouses and 19 grandchildren there are always gifts to buy—and also for many friends.

But too, I buy *"love gifts"* that are just to be kept on hand to be given out of love and sent for no special occasion. It is better to buy these when you are not upset or angry or feeling pain from another, and when all is peaceful. Though it is so difficult to do the inaneness of shopping when grieving, it is good and essential to push yourself to buy and to keep some of these small memorable gifts on hand. They should not be expensive at all, no more than a dollar or two, but just from the heart when you select them. You may not feel like giving one when someone does something insensitive or unkind in your sadness and grief perhaps even causing a quiet anger, but that is the very time when you should give a little token or surprise love gift. It is obvious they need a kindness. It could even be something from nature like flowers from your garden, a plant, or a pretty rock. Rocks are one of my favorite gifts to give or receive. A rock can be wrapped in a delicate piece of fabric or in pretty tissue, or put in a soft velvety pouch. I have found these pouches in various colors in a craft store and the dollar store in Rochester for one dollar. Immediately the rock then seems curious and a bit mysterious when presented in a lovely way. Even magical!

You will see that giving a gift will be very effective for you. Your anger will dissipate. It does not matter whether the gift is received well or not. Maybe you should keep several love gifts stored away. See, I think you are smiling now and deep in your heart you understand.

This does not mean that each spontaneous gift you give to another is to assuage your sadness from the insensitivity of another! No, no, it is always more blessed to give than to receive, and surprise presents make another's heart smile. You can tell, for the smile rises and shines through their eyes.

The eyes are the windows of the soul.

—Unknown

MEDITATION TWENTY-EIGHT

Signing

I talk to him and treat him as if he can understand, giving him
his dignity and respect. Many beautiful and intimate moments
have transpired between us because of this.
— J. G. Kolb from *Journal of Love*

March 25, 2003

*L*AST NIGHT AS I LIE IN BED READING and not yet asleep, I hear a slight
scratching in the corner that grows louder. I recognize this well for it
is a sound I have known and that grew endearing through the almost
sixteen years that Rochester did it. It is the sound of Rochester scratching
in his litter box that sits in a far secluded corner of the bedroom. That the
dark green litter box, immaculately clean, remains in its spot one year,
two weeks and two days after Rochester went to Heaven, may amaze
some who read this, but it is not a personal item of Rochester's that I am
yet inclined to remove. And for this very reason! Rochester communi-
cates to me through this scratching in his litter box!

I realize this may astound but I would not lie, and I have experienced
this communication again and again. At this point in what is happening
in our life it would be as if Rochester and I were *"signing"* to each other as
our only communication and one of us lost our hands or paws (as well as
one not having a visible body!). Yes, the litter box has remained and is
important!

You see, some years ago in the 1990s there came a point that I knew
without a doubt Rochester knew every word I said. I had been attempting

116

communication for some time and I at last could make these statements in my *Journal of Love* that we can communicate with and without spoken words. Mind to mind. And when I acted on certain things that I believed he was communicating it proved to be so. And I knew what he was saying in his love, expressions and silence, as well as the words and images I received.

But on this particular day that I truly knew he knew every word I said it revolved around his litter box and a deep concern. At this period in time before we lived here permanently in New Hampshire, Bob and I were travelling back and forth from Pennsylvania to New Hampshire every few weeks and would then remain in New Hampshire several weeks. The concern I have just referred to is because Rochester had not used his litter box after the trip to New Hampshire, nor did he use it for one full day after arrival, nor had he used the one we kept in the car for the 430 mile trip.

That day I have written about in my book *Journal*, and report on how I lovingly spoke to him as we sat on the side of the bed together and I asked him to use his litter box so I would not worry. And each time I asked—he complied. He used it twice! I asked him so politely as I always talk to him and he jumped down and went into the box and stayed awhile. I then checked it and immediately emptied it to show my appreciation, and knew he had not urinated as well. He was waiting on the bed and began bumping his head into mine and purring. Again I looked at him with love and told him I was so appreciative but I was still worried he had not done more. I asked him please to do this and emphasized the "please." Again he smooched with me, and then jumped down and got into his litter box. Again he availed himself of it, and I took the box out to clean it. This was all part of a journal entry. It was so amazing! I had talked to him just as I would a human, and he did just what I had asked both times. I rewarded him with many hugs and a clean box. It was so unusual that he used the box twice as I sat there for he rarely got into the box in our presence, using it privately if possible. And I always tried to respect his privacy for he had never failed to use the litter box not even once since I brought him home as a tiny kitten. I believe he truly was trying to tell me in his immediate responses that he understood everything I said to him, and we lived in that way, and it was confirmed continuously that we shared a deep communication.

As I wrote in *Journal of Love*:

His responses are not out of habit. I am constantly changing what I suggest to him to test his understanding of my words, and then I let him lead if it involves action. If I had talked to him and merely said the words and paid no attention, I would have missed these daily "replies" through his actions and not seen the wonder of it all. Awareness is necessary and appreciation for the present moment, and through this will come mysterious blessings.

This communication from Rochester and between us has continued after he has entered the spirit world. It is a blessing and confirmation from our Lord and an answer to my prayers. Perhaps it was all part of the great eternal plan when I felt the deep need to communicate with him in the years we had before he passed, mind to mind, and through receiving his replies through writing and journals I kept. For now this has continued ever since he went to Heaven, but yet he remains in spirit with me.

Perhaps I seem matter of fact in my opening words of this meditation but oh, that is not so! Each time since his transition on March 8th, 2002 that I have heard the action in his litter box I wanted to fall on my knees in gratitude, but I did not because the heat and electricity would come onto my legs signaling his continual presence. But I would offer up prayers at once in appreciation both to God and Rochester.

Let me tell you when it all began anew after March 8th, 2002.

You see, immediately after Rochester went to Heaven I knew I had to write a book on grieving in order to help myself and hopefully others as well. As I have written, I put aside another book I had already begun (the first nine meditations of this very book) to start at once writing to honor Rochester and to record my path of grief that followed. I completed the book titled *In Corridors of Eternal Time—A Passage Through Grief* and sent it to my publisher on October 7th, the Feast of the Holy Rosary. There was significance to this date I chose for mailing, for the Rosary was significant to Rochester and me.

On the first night of the day I mailed the manuscript a phenomenon began. As I sat in bed that first night not yet asleep and praying the Rosary a slight scratching began in the clean litter box that I could not yet part with. I was in awe. It was not that I had not had many precious and incredible things occur in regard to Rochester's constant presence to me but this was a new one. I kept thanking Jesus and Rochester. There had been the tremendous heat and electricity on my legs, then the scratching began and the heat lessened. I continued to pray five decades of the Rosary and all the while the scratching continued. Intermittently there would be a pause as there was when Rochester was in body and using the box, then the scratching would continue. When I completed the Rosary the scratching ceased and the intense heat and electricity returned to my legs until morning, indicating Rochester's return. I sat in bed and cried in joy and wonder. I felt I had just received one of Rochester's ultimate gifts of presence to me.

I believe then you may be astounded as was I when I tell you this same scratching and litter box activity continued every single night from October 7th, 2002 to January 7th, 2003. Can you imagine my gratitude? Every night as I sat in the dark with Rochester's spirit asleep on my legs and he making it very evident through the heat and electricity, this silent activity would diminish as I began to pray the Rosary for him. Then scratching would begin across the room in the corner. It was just as authentic and as loud as when he was present in real life. When I completed the Rosary his spirit returned to my legs.

On January 7th I received word from my publisher, Paul Clemens, that my manuscript of *Corridors* had been accepted. That night was the last night that Rochester used his litter box to scratch in and to tell me he was ever present. Of course I told him at once verbally during the day about our manuscript's acceptance as soon as I learned it. I sat and prayed with Rochester in our writing room in thanksgiving. And that night he scratched for the last time. He was keeping a sort of vigil with me as we awaited word of our manuscript and making his presence as evident as he could, even over the intense heat on my legs. It was his heavenly method of comfort and faithfulness and standing by. I know that because he told me so in spirit, and it is written in my journal—and I never doubt his communications.

So to have a present activity repeated through *"litter box communication"* is surprising and exciting, for especially, as I have told you, it is one year, two weeks and two days after Rochester went to Heaven.

P.S.   July 22, 2003

He is doing it again! Another night of Rosary, and scratching in response. Thank you, thank you dear Rochester. And the clean litter box remains, but secluded. How can I ever remove it? He needs it to "sign" to me!

Rochester on the windowsill in the room in which he "signs"

Silence and Meditation

The deeper we look into nature, the more we recognize that it is full of life.
Man can no longer live his life for himself alone.
We realize that all life is valuable and that we are united to all this life.
From this knowledge comes our spiritual relationship to the universe.
—Albert Schweitzer

*I*N MEDITATION #4 IN THE SECOND PORTION OF THIS BOOK I have related how my beloved little Rochester gave me a priceless gift while I was deep in prayer. Softly reciting the Rosary with eyes closed I feel his tiny mouth on the left side of my upper lip and instantly know it is him. It is the second time it has happened since he has been in spirit. But in life he often stood on my lap and with his little paws on the front of me he searched my eyes. We would be "held" tightly by this invisible connection, and often then he would bless me with his ethereal kiss. Now it has happened twice in spirit.

In life he was always with me or lying upon me, and he was especially drawn to participate when I was in prayer. He would present himself if he was not already with me, and if he was he would snuggle close and put his little paws around my hand or hands. I have written about these priceless moments in my books and in my poetry. He inspired all that I wrote. When I was praying the Rosary he often would pat it gently, sometimes holding it secure in his paw and at those times I was so moved by this I just sat in prayer quietly with him and waited until he released it. It is no wonder that the Rosary has become A Holy link between Rochester and myself connecting us now in spirit. I have written much more about this in my previous book on grieving.

It is written and said by John Edward that when we pray the Rosary for our loved ones in Heaven it is heard as musical notes by them drawing them closer and closer to us. The Rosary or other prayers of repetition of all faiths are music to their ears reminding them again and again of our deep love for them. And so I pray the Rosary in an extremely personal way numerous times daily for Rochester and we are connected by this chain of love as well as in other sacred ways.

Remembering all of this continually I was moved then to read an article in an older magazine, *Yoga International—The Voice of Silence,* in an issue that I bought almost a year before Rochester entered Heaven. I had been blessed by the story then, and coming across it again today it has new meaning in the rereading. And how meaningful I should rediscover it on a Friday following my Holy Hour I keep with Rochester. The previous Meditation #4 I have written about in this Meditation was also written on a Friday after our Holy Hour. What I have reread in this article I will relate because combined with what I have shared about Rochester I believe you will have much to reflect upon, particularly if you have not been close to animals, and too if you deeply love them and know already their great capacity for love. Either way it is memorable and moving.

When the *"St. Francis Effect"* is referred to it is recalling the legend in which St. Francis tamed the wild wolf and attracted birds and other creatures, and a very dramatic example of this was told by a woman in Concord, New Hampshire. The author of the article relating the incident is Herbert Benson, MD with Marg Stark, from his book *Timeless Healing.*

This New Hampshire woman had two beautiful Egyptian geese that she kept on her farm. The were male and female and magnificent birds, but she described them as being ornery and aloof and except at feeding time they kept their distance from her, even then stayed a few feet from her. The woman liked to practice meditation sitting by the pond on her farm in the Spring. One May day when her meditation was underway and her eyes were closed she just unexpectedly opened her eyes to find that the two geese were right in front of her and their heads were only inches from her face. Though this amazed and startled her she again went back to her meditation and closed her eyes. In a few minutes she peeked again and was in awe to see these lovely animals still very close to her but now prancing and extending their legs and wings. It seemed to her to be a kind of ritual or dance. The woman was incredulous but she returned to her meditation. What was only minutes later she actually felt the geese sit, one on either side of her, and stretch out their necks and lay their heads across her lap. To her astonishment, these normally aloof geese rested there for some time.

It would seem that when we are reflective and quiet and yes, prayerful too, unusual things can occur. Perhaps we draw these occurrences to ourselves and the animals sense a certain inexplicable mystery within us and come close to share it. It is a precious gift that I have experienced again and again with Rochester in life and spirit.

Perhaps reflect on this and spend time in silence and possibly such a gift will be given to you. Like the woman in the unforgettable story I too have experienced the unusual. In *Corridors* I write of having an early morning meditation on the sofa with my back to the sliding glass doors for approximately twenty minutes. All the bird feeders above the deck are behind me, and Rochester, in spirit just as he always was in life, is on my lap. I go deeply in spirit into my meditation and sit motionless. When I slowly end this period I speak softly to Rochester from my heart and then slowly stand. As I turn to look outside I feel like I am seeing another world! Literally dozens of birds of every kind rise up and fly from the deck floor, the railing, the feeders. Never has there been such an enormous congregation of birds as this since we owned this cottage. It is surreal!

In *Corridors* I list all the birds present that I catch fleeting glimpses of and am amazed I can capture them all in heart and mind to write down immediately afterwards. I write that this is no mere incident nor was it any mere gathering. It is other-worldly and with great significance. I have that confirmed in my heart and soul. It has everything to do with Rochester. I feel it in my spirit that they were gathered on the deck due to my deep prayer and meditation, and in ways known only to God they were drawn there through the passage of prayer, and to honor Chester. I also feel they were sent to comfort me, for only God could cause such an outpouring of wild life on one deck, all gathering behind me on the other side of the glass doors as I prayed and wept, and yet not make a sound as they normally do. I believe they were praying with me, visible signs of the supernatural, and power of prayer and assurances of Rochester's presence. They were like a heavenly silent choir accompanying me, and when our prayer ended, their voices were all freed and let loose as they flew in one giant flock! I will never forget this! Too, I have had an experience with a wild duck I have called Mrs. Mallard, and wrote of her and of this incident in previous books. I have had many experiences with her but this one I will relate was so tender. The interchanges I have with her are other-worldly, and particularly on this occasion when she came to me while I was on my hands and knees. Inches from my face she stood and stared into my eyes as I dug in the earth yet I was in deep meditation oblivious of all around me until she made herself known. I talked to her softly aloud the entire time she remained, calling her "*Dear*" or "*Mrs. Mallard.*" I feel I was permitted to experience something divine. Bob discretely observed it all. This poem tells of some of the happenings she and I shared as we came to know each other and that I have recorded in more detail in my *Journal of Love* and *Beneath the Stars and Trees*—even a night when a mating took place in the lake by my prayer chair for fifteen long minutes silhouetted against a brilliant setting sun. I spoke to her afterwards whispering to her softly as she nestled into the earth on an incline by the lake so totally exhausted with her sweet head on a rock. I comforted her and told her my love. This poem expresses further love for her.

Mrs. Mallard

I remember the day I came to call
    and knocked on your sliding glass door
        with my beak.
I had visited often before
    to feed on your seed
        but this day we did not speak.
Through the glass I could see the delight and surprise
    in your eyes.

And I remember the day you were working in the earth
    on your hands and knees—
        inside the circle of a raised rock wall—

And as softly as you please
   I again came to call,
      suddenly appearing
      and endearing
         myself to you.

I flew up into your garden
   and inches from your face—
      staring into each others eyes—
         we knew this was a sacred moment and place.
As you spoke to me
   I padded among your flowers
      never bending a one.
Then with my eyes
   I said good-byes,
Flew down—
and waddled across the grass in the sun.

It is a wonder to live in the woods and experience these precious moments and learn first hand from God's creatures. Silence and reflection bring unexpected gifts to treasure forever. I write each one down and every gift from Rochester is forever engraved on my heart as well.

Mr. and Mrs. Mallard

High Places

When something wonderful happens, pull over, step back,
take time to write it down while your heart is full.

—Unknown

March 30, 2003

I WAKE IN EARLY MORNING BEFORE LIGHT and feel the intense heat of Rochester asleep on my legs. It is so comforting and tears start to wet my eyes as I drift back to sleep. In a moment I am in the living room standing near the colorful velvet-like swivel rocking chair at the base of the living room stairs. Rochester has just leapt from its back and onto the top shelf of the nearby green bookshelf, also at the bottom of the steps. It is a far energetic leap and one I have seen him do numerous times in his life but not in spirit. He lands squarely facing the wall with his little bottom hanging over the edge and his tail descending. It is all so as in reality that when I abruptly wake I am startled to find myself in bed, the heat and electricity still engulfing my legs.

Later in the day I always write up completely these blessed events that occur if there was not time to do so immediately, even though they will not carry the same spontaneous energy of what is written in the heat of the moment. Henry David Thoreau has written: "*Write while the heat is in you.*" And this morning I am obeying his maxim, though I feel fairly certain he may not have been referring to this specific heat from my precious Angel.

126

Rochester is here, ever telling me he continues to live, play, and dare adventures to high places in his personal cottage. He has comforted me anew with a dream of truth.

MEDITATION THIRTY-ONE

Devotedness

*Six years after the death of his beloved dog, Kosins remains devoted
to her memory. And the slender, soulful tribute he penned to Maya
in the months after her death has become a surprise hit.*

—People

T HE ABOVE QUOTATION is one of several reviews and comments on the
back cover of a book you will never forget once read. It is *Maya's
First Rose* by Martin Scot Kosins and I have written about this relationship of Martin and his dog Maya in my previous book *In Corridors of
Eternal Time*, and also in my earlier book *Journal of Love*. It is a book that
became part of me from the first time I read it. I have given so many copies
as gifts, and following the passing of my beloved little Rochester it
became my constant companion. I carried it around this small cottage in
my grieving and Martin's words were one of a friend sent by God to aid me
in this unknown passage of grief. But I had read it too several years before
Rochester passed and could not imagine how Martin could survive this
loss. I knew I could never withstand the physical absence of Rochester.
It was something I could never allow myself to think about. Just as this
book helped me and others I gave copies to when Rochester was with me
in body in all his vitality and preciousness and love, so it became a
spiritual treasure to me after Rochester went to Heaven. I knew no others
in my life who grieved as I did be it for animal companion or human. The
only other whom I knew solely through the reading of his books was
author Cleveland Amory. He loved his beloved cat Polar Bear so deeply

and had written a trilogy of books about him in Rochester's lifetime and I own them and read them all. In my grief I did not see or remember that Martin knew Cleveland and that he lists his name in the beginning of *Maya's First Rose* and thanks him for his generous praise of Maya's manuscript and for encouraging him to seek a publisher. I too in turn thank Martin again for his sensitive spiritual words on the cover of *Corridors,* for they honor Rochester's existence and his precious touch upon lives. And so I feel I am in a wonderful spiritual circle of friends with Martin, Maya, Cleveland, Polar Bear and Rochester. The strength of this circle emotionally and spiritually cannot be expressed in writing or even the spoken word. As I wrote in my previous book, Cleveland is now with his beloved Polar Bear in Heaven having joined him in Fall of 1998. I can only imagine their mutual joy.

I share all these loving things that have been a tremendous support for me as a result of the quotation that begins this meditation, a quote about *Maya's First Rose.* It states:

Six years after the death of his beloved dog, Kosins remains devoted to her memory.

Now to many, in fact perhaps to the majority in the world, this may not be understandable. Often a death comes and goes and people act totally normal like it barely happened (especially an animal's death). Others deeply grieve. But most after a short period, at least those in my life, end their grieving not long after. Perhaps in solitude they are heartbroken and they keep it all hidden, but basically those whom I have known and witnessed pass through grief fairly quickly. Understandably sometimes it is not the main individual in their life or someone they deeply cherished who has passed. But whatever the reason I have not been witness to anyone in extended grief or deep grief with the exception of my own parents. I have written previously of the deep and extended grief of my Dad over our family cat, and also of my Mother's deep grief over my Dad and Uncle who died within several months of each other. She grieved so she died of a broken heart thirteen months after they did.

I realize my grief for Rochester is not understood or making mention of his name at times except by Bob, and too by my friend Chris, who was given the spiritual gift of witnessing Rochester's passing. This is recorded in my previous book. I can sense an uncomfortableness if I refer to him to others. And so it is rare that I do this unless there is a specific reason. Grief is a gift as well as a sorrow so deep. Few can understand this. I write this meditation to say that everyone grieves differently and some simply not at all, and hopefully we will all be extremely sensitive to anyone who has suffered a loss, even a year or two or much more after the death.

A recent account on a TV program touched me deeply for my heart and soul so understood their grief and the actions of a family bereaved. They told of how they set the table and acknowledge daily a place for their Mother, and on her birthday they have wine and festive food she enjoyed. The one who was told this, a man associated with grieving and the afterlife, said that what they were doing for their Mother was fine. He said that some people would think they were obsessing but this is not so. He stated they need to do this as I do for Chester when I keep his small feeding table set for him with flowers and his bowl of water and a plate. This woman's children do not feel time heals and miss her even more as time goes by and continue to share life with her. Too, they talk to her as if she were with them just as I do to Rochester, and I have learned through many bereavement sources that this is not strange at all, even encouraged. Our loved ones hear and are always with us.

Another source recently revealed of parents who set plates at the table every day for their two daughters. Their girls died five years ago. Many too continue to leave empty chairs at the table for their loved ones to share life with them (and they do!), or some even keep a room in which they keep company with their beloved's spirit and pray, or light a candle. And when one is aware and honors a loved one they are frequently rewarded with an overpowering sense of presence, and often in various and surprising ways. My writing room is such a room, but I have been blessed with Rochester's presence throughout our cottage.

It has been said by more than one and written that we should validate our loved ones in Heaven by a candle, prayers, anything to say that they are remembered. They need to know they are remembered.

I do not have to be told this for I do it constantly. And Rochester gives me his spiritual presence. I know without a doubt he is with me. We live together!

And so to read that six years after Maya's death Martin still grieves is absolutely as it should be and for myself also. I believe Martin will always grieve for Maya as I will for Rochester. It is part of who he is forever and part of who I am forever until I am with Rochester again.

> *You should talk to and acknowledge your loved ones on the other side and include them in your daily life.—Acknowledge the signs and symbols you are receiving to let your loved one know you know they are with you. Do not dismiss them. They want to communicate.*
>
> —John Edward

> *... we will understand that our grief is now a part of who we are. Like the memory of our loved ones, grief will never disappear, we just grow stronger to support the weight of it.*
>
> —George Anderson, *Walking in the Garden of Souls*

MEDITATION THIRTY-TWO

Falling in Love

But then something fairly obvious dawned on me for the first time:
if a deceased person can move things at all it is more than likely that
a good many more such happenings occur than are noticed—
especially by one like the author, who does not always have
things around in perfect tidiness.
—The Right Reverend James A. Pike

ROCHESTER HAS OWNED ME FOR MANY YEARS and because of him I have in my possession two miniature stuffed animals, both cats. They were given to me the year after Rochester entered my life and because I love him. One little guy resembles my little guy for he is orange in color, though no white fur at all. The other is a tiny Siamese cat and both are about two inches tall. These small cats have sat on the top of this book shelf with other keepsakes through the years, and daily I have enjoyed them though never removing them. This bookshelf made by Bob is behind the door in my writing room that Rochester and I have always shared. Each time I come in the room I see them, and Rochester could easily see them from the bed he laid upon there or from my desk as I wrote and he helped. These two little furry cats were permanently situated on that shelf unless I picked them up quickly to dust around them, otherwise they were immobile. They have never been off the shelf! Never!

Today I walk into our writing room and the two little cats are not sitting there to greet me. I look down and see them both lying on top of Rochester's tan carrier which I keep in our writing room. The carrier is there in memory of my little one and to hold keepsakes pertaining to his life. I am astounded to see these miniature cats lying where they never have been in their lives! I just stand there too amazed to do anything!

There are no open windows across the room allowing any strong breeze to blow them off, although through the years they were open in nice weather but the two cats never moved. And Bob never goes upstairs to my room. Another small keepsake is even in the path of the two small cats on the shelf, yet that item remains in place.

But then I know the explanation. It was Rochester who patted them gently off the top of the bookshelf directing them to his carrier and not the floor. I can envision him doing this with his sweet soft white paw.

Again he is leaving clues of his daily and continuous presence and saying *"I am here!"* What better way to get my attention than with two small cats that have been a part of our life together and who never left their positions and stance on that shelf? And he knows I know that!

Their sudden absence silently screamed Rochester's presence! I knew he was again leaving a message of love and hope! If only we are observant we will continually see and hear the many ways out beloved ones in spirit are attempting to tell us their love and that they want to be with us. They want to be discovered! They long to give us joy and solace!

Postscript

After completing the writing of this meditation I wanted to find the perfect quotation for its beginning. Though for many years I have been collecting quotations in a journal, I am in a new life now and do not have suitable ones that apply to all the mysteries, joys, and happenings that are occurring since Rochester's passing. I will need a special journal for the quotations for this new life of ours together in spirit.

I decided then to pray, and with eyes remaining closed, open the present book I am reading at random. Once opened, I opened my eyes as well and let them alight on the first passage in my view. Incredibly, the passage I have included could not have been more perfect. Without a doubt my Rochester continually guides me with God's Help.

The Solace of Plants

Plants can see. They can count and communicate with one another.
They are able to react to the slightest touch and to estimate time
with extraordinary precision.
—David Attenborough, *The Private Life of Plants*

THE ABOVE WORDS were in the *Boston Globe* some time ago in a brief review of the book mentioned above. I too wrote about it in my *Journal of Love*. This book by Attenborough is an offshoot of a BBC television series, and the author tells how plants function, compete, survive, and master their environment, be it in rain forests, mountains, or the nearest back yard. He feels they do not have as much fun as their animal counterparts, but they do lead a more varied and vivid life than they are generally credited with. Imagine then how much joy they can bring to someone who is in need of a quiet friend, a listener, one who will silently share life with you in your home. Even in a small apartment there is room for a plant or two. It is always meaningful to have something or someone to care for, but if one is downcast, depressed, or grieving a plant can be a non-invasive companion to one's sadness. A person may even find himself talking to his plants when he would not talk to other humans. I understand this. We do not always want advice or to be told what is best for us. We often have to discover these things on our own. This is preferable to me and I am certain to many others. One can come to conclusions at one's own pace, cry, or sit and stare, or meditate in the company of plants.

PLANTS

P urchased for beauty and companionship—
L iving plants languish and stand
A lways available for appreciation,
N oticing those who care enough
T o talk and pause in reflection—
S ensing their need for salutation and conversation.

Jan
2003

Years ago I copied a quotation by a wonderful man named George Washington Carver into my Commonplace book that struck my heart:

I like to think of nature as an unlimited radio station, through which God speaks to us every hour, if we will only tune in.

May these words inspire us all to tune in to all of nature. Then I later wrote about this man in my own book previously mentioned (*Journal*). This man would not have thought the opening quotation to this meditation outlandish for he too talked to his plants and had an uncanny knowledge of all growing things. When he was a child he built his own secret greenhouse out of odds and ends of material and when he was forever being asked what he was doing all by himself, the child replied, "*I go to my garden hospital and take care of hundreds of sick plants.*" He would sing in his squeaky little voice to ailing house plants and cause them to bloom. During the day he took them outside "*to play in the sun.*" After the plants were returned to their owners, he would be asked repeatedly how he could work such miracles. The little boy would answer softly: "*All flowers talk to me and so do hundreds of little living things in the woods. I know what I know by watching and loving everything.*" Carver went to college and had a Master Degree and was a brilliant man and solved many agricultural problems in the South. He believed that everyone could do the things he did and have his power with living plants if only they believe it. He believed in fairies and their work with the plants but above all he believed in God. One can read much more about him in my previous book. He has been an inspiration to me.

Luther Burbank is another man who talked to plants and nature and he felt they could comprehend his meaning through telepathy. He would talk to his plants and believe he created a vibration of love. He took plants into his confidence and he asked them to help, and he affirmed them and assured them he held their small lives in deepest regard and affection. He was a remarkable man and all his life he loved children, and he believed that most of the things that are truly useful in later life came to children through play and through association with nature. He said when he was seventy-seven that his body was no older than his mind— and his mind was adolescent. He said it never grew up and he hoped it never would. As I wrote in *Journal,* this too describes myself—one who remains interiorly like a child in many ways and who is filled with the wonders of animals and nature. You can read more about Luther Burbank too in *Journal.* He left people stunned with his words and accomplishments and beliefs.

Another man who by chance discovered the joy of plants is Richard W. Langer who writes in detail about this in his book *The After-Dinner Gardening Book* published in hard cover by Macmillan Publishing Co., Inc. and in paperback by Collier Books which I own in a fifth printing in 1974. This book is off beat and fun and a step-by-step guide to growing beautiful plants from seeds and pits of fruits and vegetables right in your own living room. It is also serious and has much useful information on soil, research, cultivation, pruning and more. He is a window sill gardener and proves that any city-bound would-be gardener with a sense of adventure and a little patience can grow his own lush plants from the seeds and shoots of mangoes, kiwi fruit, avocados, sunflowers, sugar cane, grapes, date, coconuts and the entire citrus family and more. This is just the delightful information shared on the cover but it has wonderful reviews and is intriguing for its humor. His adventure begins while he is sick and drinking lemonade. Almost choking on two seeds he places them casually in the soil of a bedraggled begonia in a pot nearby so he does not have to get up to dispose of them. You will enjoy the book as I did some years ago when I found it, but have gone back to it at times too for fun and good information.

You can not only have plants for yourself but you can grow them for others. I have given many plants away that I first cared for and my special interest was Jade Plants and Christmas Cactus. Some people like giving African Violets to others and to have them around themselves when they are despondent. If you are deeply fond of a certain variety of flower or plant you can put much love into them with care and prayer, and then give one to another who may be grieving or sad also and they will have a lovely silent companion but that can also be conversed with if they so choose.

If you do something you love like caring for a plant, you may not want to stop there. Share what you love with others. It is a nurturing of spirit for giver and receiver.

I admit to being very talkative both aloud and mentally to my house plants. Over the past six years I have collected seven Jade plants and one Christmas Cactus. The latter and one large Jade plant are the oldest. Each plant has a name and the large Jade plant is Emerald and the Christmas Cactus is Winter. The others are Sophia, Jasmine, Sweetness, Eleanor, Angela and Mary. I think of them as a little family and imagine them communicating amongst themselves. I also say little prayers for them holding my hands over them. Like George Washington Carver, I place all my indoor plants outdoors on the deck each summer for periods where they can *"play in the sun."* They truly enjoy this. I hear their happiness in my spirit and they continue to live and thrive.

I might add too that each of my plants is in a pretty pot, all identical except for various sizes, with the face of a fairy on each with greens and fruit and flowers as hair, though all ceramic. When I talk to the plants they seem even more to have definite personalities because they all have faces.

If you have an animal companion it is important that you read first about any plant or flower you bring into your home because there is a long list that is poisonous to animals. I never brought any plant in until first knowing if it was safe. Such a detailed list can be obtained on the Internet and was excellent to have.

Rochester too, has a special plant all his own, that of a tub of rye and oat grass. I plant the seed, and it grows into lush green fullness in a few days and lasts several weeks. The veggie added to Rochester's diet has given him enjoyment through the years and is a healthy, cleansing snack. It was even worthy of a poem I wrote about it that is in *Journal*. It is obtainable in containers in stores like Wal-Mart that sell pet food, and in pet stores. I still continue to grow it at intervals for Rochester's spirit. It is attractive and beautifully full and green in appearance.

It has been discovered that many people remain happier and healthier if they have living growing plants to care for. The discovery even developed into a new field called horticultural therapy.

Not all depression and sadness can be cured that easily by caring for plants, but it is a simple suggestion that might prove to bring help. And when a sad person shares a plant with another who too needs help, that is a lovely act. You may feel more in spirit with a plant also if you know that they grieve too. Winter, my Christmas Cactus went from blooming once a year to four times a year in the presence of her friend Rochester who often sat on the table by her at the window. She had just bloomed at Christmas and into the new year when Rochester passed. She has never flowered again in these past seventeen months since March 8, 2002.

Aside from the books, I have already mentioned in this meditation you may also enjoy the following:

The Secret Life of Plants by Peter Tompkins and Christopher Bird and
Talking With Nature by Michael J. Roads

Too, a video that is most enjoyable and unusual is *On a Clear Day You Can See Forever*, starring Barbra Streisand. My daughter Janna gave this to me for Christmas because she knows I talk to my plants as does the star in this movie.

Perhaps today if you are in need go to a store or plant nursery and choose a plant that appeals to you. Ask for instructions on how to make it thrive. When you take it home give it a place of honor. Perhaps even take home two. And my plants are reminding me to tell you to please name your plants and introduce them to visitors. They enjoy soft mystical music at times too, and also having their pictures taken. And my plants were especially both soothed and enlivened by the gentle presence of Rochester when in life, and now also by his spirit. Plants are magical little friends.

SIMPLY GRAND

Leafy green friends
Standing silently—
Giving themselves
So compliantly.

They touch our souls
And aid in healing—
Hearts parched and dry
That need more feeling.

They simply stand—
But plants are grand.

Jan
2003

MEDITATION THIRTY-FOUR

Falling for Me

Experiencing unusual physical phenomena definitely stretches our mind because these occurrences seemingly defy the known laws of physics.
—Bill Guggenheim and Judy Guggenheim from *Hello From Heaven*

April 15, 2003

I JOIN BOB IN THE LIVING ROOM in evening and sit down as always on the sofa with my back against the sofa arm, and my legs stretched down the length onto the middle cushion. I place my bathrobe upon my legs to await Chester's arrival upon me. I am no sooner comfortable and anticipating his presence when there is a gigantic crash in the kitchen, one so loud and totally unexpected my upper body does a little dance. Bob too appears physically jostled. *"What was that?"* we say wordlessly, our eyes open wide and staring at each other. No other noise follows. Bob gets up to look around and soon finds a pile of shattered glass and a picture frame lying on the kitchen floor. He brings me the frame minus the glass. I am floored just like the picture had been, and still yet too the glass! This is a light 5x7 inch wooden frame that should only have made a quarter of the noise that it did in falling. It should not have sounded like part of the roof crashing. Inside the glassless frame is the beautiful picture of a little marmalade and white kitten tucked into a bed with his little paws gently over the pink blanket. It is a picture I have treasured through the years, one given to me by our daughter Laurel after Rochester came into our lives, and is a work of photographer Ron Kimball. I have a journal and many book plates and bookmarkers with this same precious

140

photograph upon them. I have also given these sweet items as gifts. The dear kitten looks like baby Rochester.

Who can explain such a happening, one of so many that have occurred since Rochester's passing? This picture has hung on a narrow wall in the kitchen area next to our refrigerator since 1986 shortly after Chester became mine. It is one of five framed pictures that are displayed one on top of the other in vertical placement. Each frame holds a picture of a little kitten or cat and several have a little girl with them, each a different child. They are greeting cards sent to me by close friends celebrating Rochester in the months that follow his entrance into our lives. They are so lovely to me, the cards worthy of framing, that they have hung on that narrow wall for seventeen years! They have never fallen from the wall or been knocked off despite active play in that area by young grandchildren, nor by our constant use of the refrigerator next to the pictures. Not even by the removal of the old refrigerator after many years and the installation of a new one several months ago. Delivered by very large delivery men who were vigorously working in that area to make the new refrigerator conform next to that very narrow wall, the delivery men never caused one of those pictures to fall despite all the jostling and close contact.

But tonight the look-a-like picture of Rochester seems to leap off the wall while we are no where near it. A tremendous crash occurs far more worthy of that light picture, and upon looking again Bob sees the nail is still in the wall. After seventeen years Rochester's framed look-a-like simply leaps off a wall it has been on since 1986 while we are in another room.

And after the crash and the discoveries concerning it, the familiar sensation of Rochester's arrival upon my legs occurs, and the gradual intense heat and electrical like current builds, and I am overcome by his presence and tremendous warmth. I am being given again the gift of his constant love and companionship. That he should choose tonight to announce himself by causing his picture to flip off the wall is a glorious curiosity! I think of the fallen picture as a tremendous communication, as is the heat and currents on my legs. He was never destructive while in his physical body, but how does a little cat surprise his family now that he is in spirit? Tonight he chooses the look-a-like picture over the other four, and causes it to flip from its seventeen- year placement on the wall to say

"I'm here!" It would have had to flip up off the wall to release the wire from the nail head, and then fall to the floor. I am in awe and so grateful! And then in sweet typical fashion he comes to cuddle on my legs. I am so blessed!

This is a happening that leaves Bob bewildered for sure. He has no answer. He shakes his head smiling, indicating Rochester and I are from another world. Only he is normal. But we already know that.

FALLING FOR ME

It leaps from wall
    and down it crashes—
And with that fall
    it truly dashes—
All sensibilities
    and doubt—
That he is truly
    not about.
As it lies scattered
    on the floor—
Rochester states
    "I'm here!" once more!

For Rochester   JGK

Baby Rochester
look-a-like
picture, second
from top

Purple, Orange and White

Think of your life as an empty canvas and each thought a different color.
What are you going to create with your thoughts?

—James VanPraagh

Count among your blessings all the colors, beauties and splendors
of a living earth.

—Edward Cunningham

A S A CHILD AND TEENAGER my favorite colors were purple and orange. To my friends I was strange that I should like those particular colors individually or in combination. I realize I am different in many ways but at least I have been consistent, for these are still two of my favorite colors but with green added also and being number one for years. I have written how green has affected me in an earlier meditation.

As I sit here writing I too have just come to notice the colors in my cotton blouse I am wearing. The material is covered with very small purple and orange flowers similar to violets in appearance with green leaves all about them. All the colors that affect me are on this blouse and yet I really did not become aware of it until right now. And I have had this blouse a year!

The background is white and that too has become significant. When I bought this blouse it was just pleasing to the eye on the rack, and now I know why. My heart was grieving and it still is in the present. I needed a blouse and selected it in a hurry without scrutiny for I dislike shopping for clothes. The combination of these appealing colors drew me to it at once.

Some people need to wear their favorite colors and deliberately select them, while others choose what will cover them by the style of the items and not the color. Though I love being surrounded by glorious green in all its various shades in nature here in the woods, I tend to wear various shades of purple. I have worn three purple items, a blouse and a soft sweater, and a jacket for years, and do not intend to give them up as yet. I feel soothed and safe in them and wear them so often I am sure some are wondering when I will stop. I never ever feel attractive, but wearing any one or more of those items I feel I can pass myself off to the world and be acceptable. I know Rochester likes them too. I am wearing the sweater in the author picture of this book.

Orange or peach I have not been as fortunate to find in clothing with the exception of one pretty vibrant orange cotton shirt. Nothing more. But Rochester was always before me in the splendor of his soft orange marmalade and white fur and fulfilled everything. Why should I worry about finding orange apparel when he has the most magnificent of orange and white coats? Anything I would wear would be less.

We do however have burnt orange carpet in the bedroom and curtains I made of material depicting a Native American design of burnt orange, white and black, with the orange most prominent. Rochester in his orange fur was a precious enhancer to this room where he slept every night of his life with me.

There is no place more beautiful than New Hampshire in Autumn with our woods and trees in color around the lake, and country roads lined with the brilliant shades of orange and gold leaves. People travel on bus tours from other states to see this amazing beauty and we are blessed to live right in its midst. The brilliance of orange mirrors into our lake and I have taken so many pictures in awe. When developed the pictures can be viewed normally or upside down, for you cannot tell which are the real trees and what are reflections in the water. John Burroughs has said: *"How beautifully the leaves grow old. How full of light and colour are their last days."*

If you do not have enough orange in your life try to stay healthy by nourishing yourself with oranges, cantaloupe, tangerines, and carrots.

Squash is nice also in Autumn when the leaves are becoming orange on the trees. You may enjoy a treat of some candy corn then too.

Violet, which includes royal Purple, is the highest color vibration of the spectrum I have read. It is a blend of Red and Blue and is the most spiritual of colors. It is as if it chooses ceremony for it is in most stained glass windows in churches and is connected with the Holy. Purple is also the Christian color for Advent and Lent. Kings and other royalty wear purple, and Priests' and Ministers' vestments often are decorated and embroidered with this color. I believe aside from these facts, that Violet is a color that makes us reverent or spiritually mindful. Rochester's most recent collar was purple and each day and night it is treated with great respect and prayerful daily rituals. I chose to wear his red collar after he went to Heaven for he had worn the red for a very long period. It was filled with his essence and energy. I never remove it from my left arm. The purple one he had worn only several weeks. But purple is a blend of red and blue as I have written and so the red one , a component of purple, also is regal to me for it was worn by royalty.

Amethyst, a beautiful purple stone, is a favorite of mine also. I have many large rocks of it sitting about in the living room and the writing room Rochester and I continue to share. He would often pat a favorite smaller piece of it around my desk top. I treasure that particular piece now. There are many beliefs about the influences of Amethyst. My pieces came from mines here in New Hampshire. I have always appreciated rocks and these Amethysts are certainly ones of beauty and cast lovely auras about them. I have often given pieces of it as gifts as I do also rocks and stones from our woods and shore lines. Too, I have appreciated it so much when several friends have sent me stones from their vacation spots. Objects that are given from the natural world can often speak of God.

I have planted so many flowers in my gardens all for Rochester and so many are purple. There is low blooming phlox, a very beautiful perennial purple flower whose name I do not know but that is exquisite, pansies, violets, and velvety petunias, my favorites, of many shades of purple to border the gardens along with the pinks and reds and whites.

The last four lines of a longer poem written in the early 90s, titled "Violets," share a lovely fact.

> Shy, gentle violets sent from God
> To grow in grass and cracks and sod.
> I knew a Violet like no other
> Upon this earth, she was my Mother.

Too, we have planted two Lilac trees to honor Rochester. Lilac is New Hampshire's State Flower and the Purple Finch is the State Bird. Purple signifies precious memories to me. But our gardens are not without bright orange shades of zinnias and marigolds too, catching the eye, almost like a fleeting sighting of Rochester. I have a china Angel bird house wearing soft violet, green, and white hanging high on a pine tree branch. Perhaps a Purple Finch has visited her.

We enjoy purple grape juice daily to attain vitamins and refreshment, but at one time and for years this same purple juice was our Holy Communion received in the Methodist Church and blessed and made Holy by Christ. And as a young teenage girl one of the prettiest pieces I played frequently on the piano was "Deep Purple."

I would like to leave a small, final, poetic meditation with you about this color titled "Woman of Color."

WOMAN OF COLOR

> Dear Mother with a colorful name—
> I often wished I had the same—
> First name as yours.
> This name endures—
> Coming from your Irish background.
> More recently I've truly found
> It has a great significance—
> And I never had the chance,
> To tell you so—its afterglow
> Remains a floral cameo.
>
> A delicate leafy violet plant—
> Somehow—someway—can so enchant—

And speaks to me of you—
For you're a Violet too!
And add your Welsh last name of Gray—
Such color you gave every day!

Though I have used green ink solely and continuously since 1989, I make one exception. On my Mother Violet's birthday and wedding anniversary. I write in purple ink in my journals only.

STARS

S prinkled across the heavens of night
T rillions of infinitesimal dots of light
A stonish seekers
R everently
S ubdued

Jan

There is such beauty in the moon and the stars in all their whiteness and these were significant in the life of Rochester and myself. Many poems were written about them in our life together, and many thoughts are recorded about them in my previous book, *Beneath the Stars and Trees.*

In the dark immensity of night
I stood upon a hill and watched
    the light
Of a star,
Soundless and beautiful and far.

—Grace V. Watkins

That night I returned from the Veterinarian's office March 8, 2002 without my beloved Rochester in my arms I stood outside, head back, looking up at the moon and stars and I never felt so alone in my entire life. I was in tears and my heart was in pieces and I wondered if my little Rochester was looking down on me and sending love. I would learn such comforting news only minutes later that I have related in my book,

Corridors and elsewhere in this book. So yes, the moon and stars are very important in my life and just last night I went out after midnight to take pictures of the full moon over the lake. I have been doing that for years but it has deeper meaning now that Rochester awaits me in Heaven.

The whiteness of the snow has always been deeply spiritual to me and we have such enormous snow falls in New Hampshire leaving mountains and glorious areas all around our cottage of untouched snow. We are often snowed in for several days. Rochester was always by my side as I spent those days writing and we would look out the window together and watch each flake and think we were the most fortunate of beings, for everything was so magical. And we would write poems about it all, and cuddle together, and I cannot think of those moments and days without dissolving in tears. But they are ours forever in our spiritual memory bank to draw on again and again.

I have read in the past that white is the ultimate expression of Oneness with the Father and copied it into my journal. It spoke to me immediately of Rochester and his pure white fur. It is said white indicates blessings in the home, fidelity, sincerity, purity, honesty, pure faith and mercy. These thoughts and this list are cleaved from an old journal that has brought some comfort, and speaks of the blessings Rochester brings to my life both when he was in body and now in spirit. In the presence of his pure whiteness of fur inadequacies vanished and fears disappeared and I can attest to that in my own life when Rochester entered it. He was and is a gift from God.

When a person is close to God he has spiritual inner strengths and radiant energy and is capable of reaching his highest spirituality. Rochester caused me to draw closer to Him and pulled me up from despair for he is an Angel.

As I have written, the color white depicts fidelity and pureness, and Rochester and I were true to each other and realized that to be faithful to those we love is a precious jewel. Many think only humans are capable of this —but far more know that the love and fidelity of an animal is the highest of gifts and so very pure.

Some years ago because I am an only child and not a son, I felt the need to honor my Dad through my writing in the use of his last name and my maiden name—instead of my middle name. The name is Gray—a slightly darker shade than white, but one that has subtle colorful meaning to me personally. I can at least carry his name on until my life ends.

I share these thoughts on colors because I do believe colors affect us both positively and negatively. What can be soothing to one person can disrupt another's spirit. Colors do produce physical, mental, emotional, spiritual responses so be sure to surround yourself in the colors you know can please your soul and minister to you as well. As you learn to live in different ways following heartbreak of any kind be aware of the colors that you have around you or are wearing, and perhaps you will want to make some changes if your soul and heart are at unrest in the presence of one or more. Sense when you are more at peace and feel more comforted and learn from that if you are shown a revelation. As for myself I will surround myself in the green of these woods and all of nature, the purples, oranges and whites, and be more restful in spirit. These are the colors I share with Rochester, the colors of our own personal rainbow. One day I will cross that rainbow and he will be waiting for me at the end of that spiritual bridge. He will spot me in that purple sweater, the one so often worn through the years when he cuddled close to me. He will leap into my arms once more and I will gather up his precious and most adorable orange and white being and clasp him to me in joy unspeakable never to be separated again.

Other things I did included wearing lighter colors. I was wearing black—every day. One day I decided: that's enough. But just as sunlight and light rooms lightened my mood, so did the colors I wore. I'd feel depressed if I sat in a black room. Wearing black wasn't helping me much either. I put my black clothes away, until I felt better.

—Melody Beattie, discussing her life following
the death of her son, from *A Reason to Live*

I have set
my bow in the clouds,
And it shall be a sign
of the covenant
between me and the earth.

*... I will see it
and remember the
everlasting covenant
between God and
every living creature.*

—Genesis 9: 13, 16

MEDITATION THIRTY-SIX

Ring Toss

We cannot but speak the things we have seen and heard.
—Saints Peter and John, Acts 4:20

May 17, 2003

As I AM CERTAIN I HAVE WRITTEN ELSEWHERE IN THIS BOOK, but most certainly in a meditation in my previous book, *In Corridors of Eternal Time*, I have asked my Dad to be Rochester's friend and guardian in Heaven. Though he did not know Rochester in this life for my Dad passed away in 1977, I feel certain he has known him and been aware of him since Rochester entered my life in 1986. My Dad had always loved our family cat Mitzi so deeply, I felt certain he would cherish my Rochester too, and care for him until I joined them. In my heart is that assurance.

Because I am continually aware of Rochester's presence in extraordinary ways, and too in subtle ordinary ways, I asked my Dad in prayer to also communicate in some way with me. I did not realize many truths when my Dad passed away in 1977 for I had never been taught them, nor in my reading.

I experienced my Dad in dreams but nothing more, except in my own thoughts, or in the poems I wrote for him and about him, or the writings speaking of him in my past published books. In one exceptional instance I felt I saw him and have written about this also in my previous book, *Beside the Still Waters*. But I was so struck by what I believed to be his presence seeing only his hand up close, and the back of his figure walking

151

away from me, I let him go. I will never know for certain in this life, yet believe it was him. My friend Ginny shared this unexpected experience with me and I believe she too was moved by it.

And so anew I prayed that my Dad would show himself to me as Rochester continues to do. The day after I lifted this silent petition to Jesus, an amazing incident occurred. I was in the bedroom and about to leave when I briefly turned back to do something. In that instant an object swiftly flew off of my bureau! It came from the back of the bureau and rose into the air at least a foot from its surface, and in a half circle sped downward to the floor. I simply stood there as if glued to the spot and in awe! What was it? How could such a thing occur when no one was there but myself and Rochester's spirit? Over the initial shock I began to look for the object on the carpet and found it almost under the bed. Holding it in my hand tears came, for I was cupping a treasure I had not seen in years. I had thought it had been permanently lost and put it to rest in my mind, even though I felt terrible that I could have been so careless as to lose it.

In my hand was my Dad's gold ring, a rather large ring with an emblem of an eagle on it. At one point in his life he wore it regularly, then put it away. It became mine when he went to Heaven. Now it had made a new appearance!

As I write this now I still do not know if my Dad tossed the ring up in the air to show me he is very much alive and with me, or if Rochester, sitting on my bureau as he often did, patted it vigorously into the air with his soft white paw. He did this many times with other belongings of mine in sweetness and fun. And although my bureau was not neat and tidy, I do know my Dad's ring was not upon it all these years it has been missing! I kept it in a jewelry box in a bureau drawer, never carelessly loose on top of the bureau.

And how could it just reappear and be tossed in the air at that moment for me to discover after previously praying that my Dad would reveal himself to me? I do not know the answers. I am finally beginning to experience the treasures revealed from beyond. I only know it fell at my feet the day after I prayed, as if propelled into the air by an unknown force. Whether it be my Dad announcing his presence or Rochester, it is all beauty, truth and consolation to me, affirming once again that our precious loved ones are ever with us.

Do not miss the subtle ways your loved ones come through. Do not look for great big things, though in this particular instance it truly was remarkable. But not every time I am blessed by Rochester's presence does he toss a ring into the air! Our sweet loved ones are trying to come through so they may show you they are there all the time! How I wish I knew this all these years after my Dad passed away! How many subtle "hellos" have I missed? I believe it has taken my beloved Rochester to teach me awareness on a daily basis, and then every now and then he causes an enormous gift to be given to me from him within the walls of this cottage or elsewhere in daily life. But as to the tosser of this ring, so far it remains a mystery though I have prayed. I think Rochester and my Dad are in cahoots. They both have mischievous personalities at times. But it confirmed anew in my heart, though Rochester's spirit is ever with me here, my Dad and he are together in Heaven waiting.

RING TOSS

Who tossed that ring—
Rochester or Dad?
Who gave it a fling—
To make me glad?

Who cares which one,
It was all in fun—
To say anew
"We are with you!"

For Rochester and Dad   Jan
with deep gratitude   2003

Rochester's Birthday
May 30, 2003

God danced the day you were born.
You are loved.
You are beautiful.
You are gift of God.

—Anonymous and Jan

A Star danced in Heaven on the day you were born.

—Flavia and Jan

May 30, 2003

*I*T IS YOUR SEVENTEENTH BIRTHDAY yet when you went to Heaven you still looked like a very young cat. You never aged and never shall. It is your second birthday we have been apart physically, yet we are always together. I think back on all the others and how we spent each one, never apart. I grow a container of lush green grass for you so it is ready and full for today. I know you appreciate it. I put your prettiest plate on your feeding table and decorate it with your several pieces of Iams food as a treat. I think about the gifts I enjoyed surprising you with in the past. Many are still here and in your carrier with the other treasures in our writing room. Your Hibiscus planted last year for your birthday is standing in your garden so tall but not yet blooming. It has been indoors with us all winter until just recently. Your purple Rhododendron bought last year for you are not yet blooming either but are a lovely green and so full. Everything here where you lived and still reside celebrates you, little one.

Today we drove to your town of Rochester for whom you are named. I go to the Walden Bookstore in Lilac Mall and buy books on grieving again—and too about the afterlife. They are our books. Too, I buy a new journal for us to await its turn to be written in.

After this visit which is significant as was the one on March 18th last year after you went to Heaven, and the visit on March 18th of this year, we drive to the place where in 1986 God set you down on earth just for me. I will write in more detail about it when I write your meditation for June 23rd. This year instead of a rock, I place a shiny new penny on the cement ledge outside of the door of an unoccupied office where once the mall stood. With prayers and tears I remember that glorious day in 1986 when first we met. Because you send me pennies from Heaven I leave you pennies too, sweet Rochester.

On our drive out of Rochester we stop at the Wal-Mart where last year we bought you the incredibly lovely, tall, coral Hibiscus for your birthday. This year I select a new Lilac tree for you, our state flower. You and I love this lovely color also. Though we buy specific memory plants, all the flowers in the gardens are for you, little one.

We drive home and I spend time in the gardens and take pictures. Inside I sit and stare and cry too. It is Friday and I keep our Holy Hour at 5 PM that extends to past 6:30 PM and too, pray the Rosary as I do always. You bless me with an image of your precious face up close to mine in Hypnogogic Imagery and I am overwhelmed. We are never apart.

It has been a Holy Day. I borrow words from our journal entry last year in *Corridors* and write that *"though it is sad, it ends with the knowledge of certainty that we shall be together forever. Happy birthday, dear Chester. You made my life like a birthday every day."* Tonight we will be on the sofa together and the heat from your precious eternal being will fill my legs as always.

IN CELEBRATION OF HIS LIFE

It is the birthday now—
Of a young gentleman most distinguished.
Long ago I made the vow
Of love—and relinquished
Heart and soul and holy space—
To this companion with the beloved face.
Through deep, silent gazes our love is spoken—
This bond created above cannot be broken.
It is with gratitude that I thank God for this priceless friend—
That I was chosen for this honor—I shall never comprehend.

Dedicated to   Jan
Rochester   May 30, 1996
on his birthday

Taken on Rochester's birthday

My Little Comforter

It is as important to them to communicate with us as it is to hear from them.
Your pets know how much they mean to you, and they are still with you.
Your pets will be waiting for a happy reunion when you cross over.
—George Anderson, *Walking in the Garden of Souls*

June 8, 2003

*I*T IS ROCHESTER'S FIFTEENTH-MONTH ANNIVERSARY of entering Heaven and I have been so aware of it all day. How can it be when it always seems in the present as I had prayed for? Sitting on the sofa as I do at night with my back against the armrest and my legs stretched down the middle cushion, I settle there to read and watch TV. Not long after getting comfortable some words were said on a program by someone that caused painful memories to rise up and surface within. Tears came, and immediately the heat and electricity on my legs from Rochester's spirit began to intensify to great and unusual proportions to tell me he understood and he sympathized. He had been present in body so many times when I was in emotional pain about this issue in the past. It was incredible and so deeply consoling to realize anew that he was showing me how aware he is of everything in this life we share.

Just several nights previous on June 2nd Rochester made himself present in still yet another dimension, that of Hypnogogic Imagery. I have seen Rochester before in this way numerous times, yet before he went to Heaven I had never seen anyone I ever knew in Hypnogogic Imagery. As I have written in a previous book, I saw many clear and amazing scenes and people that I described in this unusual dimension but never anyone I ever knew. But this all changed when Rochester passed, for then he began to appear to me in this visual form. It was both startling and utterly consoling and I am so grateful. It is quite possible that all I received in these visions before his passing was in preparation for me to have the awareness of this other world and dimension so I might be totally prepared for the gift of Rochester to come through and appear.

On this specific night on my Dad's birthday when in bed in the dark and before sleep as I prayed, I saw Chester up close. Just his precious face was so very close to mine, his big golden eyes looking into our one soul. It was so detailed and beautiful exactly as in real life, and all the while his heat and electricity were being generated on my legs as had been before his handsome countenance appeared. It was such a gift—and I felt it might be such from both Rochester and my Dad, a divine gift on my Dad's birthday.

Often in prayer I have to wait for images to appear and some never do. But this night as soon as I closed my eyes my beloved little Rochester appeared an inch or so from my face while I was lying in the dark. How often in real life he would come up close to me like that to bump his little head into mine numerous times while his paws were on my shoulders. And then we would settle down to sleep as he laid on my legs facing me, his little paws in my hand, just as he did this night of June 2nd in spirit.

Life is not measured by the number of breaths we take, but by the moments that take our breath away.

—Unknown

Our Black Bag

What a lovely surprise to discover how unlonely being alone can be.
—Ellen Burstyn

*I*N A BOOK I BOUGHT OVER TWO YEARS AGO there is an interesting story of
an author and lecturer who dramatizes very graphically what it looked
like to carry our past with us. As he walked across the stage hunched over
with the burden of the heavy sack he was carrying over his shoulder
someone asked what was in the sack. His response was *"My Mother."* He
was asked if she was heavy and he indicated definitely so. Then he was
asked why he did not put her down and he replied *"I can't."* When asked
why he cannot stop carrying her he replies that he does not know. He has
always carried her.

It became obvious to those present that it was such a waste of time
and energy to carry the heavy burden of the past with us. Our present
moment is destroyed by guilt and shame, and resentments truly make it
impossible to have healthy relationships. This small account was spoken
of in a book *Precious Solitude* by Ruth Fishel, an author I have read
through the years. The title had appealed to me for I had already begun
to write my book on solitude back in Fall of 2001.

Almost two years later the small account has new meaning for me for
I am a different person than when I first began to write this book, and I
have dramatically but piece by piece discarded the baggage I carried
through the years. I too had a large black bag. I knew I could no longer
live that way any longer. We only have the present moment, and if we are

fortunate the present day, and we cannot afford to waste this time. Rochester's passing has taught me a great deal that no other death has, simply because our love and relationship is so deep and of God. Also because I had not been given time to grieve in the past. I was told untruths, and rushed through the passage of grief for my parents and uncle because it was said I should not cry, and I was scolded when I did. Since I had children to care for the grief was not expressed fully nor did I work through it or deal with it in any way except to occasionally journal about it. Even then I felt this was wrong. Though these specific words were not being said to me along with the other words, it was as if I heard the scathing rebuff "*Grow up!*"

Well I have grown up and I truly know the importance of going at your own speed through this passage of grief. For some it will end at our own deaths. That is how it shall be for myself. No one can tell another to grieve or not to grieve. The heart directs this sacred passage, not another human being. It is a passage so sacred it can barely be written about though I have tried. Some portions of it can never be put down on paper or spoken to another, only to your precious loved one that has passed and awaits you.

Often people think that we can push memories away and by keeping busy they will disappear. But they do not and they will continue to haunt us if we do not let them just surface. By prayer and thought we can spiritually deal with them. Though they can be painful it should be our joy to meditate on them giving them special time. Were not these beloved ones that you loved? And still love?

Some memories would bless us if we could let them go. Their absence would be healing. Other memories we never want to let go. They are like a string of pearls—each pearl a special moment to place on a chain and wear forever close to our heart.

If we can go at our own pace and pray, and in recollection cherish our loved one and the memories we shared, then we will indeed be in a precious solitude. Writing in our journal we can record memories, ask questions, talk to our loved ones, and gently go moment by moment through this passage.

Our town dump, fifteen minutes away, is an intriguing place with many sections, deep holes in the ground, and huge containers for every kind of refuse that must be separated. It has become so complex that even the term "dump" has been replaced by "transfer station." It is an experience to be there with the sea gulls calling, and circling the entire area above. It is all like another dimension. I often dump various things of a "non-material" quality while there. You too can do this in a dump you create through imagination. A poem I wrote some years ago explains a visit there of this sort.

DUMPED

> Today—I am at the town dump.
> Most appropriate—for there is a clump—
> Of balled-up debris—within me;
> With roots just like that of a tree.
> It's made of junk clinging there—
> It is nothing I want to declare.
> But it causes such sadness and woe,
> I desperately want it to go!
>
> Right here on this spot in this dump
> With the Sword of the Spirit—that lump—
> I'll cut free and jump on and smash—
> And leave it right here in the trash.

> Jan

Some things we will be able to let go of as I have, the things that tortured for years and entered into my sacred grief concerning Rochester. Paper is a willing, quiet listener. Writing is sacred and meant for solitude when your heart is aching and trying to be at rest. It is good to experience the joy of solitude with your beloved one in spirit, and the pleasure of quietness as you commune, pray, and write. It is time now to put down—

THE BLACK BAG

Put down that bag
It is breaking your back—
Empty the contents
And discard that sack!
Address, then toss the problems and pain—
And never carry that black bag again!

Jan
2003

MEDITATION FORTY

Just Beyond the Veil

Most visitations are greetings, but with a purpose.
That our deceased loved ones are able to return to us, however briefly,
proves that a bridge of consciousness, of love, of light,
connects this life and the next.

—Joel Martin and Patricia Romoroski,
Love Beyond Life: The Healing Power of
After-Death Communications.

Friday, June 13, 2003

TODAY AS I AM PRAYING THE ROSARY during Rochester's and my Holy Hour of 5 to 6 PM that extended to 6:25 PM, I ask again that I experience Rochester during this period. I have experienced him during this prayer time frequently and in different ways.

I am so happy because I do have a visit from him again today. In our writing room and while praying the Rosary I always envision Chester lying on his quilt across from me as I also hold his flowered tin that contains his ashes. Envisioning him with eyes closed but fully awake is exactly as if my eyes are open and I am looking at him directly in reality.

Suddenly I am given a beautiful clear vision of my little beloved Chester! He broke through! The image is this—all completely life-like and as if it is taking place in the present moment.

I am sitting on the sofa in the living room only I am facing the other direction toward the door, and not the window and TV that I face at

163

night while Rochester lies on my legs in spirit. The papers and book of mine that are on the sofa leaning against its back on the middle cushion are there in this vision. On my legs, instead of the bathrobe that Rochester always lies upon, is the wildlife guilt of his folded in quarters just as it always is on the bed in our writing room, the quilt he loves so to be in. Rochester jumps up on it now and stands on it looking at me with his beautiful golden eyes just as in life. Then he moves a little while still looking at me with eyes that hold me fast, preparing to lie down upon the quilt that is upon me.

It is absolutely as in real life. I can see the trees and small wooden table outdoors on the deck through the sliding glass windows as well as Chester.

The only things I inquire about in my mind are why I am sitting in reverse on the sofa, and why is his wildlife quilt upon my legs instead of the quilted bathrobe? I am so overjoyed to be given this perfect vision as if taking place in reality in the living room, as I sit in the chair in our writing room keeping my Holy Hour and praying for my precious Rochester. Another unexplainable connection! He is just beyond a veil and continues to cross over.

CONFIRMATION ANEW

On this day in a vision
I am in joyful collision—
With hope and reality
Not death and finality!
For he is well and alive—
Confirming—he does survive!

For Beloved Rochester   Jan

A Rock in Your Pocket

*We use the earth and its materials to create a life full of
materialistic wonders, but we have lost the appreciation for the earth
as a source of our spiritual development and the life of our soul.*
—Thomas Moore, *The Re-Enchantment of Everyday Life*

ROCKS HAVE ALWAYS HAD GREAT MEANING TO ME ever since I was a little girl growing up in the city of Philadelphia. Now that I am a big girl grown and living in the woods of New Hampshire I am surrounded by rocks and in my glory. New Hampshire is known as *"the Granite State."* I could share many of my experiences and thoughts concerning rocks but have already done so completely in a lengthy but very interesting chapter about them in my book, *Beneath the Stars and Trees—there is a place.* Our granddaughter Julia visiting here recently expressed awe at the long length of that rock chapter wondering how I could have so much to write about rocks. We both laughed at that but I encouraged her to read, for though she had the book because it interested her, she had not as yet begun it.

As I have written before, so many people seem to have lost touch with the earth or simply have no interest in the natural world. Rocks seem to be included in this thinking. This can easily happen to those born and raised in cities and who often remain there the rest of their lives. Some also feel no accountability to the earth. This is perhaps understandable, for those who live in cities or even suburbs—are concerned with their own responsibilities and interests, and many have not explored in thinking, reading, or actuality, territory that is totally unfamiliar to them. Perhaps there has been no time in their busy lives to do this, or nothing that sparked the interest to do so. Perhaps there is even a dislike for any other way of life except for city living. It is a combination of many things really that causes indifference or unawareness.

Rocks, however, can be incredibly interesting. They carry stories from millions of years ago and are conduits to another reality. In another meditation in this book there is an account of an amazing rock formation that was ten thousand years old. It touched hearts and was a center stone for many area residents and those from other states. Rocks have a sacredness about them through all time that some cultures respect and others disregard. Author Thomas Moore suggests we make an amulet out of a rock or stone and that we wear a stone around our neck. Stones also seem to teach in so many cultures.

Thich Nhat Hanh, a Buddhist monk, a peace activist, a seeker of the way, and a respected author I read, suggests that it is good to keep a pebble in our pocket, a beautiful pebble we may find in our own yard. To read this just this week in a new book of his gave affirmation to a practice I have been doing for years and also wrote about it in the lengthy chapter on rocks I referred to earlier that is in my own previous book *Beneath*.

I relate how I had a rock in my pocket frequently some years ago that I found here on *Higher Ground*, one I treasured. I also carried stones from our property in my pocketbook so that while living in Pennsylvania I always had these rocks from our beloved property in New Hampshire with me. But the one that was always in my pocket was special, though I would transfer it to my small Rosary purse at night that went along to bed with me. This brown and white purse became lost once in a town in New York when our van broke down while travelling from New Hampshire to Pennsylvania. I could only imagine what thoughts might go through the finder's mind when first they opened it and discovered a rock and a rosary. I had been so concerned about seeing to the safety of Rochester in a strange motel room I left the purse under my pillow.

A woman who worked in the motel to which we had been towed, lovingly returned the purse and contents by mail, learning my address through the motel registry. In writing her a letter of appreciation, it began an exchange of many letters. She apparently did not think the rock strange, perhaps it revealed ancient insights to her, and when she later made a spiritual visit to Medjagorge she surprised me by sending a Rosary of black stones. God often sends *"alike persons"* into our lives in strange ways. I still use that Rosary nightly and Rochester's little paws are still upon it as always. Rochester was always attracted to my Rosary. I wrote several poems for him in this regard. And it is unusual that this kind woman of the Rosary is named Rosalie. I think of her as *"Our Rosalie of the Rosary."* Too, I think of the rosary and the rock as Rochester's

To keep a pebble or small rock in your pocket, one that is picked up perhaps from a place of meaning to you, is a lovely practice. Washing it first and examining it to see its special features if it should have any, and then saying a prayer over it can give it significance. It becomes a prayer pebble, one reminding you of a beloved place or companion and also to pray often. A quick touch of your hand upon it may center your mind upon God if only for a moment while in the midst of activity. There is a beautiful true story about a boy and the rock he carried in that same chapter about rocks in *Beneath*. Thich Nhat Hanh also states that just holding the pebble, breathing in and out calmly and smiling, can help you tremendously. It helps us to practice mindful breathing and we feel very peaceful.

He states many people invoke the name of Jesus or Buddha Amitabha with a Rosary, and I would reverently add the name of Mary also, for she is my Blessed Mother and causes a deep spiritual connection with Rochester and myself in the praying of the Rosary, one of numerous connections. Many Rosaries are made of real stones and not beads.

And so the pebble is a kind of Rosary, a reminder that the Lord is always with you. Every stone is a unique spirit. Each stone has its own story to tell. Perhaps today you may wish to find one for your pocket. A simple stone can bring solace. After all, we have it on the authority of Scripture that—*God is our rock.*

Nourish Your Soul

We each have within ourselves what we need for our own journey.
The answers aren't out there, out in the world, but within us.
And we will only hear those answers if we are quiet enough.

—Unknown

*T*HERE ARE MANY WAYS IN WHICH TO NOURISH YOUR SOUL and this is so important that I tend to repeat it. You need this nourishment in everyday normal life, but you especially need it if you are despairing, depressed, sad or grieving. Many have found ways to accomplish this nourishing.

Simply sitting quietly and meditating and realizing all that you have to be grateful for can lift your heart. If you are further inspired you can write in your journal all these things that come to mind. Doing this on a regular basis will help you and if you have written you will have pages to turn to refresh you and to give thanks for in your life.

Many of the thoughts that follow can be adopted into your own life to be used on occasion or often when you are in need. Perhaps some will prompt other ideas in your own heart to rise up.

Giving flowers from your gardens or plants you have tended is a loving gift. Lighting a candle each night at mealtime to nourish giver and recipient, and saying prayers that also include family or those in need is uplifting. Put on some meditational music, or classical, jazz, the old lovely Big Band songs of the 40s and 50s or even children's music. (I lived listening to that for years with my six children and loved it) A particular type may strike your heart and cause you to cry but that is okay too. For years Christmas music fed the hearts in our family and we would begin playing it continuously at Thanksgiving.

I have had very significant music in my life in certain periods and have written about it previously. It was surprising the music I turned to at different times and that I absolutely needed! I would often make tapes of only one song ("Morning Has Broken") that fed my soul but drove my children crazy, and too, *Italian operatic music!* I would only play these tapes when driving our green van and get lost in their beauty while trying to heal from things in my life. Another car I associate with *Vivaldi's Four Seasons,* for it was all I ever put in the cassette player in the two years the red Ford Mustang was mine. Over and over again it played. This was the music I played while driving my children around, doing errands and going to Church. But inside our home Johnny Cash could usually be heard singing. He ministered to me again and again. Now I play no music.

Take walks to lift your spirit and see what treasures you can find along the way be it on a sidewalk or in the woods. You will be surprised. The tiniest thing may bring an answer to a question you carry within or something under a leaf or behind a rock may be the very thing God hoped you would find. Merely looking at puffy clouds can be inspirational.

Go places occasionally where there is wildlife if you live in the city and relish it. Take notice to each detail about the little creatures you meet. The wildlife here in our woods and property and out front on our deck has been pure inspiration for me through some of my most sad and difficult days. To feed the Mallards, squirrels, chipmunks, birds and raccoons and see the wild blue heron and hear and see the crows communicating touches me so deeply. I talk to them all and receive the dearest responses, and surprising ones too.

And likewise, if you live in a remote area perhaps a change of scenery in a busy town will revive you. Just walking, or even sitting on a bench watching people can shake up your saddened spirit if only for a brief period.

When you feel sad or discouraged I have found praying for others can help you draw close to God. I write many letters and cards and this is a joy to do and helps me, but also the recipients of these love missals are hopefully revived a bit too. Too, you can write your own prayers for yourself or to include in letters or cards. As I have written in a previous book in detail you can create your own prayer book in so many and different creative ways. You can choose a lovely cover, or cover a plain book with material of your choice. You can write prayers or quotations in it, and glue in lovely nature scenes or pictures that move you with your written entries. And always use a pen or pens that you enjoy, perhaps with different colored inks. All of these thoughts can apply to your journal as well, but to have a book especially for prayers is lovely. Just holding it is a comfort.

Holding too your precious animal companion and petting and stroking him is a treasured way of nourishing your soul. Rochester was my dearest comfort and he always knew when I needed him on my lap to cuddle. He still does! Even our larger animal companions who think they fit on your lap but do not, still need to be held and comforted as you do, and in perhaps sitting on the floor with them to do this or having them cuddle next to you on the sofa, can all be so precious to you both.

Having pictures around of loved ones you love but are in Heaven can be soothing. Keep them out where you can see them and talk to them and you will begin to realize they are very close in spirit and are encouraging you from beyond. Photos mean a great deal to me in this way. I carry two of Rochester always and have others in frames. In my writing room I have small framed photos of him as well as of my parents, uncle, and my wonderful friend I call *"Friar Francis"* whom I have written about, and a kind friend Barry. I know they are in Heaven but hearing my every word to them just as Rochester does.

Choose reading that will bless your soul and you will be led to the right books if first you pray. I have written elsewhere the significance of books and reading in my life. You can read anywhere, indoors or out, and perhaps with a cup of coffee or tea. Speaking of coffee and tea, there may be some foods that are comfort foods to you, perhaps even something from childhood. Wrap yourself in a blanket if it is cold and have tea and cookies or anything that will soothe your soul.

Watch a beautiful sunrise when you can or a sunset. We have sunsets on our lake of such incredible other-worldly colors that they are inde-scribable. I catch as many of them as I can with my camera and have sent many photos to friends. Often I take a sunset on a friend's birthday if the sunset is glorious over the lake and send it later. In the city or suburbs people do not always take time to look at sunsets. Last night I took a picture of the full moon. I do that often as it sits out over the lake. It is comforting to see and you feel a heavenly presence. Look at the stars and talk to your loved ones in Heaven. They are listening as you stand there alone with their spirits in the dark.

There are so many, many ways to nourish your soul. You will discover many yourself. Some of these thoughts may have prompted some deeper thoughts on your own. Reaching out as well as going within is good. But you cannot reach out if you are so in pain emotionally. Try to nourish yourself first. That is important. The other will come gradually. If your own soul is in pain you need God's touch in aloneness and peaceful silence.

Our daughter Jessica has been involved here in her town of Center Ossipee, New Hampshire with the Pioneer Club, which is for girls. They have done many loving things and one is to deliver a bag of canned goods to people in need. Each care package is individual and contains a stone (ah—see how significant stones and rocks are?) and a story. The story is the recipe. I will include it at the end of this meditation in case you may be inspired to make up one bag or more of these care packages. It is such a wonderful thing to do. You may have to slightly change two ingredients if the person you are giving your care bag to is a vegetarian. These bags can be made up ahead of time to have on hand and the story also. Perhaps you can type it or write it out from this book to share with others. Always include it and a stone in each bag. All of this will nourish your soul while it nourishes the bodies of those in need.

Another thought in closing to be used perhaps when you can reach out a bit as in giving the care bags is to deliver another kind of a bag, basket, or box to someone hurting emotionally as you have been, or similar.

In this delivery will be comforting items. The surprise of a gift when someone is down and depressed can be invaluable. You do not have to stay or visit when you deliver it unless you honestly feel the person wants company. Do not stay if there is even an inner twinge of the opposite feeling for then your presence lingering will even take away from the original idea of bringing comfort. Your giving time to create the gift is evident and will be present even when you have left the doorstep so they can be alone to enjoy your kindness.

In the comfort bag or basket you can put an inspirational book, chocolate kisses, a small journal and a pen, scented lotion or soap, shampoo, fresh coffee beans or some herbal tea bags, a snapshot from a shared happy day or one that makes you smile, a magazine, and top it all off with a cute small toy of some kind or stuffed animal for the child in them. An added lovely touch would be to write a letter telling the person of what they mean to you and all the qualities in them you respect. The letter alone would be sufficient in most cases, but for someone you know is deeply grieving or depressed the added gifts might be very comforting. You will think of other choices to make replacing the ideas above.

In solitude and silence we are led and nourished on our own journey. That is the answer—and once you discover this you will find your hopes and strengths and all you need. Let your soul rest like a child in the arms of its mother, like your little cat or dog asleep on your lap so trustingly.

The ingredients for stone soup follow as well as the story, "The Soup Stone," which is the recipe.

Luke 9:10-17   Luke 10:27

FOOD

canned potatoes	large canned chicken broth
canned carrots	canned green beans
canned onions	canned chicken

The Soup Stone
Retold by Iris Van Rynbach

There was once a soldier who was on his way home from the war. The distance between villages was great, and he had little hope of finding shelter before the night set in. But at last he came to a farmhouse on the outskirts of a village. The soldier stopped at the house and asked the farmer for shelter and something to eat. "I'm sorry, but what with the war and the poor harvest, we have little food to spare," replied the farmer. "Have you got a large pot and water to fill it?" asked the soldier. "Yes, of course," replied the farmer. "I have a soup stone with me," said the soldier. "A soup stone, what is that?" asked the farmer. "Fill the pot with water and put it on the fire, and I will show you," replied the soldier.

When the farmer's wife had filled the pot, the soldier said, "This is a recipe cherished by my family." He took the stone out of his pocket, turned it three times, and tossed it into the pot. The soldier stoked the fire and the whole family gathered around to watch. "This will be a good soup," he said, "but some salt would help the flavor. Could you spare a bit of salt?" "Of course," said the farmer's wife. She took the salt box out of the cupboard, and the soldier took a fistful of salt and threw it in the pot. "I've used the soup stone so many times, the soup may be rather thin." You wouldn't have a carrot or two, would you?" asked the soldier.

The farmer's wife told the oldest daughter to run out to the garden and pull up a few carrots. They were cleaned and put in the pot. While the soup boiled the soldier told them about his adventures. "If only we had a handful of potatoes this soup would be just right," said the soldier. The farmers wife came back from the root cellar with a handful of potatoes and some chicken. And into the pot they went. "What a grand soup this will be, and all from one stone," said the soldier.

"If only we had an onion and some green beans this soup would be fit for Christmas dinner." The farmer said to his son, "Run down to the neighbors and ask if they could spare an onion and green beans. And ask them to join us." Soon the son arrived with the neighbors and the food, and put them in the pot. While the soup bubbled away, they set the table with their best plates, bread and cider. At last the soup was ready. The soldier, the farmer's family and the neighbors all lined up with their bowls and the farmer's wife served them all. They sat and enjoyed their meal together and it was the best soup ever. After dinner the community sat and told stories and sang songs. They gave the soldier shelter for the night and when the soldier was ready to go he gave the farmer the soup stone so that they could have many more community soup gatherings. The solder told them, "Families helping families make all the difference."

The soldier waved and picked up another stone as he entered the next town.

The End

MEDITATION FORTY-THREE

Forever and Ever

1986

Today I journey back in years—
To a town not far away.
I fill with yearning and with tears—
Thinking of that joyous day.

For Rochester   Jan
                                 June 23, 2002

June 23, 2003

*L*AST YEAR ON JUNE 23, 2002, the anniversary of the day in 1986 that
Rochester entered my life, we travelled back to that spot in Rochester, New Hampshire. The original small mall that I had once entered and
found my beloved Rochester on a bench in a carton next to a man, is now
a building with numerous offices within. It is no longer occupied. Over
the years since I adopted him, each and every time we entered the town
of Rochester, or shopped in that mall, or rode by on the highway, I offered
up prayers of thanksgiving to God for allowing this precious little one in
my life. I never failed to do these things.

When in the mall I would go to the bench if empty, and lay my hands
upon it, and thank God for Chester. If someone was sitting there I would
stand to the side and pray.

Last year I prayed and prayed in thanksgiving for Rochester telling God and Rochester once again that I am broken hearted but so appreciative he is ever mine and I am his.

Before I turned to go I looked for a correct spot to leave a rock that I had selected from our grassy yard before Mass. It was a rock broken and cracked open like my heart and from a spot beneath the shelf on our porch where Rochester loved to sit. He viewed his world filled with beauty from this shelf. I knew his precious eyes had seen this rock in the grass below his perch. I dug it from the earth and took it with me to keep in my pocket while in church. Then I placed it on a cement foundation that runs the length of the base of the building as a trim. There was no other place to leave it. With more prayer I told Rochester again that he is like a rock in my life, but like this chosen rock I am broken and shattered. He already knows and continues to send me comfort. I felt the rock had more chance of remaining there indefinitely than if I had taken a bouquet of flowers. And so I left the doorway in tears, an area I once left with a carton sixteen years earlier, containing the deepest of joy in the form of a precious marmalade and white kitten, my feline soulmate.

On this June 23, 2003 one year later we again go the town of Rochester. I look at the many signs on the road bearing his precious name, the first one being at an intersection in our own town of East Wakefield. Today instead of going to church I visit the Walden Bookstore in the Lilac Mall. It is a place I found solace and books on grief to help myself ten days after Rochester went to Heaven and have returned to it other times. I go this anniversary to buy books again on this same subject and too, on the afterlife, just as I did on his birthday May 30th.

After this Bob and I drive to the same small mall in Rochester on the other side of town where God had placed Rochester down for me, the same mall that we visited May 30th. Birds are still flying about and several are in the eaves of the broken ceiling of the overhanging roof. I greet them and go to the door of the building as before. I look down at the cement foundation outside the door and through blurred vision I see my penny that I left there May 30th in its same spot. How wonderful! With prayers and continued tears I place another shiny penny down next to it. I will send pennies to Rochester just as he sends them to me. It is a sacred spot and moment and day. It is ours! And too—I write and dedicate this poem to my

ETERNAL ANGEL

Each day your life is celebrated—
All through the years for you I waited—
    Though I did not know.
But when God placed you down for me—
    I acted most emphatically—
    I could not let you go!
The box was carried with great care—
Your little head soon popped from there—
    And then we fell in love.
I placed you in my heart and soul—
Your precious presence made me whole—
    My Angel from above.

For Blessed Rochester   Jan
17th anniversary of
our meeting—2003

O dear faithful companion—all love and purrs—
At your ever constant presence—my soul stirs.
Thank you, Lord—for the gift of Rochester.

Conclusion to the poem—   Jan
"Inexpressible" written on
the 5th anniversary of his
entering our lives.
June 23, 1991

Our Mystical, Magical Tree

From an early age I have recognized a connection with Nature,
a mystical thread moving beyond mind and heart, connecting me to some
mysterious, unknown element. That I am not alone in this connection
is proven by the mystical writings of the ages, yet for some reason
mankind as a whole has failed to realize this inner truth.
—from *Talking with Nature* by Michael J. Roads

June 26, 2003

FOR THE ALMOST EIGHT YEARS we have lived in New Hampshire and several years before when not yet here permanently, our Christmas tree was placed on a small low table in the living room. It was in front of the sliding glass doors so that it could be seen from outside, and between a chair and a sofa arm. Rochester created two special areas for himself during the holiday season, one on the back of that chair and the other on the sofa arm. On the chair he could view the tree and ornaments near the top, and on the sofa arm he would be under a branch that always seemed to extend out over the arm. He truly loved being near the tree and patting the ornaments. At night he would lie on my legs as always as we sat on the sofa together my back against the other arm, my legs extended down toward the tree that we could admire together. Years before as a kitten in our former home in Pennsylvania he actually would climb up inside the tree before the ornaments were ever placed on it. Being a little cat that always remained indoors, these live trees brought inside he thought were for his pleasure, so filled with the good scents of the natural world. His trees in New Hampshire seemed especially meaningful to him. He enjoyed the entire process of our decorating each one and kept them company in the couple weeks that each tree was with us. And for the last several years our granddaughter Sarah would name each tree, adding to each tree's personality. This year she was not here to see our tree. I have written poems about the trees and the love and sentimentality about each. Though the trees in New Hampshire would stand on a low table they always reached to almost the ceiling. We would allow space for either an Angel or Star at the top. The trees in Pennsylvania stood on the floor and were larger because our larger home there had more space.

This past Christmas of 2002, our first since 1986 without the full presence of Rochester, we decided to put our tree out on the screened-in-porch. It is a place Rochester loves as do we, and it is where I had wrapped all the Christmas gifts that were displayed. I felt I wanted the tree in this new place because I was so sad, and though a change, it was still a spot Rochester would approve of because he loves being on the porch. In the warmer months it is his great contact with the birds and squirrels and chipmunks as they encounter each other daily through the screens.

We placed the tree on a long table out there he loves to lie upon and decorated the tree as always. It looked so pretty at night shining out from the porch onto the snow and wooded areas. I knew it could be seen by snow mobilers on the lake in the evenings, and too from across on the island. I would go out and say prayers there nightly and frequently during the day, and I knew Chester was always with me. With Rochester's inspiration I named her "*Radiance.*"

Often as I stood there seemingly alone in the still cold night with the lit tree as my only light its bulbs alternating in brightness creating a visual dance, I would see a Christmas ornament move. Several not only just moved gently, but often one or another would swing more noticeably or vigorously for a moment or two or much more. The normal conclusion would be to attribute this to a breeze or wind, but our porch is enclosed in glass in winter. There is never a breeze on that porch in winter. Everything is still and cold. And no ornament would swing as vigorously and for so long a time as several of these did due to a wind. They were not blown. There was a pattern to the movement.

And so on many nights as I would admire the tree or say a prayer I would stare at a swaying ornament, sometimes a little bear or cat or angel, and occasionally one of the satin balls. I knew who was causing these decorations to swing. For years I had watched a small soft white paw gently pat these same ornaments, and more.

It broke my heart he was not visibly here but it gave me such joy that he is ever present in daily life doing all that he did with me through the years. The tree became a most wondrous gift to me because it allowed Rochester a place to express himself and to reveal to me again and again he is always with me. Each night I lit Radiance—and prayed—and watched.

And so the weeks passed, and the time when we would normally take the tree down had long since passed too. Each time Bob wanted to do that I would object and request it remain. After all, no one was around but us to see that it was long overdue for disassembling except the snowmobilers, the birds and squirrels, and an occasional UPS delivery man or family member. People in New Hampshire often leave their lacy Christmas lights up year round, ourselves included. Living in the woods allows for some eccentricity and if not in the woods where else can a Christmas tree be kept up and lit every night until May? Yes, May!

She would have stood there until Rochester's birthday May 30th, if I had not gone out one day to suddenly find a pile of Christmas ornaments on the porch floor but no tree. When I was upstairs writing in Rochester's and my writing room, Bob had surreptitiously removed the tree. I realize his patience with the situation was commendable, but the tree was in no one's way, and he had taken it down only one day before Chester's birthday. It made me sad I had not had a chance for a special *"final night ceremony"* the evening before with Radiance and Rochester, or that she could not stand there one more day on his birthday. Because Bob and I are quite different, he just acted on impulse while I was not there and removed Radiance without a *"by your leave,"* as he would say. He is also not one who remembers birthdays.

He would not tell me where she was at first. I think he thought she would return. But finally I found her tossed on the ground behind some larger trees and was horrified. I picked the tree up and talked to her all the while, and propped her between two Birch tree trunks so she could stand.

She still looked so beautiful to me even in her plain and natural state without her ornaments.

One would properly think that this is the end to this tale of our tree, but it is not. She had given us a great lesson and only when she no more stood on our porch adorned in all her beauty, did I realize her message. This dear tree had stood from mid December 'til the end of May, five and a half months, and only in the two weeks before Christmas was she given water. I never refilled the water in my busyness and Bob had never replaced it for he intended taking her down by January 6th or so.

It was then I realized anew the tremendous power of love. Each day and night that tree was talked to and admired out loud. She was touched, called by name, and had the company of Rochester and myself telling her of her beauty. Bob too would comment on her prettiness at times. At night I said prayers for her and others as I stood before it. Often I would hold a branch in my hand as I prayed. And for five and a half months Rochester had been patting the ornaments at short intervals to make the tree feel special, and to tell me *"I am here!"* as they swung to and fro in the absolute breezeless stillness of the cold winter air.

This tree knew she was deeply loved and appreciated. When the water was exhausted, she lived on love and tenderness alone in the presence of those who deeply desired her sweet presence. She supernaturally survived on love when in reality she should have died! Not one needle dropped on the porch floor or table in those long months.

She basked in love, radiating it back to us in all her greenness. To stand in front of her made me feel loved too—because it was Rochester's tree. It was totally energized and saturated by our love.

But when she was taken down suddenly, without our good-byes and touches and regular prayers, and tossed aside and cast away, her spirit was broken. Though I found her and stood her up and prayed and talked to her, I did not continue to visit her as many times *daily* as I did when she was on the porch. I truly failed her and I am ashamed. Within a couple of days I was so saddened to find her totally brown. I was crushed! I felt like I abandoned her after all the joy she had given, even though I touched her and expressed love to her each day. She is a beautiful bronze color, and the bronze has changed to an iridescent bronze there amongst the green pines as she leans on the Birch trunks and I daily visit her and pray.

But it took awhile for me to forgive myself and only after I felt the tree understood and knew she would always be loved and remembered for all the consolation and peace and joy she had given. I still hold her branches in my hand and speak love to her. I still take pictures of her periodically just as I did when she was on the porch so green and soft. During that period since Christmas I had taken several photos each month to record her everlasting beauty. The bronze needles remain and do not drop off.

I do not feel I can relate the truth of this relationship Rochester and I had with this Christmas tree in any more depth than I have. The lesson to be learned from it in our relationships of life is very evident. Love is a miracle in any life! It continues to be in Rochester's and my eternal relationship even though his physical body is not present. And love was a miracle in the life of a dear little Christmas tree. She survived on love alone!

What miracles can be wrought by love!

To think upon:

My very spiritually insightful friend Chris attempts to create gardens that he envisions would be like gardens in Heaven. He believes that in setting up such beautiful prayerful places they often are created in the heavenly realm in which we shall spend eternity. His inspired vision combined with my own meditations and thoughts have blessed me. I love to garden and try to create unusual arrangements and color through placement of the annuals and perennials. Surrounded by rock walls they truly are heavenly to me, and always I would plant flowers in them for Rochester even before he passed.

With this mystical and ethereal vision in mind that I believe to be true, I have asked God that this dear Christmas tree be given new life in my gardens of eternity for Rochester that exist now, or possibly that still are in progress in Heaven. Too, that he may enjoy his tree green once more and nourished by heavenly soil and rain and sun. One day I will be there to see his green tree with him, but for now will continue to whisper to her bronze-like spirit standing here between the birches. May others in Heaven too be blessed by Rochester's tree and gardens, as I am by the flowers I continue to plant in his gardens by the lake.

HEAVENLY GARDENS

Soft and gentle flowers enhance
One's inner life at merest glance.
I walk beside them to admire
While inwardly I do aspire—
To loftier thoughts
And lovely dreams—
Of heavenly gardens
By celestial streams.

JGK
2003

*Radiance, our
Christmas tree, now
a beautiful bronze
amongst the white
birches*

Stopping Anger

*Speak or act with a pure mind
And happiness will follow you
As your shadow, unshakable.*

—Excerpt from *The Dhammapada:
The Sayings of the Buddha*

WHEN YOU ARE IN SOLITUDE there are ways you can learn to handle some of your problems. You may only have one or two, or you may have many. Or the entire matter could seem exaggerated if you are still in sadness and may too, seem overwhelming. You may just feel like crumbling.

Many in this world and in our own families do not know how to handle their own lives and problems and allow their anger and pain to touch others. It spills over to people that are around them, and yet to some in their lives they can control it and come across as being sweet and understanding. They are often selective in their anger. But you personally have to learn to control your hurt in response so that it does not in turn spill over onto others and be spread to everywhere you are.

Often when someone has made you suffer because they do not know how to discipline themselves, we begin to feel they deserve punishment, that they deserve to feel how they have made you feel. They have never tried to deal with their own anger successfully. But of course, this person already felt badly before they decided to attack and cause the same suffering in you. Actually this angry person has caused this same feeling in others too because they cannot control themselves. They often secretly play people against each other and then act innocent and stand back to see the result. They may be someone close to you. Even when they periodically calm down and go through a phase when they are not striking out, anger is still collecting and building up in them that will eventually be vented somewhere down the line. They cannot help themselves for they are always right. Always!

This is where you can make a difference, you in your solitude, and even if you are in sadness and grief. For it is much better to try and help than to suffer. You have learned how to be compassionate.

Because you are being touched in your solitude and are a different person through the grief that has transformed you and that you will always carry in your heart, you have learned how to calm yourself in anger. You can see more clearly how this other individual suffers. This is your chance to help and not strike back. Anger can be transformed through forgiveness. You become more calm and loving.

The suffering you see them going through motivates you to compassion and kindness and it is an entirely different way of thinking and causes non-action. You no longer wish to retaliate. This foils their plan but can be the compassion that in time can turn their life around.

The only way I feel that you can come to such conclusions when you are in pain is through prayer and meditation. Even if it is only in a short period of turning to God for help you can be changed and liberated from anger in the sacrament of the moment. You can once again be a loving individual interiorly and outwardly as you were before this person struck and wounded you. Respond to this person in love if they will allow it, but whether they permit it or not leave the person who attacked you in the Hands of God. Your anger will be dissipated.

Therefore, I say unto you, if you have faith and doubt not...
Whatsoever ye shall ask in prayer, believing, ye shall receive.
—Matthew 21: 21,22

STOPPING ANGER

If another attempts to hurt you—
May I try please to alert you.
Show compassion and astound—
Forgive and smile, you will confound.
And God will bless this right decision—
While your heart sees with clearer vision.

Jan
2003

MEDITATION FORTY-SIX

Everywhere

If your mind is closed, you cannot learn anything new.
Closed minds reject anything different, anything that conflicts with
their old beliefs, beliefs that may be false. They have forgotten that
experience is stronger than belief. Fear is the force that keeps minds closed.
Only open minds can receive and process new knowledge.
—Brian Weiss, M.D.

June 28, 2003

IN PROOFREADING MY PREVIOUS BOOK, In Corridors of Eternal Time, for my publisher I am in tears. While reading it I realize that it is a strength to me, my very own words. For you see these words were written one year and one week ago today, and all that I read in this meditational journal entry I can rewrite this very moment with the same conviction and say to you that it is completely true. I have lived one more year of life and without the physical presence of my beloved Rochester. It still feels as if it is last year this time for I am living in the present moment continually as if Rochester just left. I prayed this would be so, so that I might live on the brink of two worlds. God has answered my prayer. I live life still with Rochester, except he is in spirit. My grief is as intense as I prayed it always would be. The words written in the meditation that follows will further make this clear. I am living out the truth of this gift.

I pray that if you should ever lose a beloved animal or human that you will not relegate your beloved one to the past, be ashamed of grieving, and move on, not keeping your beloved very present to you. Often grieving is seen as a weakness. It is not! It is a precious strength! Only until you realize it in its full capacity as I have and have others, and allow it to be an integral and enormous part of who you are now and every shall be, will you truly ever know who you yourself really are and experience this transformation. May the meditation that follows speak to your heart and soul.

EVERYWHERE

He had ceased to meet us in particular
places in order to meet us everywhere.

—C.S. Lewis

Friday, June 21, 2002

The love I shared and still share forever with Rochester is a gift. I carry this grief gladly, for without it would mean I had never had Rochester in my life. It is a gift from our one life lived together. I cannot ever comprehend life without Rochester, and I would not trade one moment of this sorrow, even with all the pain, in contrast to never having lived and loved with Rochester. It was a spiritual dimension of living that defies explanation, and now it continues on still yet another plane until we are together in Heaven. Without Rochester I cannot imagine what the past almost sixteen years would have been.

Perhaps there are some who have lost human or animal companion loved ones who wonder where their loved ones are. Please pray and find a peace in the certainty that they live on. I am secure in my belief of sharing life with Rochester in Heaven, and that my Dad is caring for him until I join them. Yet I know too, as many do, that my loved one is still *here* with me, for I experience him and sense him. His spirit never deserts me, never departs. He is around me, beside me, within me, and slumbers on my legs. This will always be so. It is an unfathomable comfort. It is a solace beyond words.

Losing my loved one's physical presence changed me. I see the world differently, and a sense of solid individualism has strengthened me. I do not have to answer to others about my grief. I am changed internally, spiritually, and in mysterious ways. There is a new person within that has stronger beliefs and an endurance level I did not know was ever possible.

I believe Rochester's Anima, his breath and soul within me, his eternal gift to me, is this underlying strength. And yes, God's grace, — and His Holy Spirit bestowed on me at conception. I have resources and power within me that rise up and sustain even in my most anguished moments of depletion, and of experiencing Rochester's physical absence. I believe it is my most devastating loss, yet I know it is imparting a wisdom to carry me through what days of my life I have left until I am in Heaven with Rochester. The life we had together cannot be duplicated. It was and is a divine gift. Both Rochester and I are transformed. You who read may come to know this transformation too, if you are deeply grieving for one who was and is a special world unto itself for you alone.

EVERYWHERE

He is near
My little dear—
He is far
He is my Star.

He is without
He is within—
In the silence
In the din.

He sustains
He ordains—
Removes fear
He is here.

For eternal   JGK
Rochester

Another Friday. Another Holy Hour from 5 to 6 PM in solitude, remembrance, prayer, tears, and eternal love. He is here.

MEDITATION FORTY-SEVEN

The Solace of Gardening

Mine is just a little old-fashioned garden where the flowers come together to praise the Lord and teach all who look upon them to do likewise.

—Celia Thaxter

I FIND THE SWEET QUOTATION ABOVE VERY MOVING. Though I have mentioned our gardens here and there in this book and others, I need to express the solace of gardening and being with flowers. Gardening has helped me so much since Rochester's passing and I have written in detail about memory plants in my previous book, *Corridors*. Gardening has touched my soul as I have touched the soil. I can only hope that you too can create a garden where you can drop on your knees and be amongst the flowers. If only a small patch of earth is yours, please create a garden for your soul. If you are not living where this is possible and you have no earth in which to work, then visit other gardens as often as you can in nice weather. I feel you will find one if you seek one. Too, you can grow some flowering plants indoors, but being outdoors with the flowers under the heavens is very healing. I know for I have been gardening all summer and in the past.

If you prefer an alternative for an outdoor garden there is the Zen garden. I have seen several and they were beautiful. Combined with my own thoughts about this, are lovely thoughts by author Ruth Fishel. A simple way to create this type garden is to use a flat box and fill it partially with sand. Collect small stones and pebbles of various sizes, color and shapes. Different texture of sand can be used or various colors of sand.

189

When you add the small pebbles and stones it will need raking. A twig or other natural object from nature can be this instrument, then you can rearrange the stones and form the sand into designs. You could put a tiny meaningful object in connected to your loved one. You can change the arrangement daily or anytime you please and spend time in meditation sitting by it. It can be on a table in your special room of prayer or where others can see it. Zen gardens are known for their simplicity and are very delicate and lovely. I have always remembered the one I saw at a garden show in Philadelphia and the creation of one done on a television program.

These words following written in my chapter on "Gardens" in my book *Beneath the Stars and Trees—there is a place* tell succinctly about the gardens here on "Higher Ground."

> *Moving permanently into our cottage in January 1996, I became a true gardener that Spring and ever after. The seven beautiful rock walled garden areas Bob created, I complete by filling them all with flowers year after year. I am partial to petunias of every hue and they are interspersed among all the other blooms, as well as having one entire small garden to themselves, filled entirely with their glorious gentle blossoms. This is the "Prayer Chair Garden."*
>
> *Each rock walled garden is named; The St. Francis Garden (His statue stands in it), The Path Garden (The path leads to the dock), The Beach Garden (It overlooks the beach), The Deer Garden (It has a sweet statue of a reclining fawn I named "Dawn"), The Lake Garden (Right above and at the water's edge) and The Gnome Garden (Due to the gnome figures in it and the tree I refer to as "The Gnome Tree" because of its curious and dramatic openings in the massive trunk).*
>
> *Each year the gardens are different because although I plant perennials that should be here year after year, they are not always here. The harsh winters destroy some of the plants, but I always replace them. Also bulbs are often dug up by the little squirrels and chipmunks, but this is all part of nature.*
>
> *As we experience the riot—*
> *That came in silence and in quiet*

Lining paths of rock and earth —
We welcome you—wildflowers of worth!

Jan

Beside the gardens that God and I create together, He does an exceptional work without me in scattering large patches of wildflowers. Large dandelions, buttercups, and other varieties unknown as yet to me abound, and blue delicate asters so sweet. Wildflowers are so beautiful to me!

It took me years to get Bob to respect the wildflowers. He considers them weeds, and to me, some of the prettiest flowers are weeds. He would mow them down! He respects my wishes now to let wildflowers grow any place they please. Because of this ongoing debate I wrote this poem that appears also in *Beneath*.

Dandy Flowers

We've chosen here to be exiled
Where lovely flowers grow so wild
Along the path and by the rock.
He says we'll be the laughing stock—
To keep those long stem flowers there
Blowing in the summer air,
Because they're dandelions tall
And should be cut down one and all!

I said he had a "city mind"
Permitting him to be so blind.
In woods all things grow wild and free—
I became a referee!

We parted then—I said a prayer—
Soon he called me out to where—
The flowers stood by rock and tree
He left them all there just for me!

He thinks I'm strange and yet some how—
I know he sees their beauty now.

Jan

Earth laughs in flowers
—Ralph Waldo Emerson

I have planted rose bushes too along with other flowers for Rochester because the rose symbolizes love and is given as a message of affection.

It is Rochester who watches his roses and flowers grow and who makes my life bloom in a garden of memories. I have written in detail in *Corridors* of how Rochester presented me in a store, with a bouquet of pink silk roses that contained five large blooms and two buds. I have read in a spiritual book and been told by a spiritual man named John that pink roses are a way that our loved ones in Heaven often express love to us. Because it is a mystery there is no explanation as to how they appear when they do, but they are a gift from a beloved one. You may wish to read more about this in *Corridors*. Other things have happened similar and I treasure each one. Like the mysteries of the Rosary Rochester and I share, these mysterious pink roses bring me great comfort—a gift from him.

An ancient flower of the goddess, roses often surround Mary in Christian imagery and Mary is know as *"The Mystical Rose"* under one of her many loving titles. The scent of roses can open your heart and their beauty overwhelm. A Rosary is used to prayerfully count the prayers to Mary, and Rose windows in Cathedrals are often dedicated to Mary. She is Rochester's and my Holy Mother and companion and so I plant roses for her and Rochester.

After you buy flowers and plants and get them situated in the gardens you should take a few minutes to stand back and look at your new guests. Make sure they are not damaged and tell them how pleased you are to have them come stay with you and that you hope they will be comfortable. I talk to them as I am planting them too—and always when visiting them or watering them. (Sometimes with my tears)

Tell them how pretty they look. I talk to them about Rochester and many of the things on my heart and say prayers over them.

Author Jerry Baker writes in *Plants Are Like People* that if more people would walk into Mother Nature's living room and talk to the Almighty through plants, people would not need to take drugs to be happy. Happiness is all right there, and he says he gets high just mowing the lawn or tending the roses. He gets his troubles off his chest talking to the friends in his garden.

As I have written elsewhere in this book and in my *Journal of Love* I personalize my plants indoors by giving them names. This is true also for some of my permanent plants in my gardens outdoors. Bob, who normally does not want to be involved in any of what he considers my eccentricities, and keeps far removed from them (it is a shame for him) surprised me by immediately naming the very beautiful coral hibiscus plant I bought as a first memory plant for Rochester last spring. Once in the ground he said to her "*hi—Biscus,*" and so this glorious plant has kept that name of "*Biscus.*" She lived indoors with us all winter and is now outside again. Other plants are named also but I call all the unnamed ones affectionate little love names. The author Jerry Baker mentioned earlier gives his outdoor plants mostly Indian names. He feels you can not call a plant "hey you" and I agree. He even labels his plants' names onto white sticks. People love to see this and his gardens!

There are many statues in our gardens of Angels, animals (also angels) and St. Francis. Too, a new lovely bird bath from our extended family the Clancys, and an Angel bird bath from them also some years ago, and too, bird feeders and bird houses. Wind chimes too are ethereal and all about. All of these provide solace and inspiration with the flowers. Angels are so meaningful to me and are direct links to God. Rochester is an Angel—not just since his passing but from the day he appeared into my life. Guardian Angels that are not animal angels have wings to allow them to fly into the heavens and legs to allow them to walk the earth. My little one had four precious little legs with soft white marshmallow feet that padded around this cottage. He was and is a protector. Animal angels are messengers from God and they exhibit spiritual qualities.

As I close this small garden meditation I am inspired to ask you "Have you ever planted a flower or shrub in memory of a loved one?" Perhaps if you decide to do it after carefully selecting it, you could have a little ceremony by yourself as you plant it. I do that, and continue in the days after to pray near each plant and talk to them.

If you have absolutely no place to plant flowers, then perhaps draw a beautiful memory plant that is meaningful to you and your loved one using your colored pencils. Respect it greatly and think of it as the real thing. Perhaps display it to honor your loved one. If you take a picture of it you can glue the photo into your journal to honor your loved one also.

Too, through imagination if you live where there is no garden or it is winter, you can sit in a lovely garden of your creation with your loved one, enjoying all the color and mysteries of the garden. After spending time in meditation there record it all in your journal. Perhaps write poems in your journal about your garden, real or imaginary, and your loved one. I have revealed a secret in my book *Beneath* telling about a flower name I was given when I was a little girl and I belonged to a Brownie Troop, an extension for younger girls of the Girl Scouts. This name is so lovely to me and is a part of my love of gardening. You will learn the name in reading that book and may wish a Brownie name of your own.

We become lost in a heavenly and healing realm when we are tending a garden and down on our knees. It is in this attitude of prayer that we are brought closer to the loved one we cherish and to our God. May you discover the preciousness and significance of gardening.

Hibiscus, Rochester's first memory plant

MEDITATION FORTY-EIGHT

A Picture's Worth
a Thousand Words

The death of a beloved pet can strike humans at the deepest levels.
The human-animal bond can be as intense and meaningful as any
human-human bond, and it must be accorded the same respect,
both in life and in death.

—Therese A. Rando, Ph.D.

The artist is a receptacle for emotions that come from all over the place:
from the sky, from the earth, from a scrap of paper,
from a passing shape, from a spider's web.

—Pablo Picasso

July 17, 2003

A S I COMPLETE THE FINAL PROOFREADING this day of my latest book *In Corridors of Eternal Time* for my publisher before it is about to be printed, I receive a package in the mail. It is from my new friend in Colorado, Sue Peterson. In January 2003 when *Corridors* was accepted for publication I too met Sue at that time via e-mail. Rochester introduced us through our book, his and mine, *Journal of Love* which Sue had ordered and read. When she wrote me in response to it, a unique correspondence began. She too loves animals, and she and her husband

Tom have numerous animal companions, and I am fortunate to now have sweet pictures of them all. Sue went on to read other books of mine that also have Rochester in them but it was *Journal of Love* that initiated our friendship. As I have written throughout this book and *Corridors*, Rochester is a gift to me and he has also bestowed many gifts on me in his physical life time and in his life in spirit here with me. Today as I complete the final proof reading of *Corridors*, I open the package from Sue after making myself wait two hours to do so. I sense that what is within is significant and I need to appreciate its mysterious presence first unseen.

At last I lift out the gift within and simply dissolve. I hold it to me and cannot believe that two people I have never met would be so loving as to do this.

In my embrace is a 5x7 portrait of Rochester in the medium of a pencil drawing done by Sue's husband Tom. It is completely life-like and Rochester's beautiful large eyes look deeply into mine. It is as if he is once again and ever saying, *"I am here."* Even his pewter St. Francis medal is in detail about his neck and he is within a handsome brown frame with a thin geometrical design toward the inner edge. That he should inspire my new friends to create such a gift for me reveals anew what I have been trying to continually express. He is an Angel and he is ever with me. For this portrait to have been created by a loving man I have never met indicates the power of love and inspiration my Rochester causes to emanate to others. How precious that Tom Peterson should be inspired and make the time to draw this life-like icon of Rochester that arrives on the very day that Rochester's book *In Corridors of Eternal Time* is finalized. It is a keepsake of love from my little beloved Angel and eternal companion through Tom and Sue Peterson and their love and kindness. Thank you, thank you.

Enclosed also with this life-like work of art is a pale green candle. A green ribbon designed with tiny black paw prints upon it is tied around both the candle and a scroll-like paper it holds in place encircling it. This candle is from an animal support group and a moving tribute is printed on the scroll that I will claim personally for Rochester each time I may light the candle or that I simply pray the prayer.

I light this candle for you. You always have a home in my heart.
This candle represents the light and joy you bring into my life.

*I bless you in remembrance and gratitude
for the blessing that you are.*

I share Tom and Sue's gift of the portrait of Rochester here with you to bless you too.

Just as the handsome portrait of Rochester arrived in the mail the day that *In Corridors of Eternal Time* is completed, so today I receive another package from Tom and Sue. It arrives just as this very book is finished and ready to be mailed to Blue Dolphin on December 23rd. How can this occur again!? It is an unbelievably precious personal remembrance. A large white glazed mug with the beautiful drawing of Rochester on its side. I carefully take from the carton a companion piece to the framed portrait.

Again through my friends in Colorado, Rochester has sent me an enormous symbol of his presence and love, and blessing on this book and my life shared with him—on this most significant day.

Thank you, Sue and Tom.

Nature Journaling

"Look what I found in the grass!" cries a five-year old
running through a field of wildflowers. What is remarkable is not
what he found, but his enthusiasm, which has transformed a marble
into a sparkling, magical conveyer of light.
Enthusiasm, like the breath of God, transforms everything.
—Gail Sher from *One Continuous Mistake:*
Four Noble Truths for Writers

*T*HOUGH I HAVE WRITTEN ABOUT JOURNALING, there is another form that may be of interest in your solitude or on nature walks. This can be separate from your other journal you keep.

Use a notebook of your choosing and in doing this type of journaling you can bring the outside inside with you. Around your home or on walks in the woods bring this notebook. It can be small to put in your pocket or any size you wish. You can press leaves between the pages, draw pictures of things you encounter, just quick sketches—or add photographs if you have taken your camera with you. Some people do only this form of journaling and I own several fine journals of this type written by others that have been published. Try to note the time of day you made your notes and sketches, the date, and the weather. Later when you go through your journal carefully you will be able to read your version of the changing seasons.

If there is a special area you are checking out regularly you could make a map of it in your journal. Too, nooks and crannies and special bushes or trees within the area you could give names. It is good also to write down any animals or birds you saw and to mark on the map or write in the journal any burrows or nests you came upon. Also it is fun to record the plants you see growing there. Too, note different rocks and mushrooms. There are such a variety of these non-edible mushrooms growing in our wooded sections now and even in my gardens. It is like an explosion this time of year! One variety even grows out of my rock wall and is strong enough to force a rock onto the ground. Some are like the ones you have seen in story books that look like tall hats with red dots all over them. In another book that I wrote I have a photo of a large flat mushroom adorned with a miniature tea set with two garden gnomes standing having tea. Other mushrooms are dark gold and cluster.

I mentioned wild flowers in my meditation on gardening and they are very important even though some may think they are merely weeds. Every plant has a purpose and place. What someone may call a weed may be the very plant putting vitamins or minerals into the soil. Also the wild animals may depend on the wildflowers as food. Too, that wildflower someone may call a weed could be attracting bees and butterflies, and this in turn helps the plants near the weed to grow nuts and fruits.

I just learned recently that one of my favorite wildflowers here, the dandelion, is from a different country and out of its habitat. Dandelions came from Europe! I have enjoyed dandelions since I was a child and found them on my front lawn in the city. I like a definition of a wildflower to be simply a plant whose job has not been noticed yet, or it is simply a lovely flower out of place. If you think of them that way perhaps you will respect them.

If you read about wildflowers they are fascinating and they can be in vacant lots or roadsides or ditches or in the woods or growing out of a crack in the sidewalk. Maybe you could get a little guidebook on them at the library to look at and read, but also you could record a few things helpful in your journal about them. Sketch them and their leaves. One of the first drawings I made in my nature journal, a number of years ago, was a clump of wildflowers and I felt so good about the results. Then I drew some down by the lake as well.

I read in a nature book to avoid picking rare wildflowers or collecting the plants. Just let them remain in their plot, for sometimes it takes years for a plant to make one flower. That is something I did not know until recently.

BUTTERFLY WEED

O sunny yellow butterfly weed
    bring me your innocence
        and cheerfulness—
            your sense of the wild—
That my heart may nourish and spring forth
    with simple joys
        and a sunny nature
            and the spirit of a child.

Jan

I learned also recently that one of the biggest cities in the United States is named after a wildflower—the wild onion. This plant grows in the Midwest and the Winnebago Indians call it SHI-KA-GO—Chicago!

I find it is fun to own a nature book geared for children's learning, also with illustrations, for when we are first starting out to take walks in nature or just to observe in our own yards we are child-like, or I certainly am.

Please consider keeping a nature journal but if you think you can only keep one journal, then it would be best to write in the one that will help you in your sadness or grief or daily living for that is most important. But even in that you could put some nature notes to bring yourself cheer. Only you can know, but I would feel remiss if I did not at least mention the idea of a nature journal for I love nature so much and know how I have needed to be outdoors in these woods these past months and always.

Perhaps as I said in the earlier meditation about journaling you can simply keep only one journal for everything. The only drawback I see to this is I would never take my personal journal outside on a walk with me for fear of loss. I would only take a smaller journal or notebook. But you could later transfer your nature notes into your main journal. Perhaps that would even be a special therapy, and you could enhance the notes and draw the flowers or other observations and color them if you wish.

Only you will know what is right for you. Part of deciding and then beginning to do it is all part of ministering to yourself in solitude.

This seems the appropriate meditation to mention that my lovely Christmas tree Radiance written about earlier, is still standing with all her bronze needles.

Too, it seems a right time to share with you a poem written during a period when nature truly entered in dramatically in a storm and affected the electrical power with its own electrical force. I combined this authoritative touch from nature that we experience here frequently, with writing in my journal. And Rochester was by my side and often on my lap. He and I never like thunder storms and lightening.

POWERLESS?

The electrical power went out tonight.
I sat with my journal and began to write
By candlelight—and as I wrote
I dreamily took note
Of the flickering softness about my journal
And the darker shadows. And this nocturnal
Hour or more caused me to think
Of simpler days—creating a link
With simpler ways of long years past.
And I wanted these moments to last
For retrospection—and to absorb the connection
In gentle glow—and reflection
Upon this former unknown time and place—
With the warmth from the candle upon my face.

Suddenly—all lamps went on and motors hummed
And I was forced to swing like a pendulum
Back from candlelit ways
To be with these modern displays.
But in my heart I felt blest by that hour or two—
In my secret time-warp rendezvous.

Jan
November 29, 1994

Hail Mary

I'm certainly not the only person to have asked in advance that a loved one
continue to communicate after he or she has passed over.
Fortunately, that isn't a prerequisite for maintaining an afterlife connection.
It is however a way of letting the person know that his or her contact
will be welcome, and of helping to ensure that you yourself
will be attuned to receiving it.
—*The Afterlife Connection* by Dr. Jane Greer

ODAY IS A DAY WE GO TO SANFORD, MAINE. Whenever we go there or anywhere, before leaving our cottage I ask Rochester to please show me himself or direct me to see things he wishes me to see. It is something I believe he leads me to do to teach me to be aware and that he is always with me. I have shared in my previous book also of small treasures discovered on such outings that are gifts from Rochester.

Today we enter Mardens in Sanford, a favorite outlet store with a great variety of items, and I have several gifts to buy for grandchildren. Here you can expect to find the unusual. Remembering always my words to Rochester I take a cart and start at the right side of the store, as always going aisle by aisle. A few items for the children have been put in the cart and a few aisles travelled when my interior alarm goes off. I place my hand over my heart where Rochester resides and also his plasticized picture is tucked beneath my blouse. I ask him to show me what he wants me to find.

I stand quietly looking all about me on the shelves but see nothing that seems to light up. But I just cannot seem to move on. I feel something is here waiting to be discovered. Then I notice just a few feet away a huge carton filled with indiscernible items and balled up paper, a carton big enough for me to climb into if empty and a friend or two as well. I check out the objects on top and they are all somewhat heavy and what seem to be animals and creatures from another planet, fictionalized and strange, not of this earth. I feel certain they must be lawn ornaments for they are cheery in their unusualness. My own animal lawn ornaments at home, a fawn, a rabbit and cat are very life-like. I keep digging in the huge carton, laying the top items temporarily here and there on the nearby shelves so I can go deeper. It takes a long time to go through it all and trying to place the upper things aside gently. There is a determination to get to the bottom of this in more ways than the obvious. Finally I do, and leaning way in I push as much aside as possible to draw up the last buried pieces. I do that one by one. All are these strange creatures, an entire community of them! I feel one last thing in the bottom within the newspaper wrapping. What was this search all about?

I draw the wrapped piece up, take off the sheet of paper and oh, there before me in my hand stands someone Rochester and I love so much. Emotion floods me as tears also flood my eyes and stream down. Rochester has given me a gift most significant! It is a dark gray statue approximately 14 inches high of Mary—Our Blessed Mother. Her face is lovely and peaceful and her hands folded. Her appearance just stirs up so much within me. How could I ever deny Rochester's leadings and activity in my life when he has just caused another to occur? I could have stopped digging in that carton shortly after I had begun because there was absolutely no evidence that it held anything but the lawn creatures. But something within kept me from leaving. Rochester led me there and caused me to persist! He knew my reward would be to again have confirmed that he is ever present to me and communicating by drawing me to Mary, our Mother and intercessor. He knew instant understanding of his constant presence within me and to me, would again be validated. I write this all calmly to share with you, but the overwhelmingness of it all cannot be written.

And now to the practical side of it. Mary has no price tag as did all the lawn ornaments for I had looked at those. It was similar to when the TyToy stuffed pale gray cat appeared as a sign to me in our local grocery store and no one could account for its being there and it had no price.

I take time to quickly put all the lawn creatures back into the huge carton and with great love I take Mary to the check-out counter with my other items. She rides in the seat portion of the cart with my left hand always on her. She smiled at me, and I was talking to Rochester all the while.

The check-out woman does not know her price (Mary was priceless to me) nor do several others she calls. Finally one woman takes her to a manager. This person begins to look around the store to see if there is another like her to get a price. But I know there is not. This is a gift from Rochester. Finally the manager returns puzzled and asks, "Will $4.95 be all right?" And I answer, "Of course."

Such a day Rochester and I had!

Mary has been standing for some weeks on the wide windowsill in the living room to the right of the window Rochester loves to sit at and look out on the woods and lake. Next to her is a handsome life-like cat very similar to Rochester and whose face and eyes have his gentleness. I always felt it was as close to Rochester in appearance that any almost life-size cat candle could be. Naturally I never used the figure as a candle. It was given to me shortly after Rochester became mine and I his, and I always had it displayed. Now Mary is companion to the symbolic Rochester on the shelf, and as I sit on the sofa each evening with Rochester on my legs, they are smiling and looking down at us from across the room.

I believe too this gift from Rochester has an additional significance for us. Perhaps it is indicating that we should always take the time to look beneath the surface of the creatures and humans and situations that come into our lives. For what might seem like an entire crowd of somewhat frightening lawn gnomes, could instead be something Holy and precious beneath the surface that we are meant to meet and embrace into our lives.

*Statue of Mary with
"Rochester candle"*

MEDITATION FIFTY-ONE

Let There Be Light

Last night I saw him way up there,
A little cat who wasn't there.
He wasn't there again today
But I know that he's back to stay.

I often see him, I declare—
On the stair or on the chair.
He's my Angel ever near—
Ever dear and ever here.

For dear Rochester   JGK

July 22, 2003

*T*ONIGHT WE HAVE BEEN READING and watching TV and just as the 11 PM news from WMUR begins, Bob stands to go to the kitchen. Rochester's spirit has been lying on my legs as always that are extended down the sofa length as I lean my back against the arm. I am facing the two Lava lamps, one on the TV and one on the high green book shelf, and realize I did not turn on the latter one. The other has been on several hours. Each night I light the two mystical lamps. Since Bob is standing I do not want to move and release Rochester's spirit from my legs. I ask Bob if he would please turn on the Lava lamp before he sits down again.

The request is barely conveyed and an answer from Bob has not even had time to come forth. Suddenly in a minute or less the Lava lamp turns on by itself! I am just overcome with emotion and then feel the heat on my legs intensify as Rochester settles down anew. Such a phenomenon! Rochester continues to comfort and surprise me.

That he should be on that shelf is not unusual. He often jumped up there from a nearby chair and I have taken pictures of him up there. Too, in past weeks I had a dream of him as clear as day jumping from the chair back onto this shelf and it is recorded in this book.

He knows how I enjoy the Lava lamps each evening, one being authentic and larger from the 60s, and the other a bit slimmer and bought in more recent times, the one I had neglected to turn on. And Bob's reaction to the lamp turning on? It is simply one of those things he will not discuss. He did smile, but he also muttered something as he sat down. It is only a matter of time that Rochester will win him over, just as Rochester did when he was in body.

I have learned from several sources that electrical disturbances or interruptions (or lamps being turned on) are frequently reported as direct after-death communications from Heaven. Others than myself receive lighted communications from loved ones too.

I have experienced a dramatic incident with the television also through Rochester's attempt to communicate that I have reported in this book. I am fully convinced and am so very grateful he is constantly expressing his presence in so many varied ways. As when he was in body, he continues to light up my life forever.

It is quite common for spirits to manipulate electricity in various ways. For instance, they are able to cause light bulbs to flicker, telephones to ring, radios and televisions to turn on and off.
—James Van Praagh, *Healing Grief— Reclaiming Life After Any Loss*

Old Man of the Mountain

Men hang out their signs indicative of their respective trades;
shoemakers hang out a gigantic shoe; jewelers a monster watch, and
the dentist hangs out a gold tooth; but in the mountains of New Hampshire,
God Almighty has hung out a sign to show that there He makes men.
                                                    —Daniel Webster

July 27, 2003

ONE OF NEW HAMPSHIRE'S MOST PHOTOGRAPHED NATURAL WONDERS, "The Old Man of the Mountain" has attracted millions of visitors since the 1800s. The profile was scenically set about 1,200 feet above Interstate 93 and Profile Lake and about 65 miles north of Concord, New Hampshire in the White Mountain National Park.

Daniel Webster, a 19th-century New Hampshire statesman, once wrote, referring to the old man, the words that open this meditation. That symbol is gone from the mountain now but the beauty of this region lives on. We are all reminded by his spirit that change is inevitable and often arrives without notice breaking hearts.

We will always remember the shock of hearing the news early Saturday morning, May 3, 2003 that sometime in late evening of May 2nd or very early hours of May 3rd New Hampshire's symbol of freedom and independence vanished. It is believed that the famous profile could have been loosened by the late Spring thaw. It is written that on Thursday and Friday the profile was obscured by clouds so that the exact time of the *Old Man's* departure is not known.

He was so significant and so loved we heard on TV of people arriving from other states to make a pilgrimage there, people who had visited him as children or who still came regularly in summer or other seasons to see him. I remember well a Sunday drive there with several family members in the early 1980s to get my first glimpse of him, and now I am grateful I did for not all of my family ever had the privilege of seeing him.

It is said that on Sunday, May 4th State of New Hampshire workers could be seen examining the ledges that once were know as "*Old Man of the Mountain.*" Meanwhile below the site visitors began arriving shortly after sunrise to this well-known attraction. Some came to pray, some to photograph, some to leave a message, and others to see for themselves the emptiness on the mountain and the departure of this famous figure. Many thought this profile would be a lifelong reminder of New Hampshire. Instead the site of what was "*The Old Man of he Mountain*" is now a sheer cliff. He was also nicknamed "*The* "*Great Stone Face*" or "*Profile.*"

However on the news of July 26th it was reported that tourism is still standing up even though the *Old Man* fell. It is said that interest in the *Old Man* is higher.

Facts concerning this famous profile are so interesting, the most amazing being that he was ten thousand years old! From his chin to the top of his forehead he was 40 feet, 5 inches. His forehead ledge measured 45 feet by 10 feet and was 300 tons. The Old Man's nose was 10 feet long; upper lip 7 feet; chin, 12 feet, and a brow of two granite layers.

It is written too that the *Old Man* gazed to another time. His face bore a slight smile as he remembered the delicate forehead, scars and metal stitches. It was thought he would not fall in our life time. *The Old Man* was carved by nature not by man and was considered the most anthropomorphic gem in the whole world. There is nothing else like it.

I have learned through reading there are several heroes in the *Old Man's* biography. Niels Nielsen, whose ashes were laid to rest in the *Old Man* last summer, made preserving the profile his life's labor of love. It is said that each year, as long as he could, he dropped on ropes, suspended 1200 feet above Profile Lake. In doing this he would access, measure and repair the inevitable damage done by ice during the winter. In 1989 his son David who had worked up there with his father since he was a boy, took over the job. He has since retired as police chief of Belmont and was caretaker to the fine granite ledges that are *The Old Man*.

These men were not alone for many private donors and local businesses provided equipment and the Director of White Mountain Attractions Association, Dick Hamilton often joined the Nielsons.

There is a museum for the *Old Man* and many things can be learned there. Too, we bear the *Old Man's* profile on our New Hampshire license plates and I hope this will never change. He is also pictured on a quarter coin and too, he inspired Nathaniel Hawthorne to write one of his best known short stories. He has appeared on paintings, postcards, road signs and company logos.

It is reported he was more than an accidental arrangement of ledges left after the glaciers scraped away the tops of the mountains that once covered northern New Hampshire. Barbara Radcliffe Rogers and her husband Stillman Rogers are co-authors of *New Hampshire—Off the Beaten Path* and she has written a lovely eulogy for the *Old Man*, some of which I have shared here, as has George Geers written wonderful information.

Whether you feel the *Old Man* was created by the hand of God as Niels believes or is a series of nature's coincidences as his son David believes, it is a natural wonder and its spirit has affected thousands. David too had found the nook there to hold his and his family's ashes, just as his fathers ashes had been placed inside *The Old Man*.

As I listened to the news concerning *The Old Man* in May and periodic updates in other months, and thought about it all so often in quiet moments, I came to several symbolic conclusions that apply to my life now and to many other lives.

Sometimes we find we cannot live life on the mountain top any longer. Our face falls and our life seems to crumble around us. We end up in the valley below. We are not the rock we thought ourselves to be. We have to symbolically pick up the pieces and begin our climb up from the valley of despair. People see us when we are on the mountain, but they do not always notice when we are shattered and in pieces in the valley of despair. We must pray and seek our way, and make our ascension back up the mountain into the Light.

Animals Are Forever

A pet is a lifetime commitment.
Visit your local animal shelter
and adopt a pet for life.
—The Humane Society of the United States

All life is one and even the humblest forms enshrine divinity.
—Anonymous

OFTEN WHEN WE ARE SAD OR HURTING we are in need of a consoling companion, one that will share life with us. Though we may already have a human spouse or best friend, there is nothing quite like an animal companion. I adopted Rochester at a most difficult period of my life as I have written and shared about numerous times previously in other books and he truly was and is a gift from God. My life was changed by his surprising entrance into it in June 1986 and was dramatically altered also when he passed in March 2002. A precious animal can expand your knowledge, compassion and world, and enrich your entire life. I was never the same after Rochester became mine and I his. We belonged to each other and lived every day and night together. I am thankful I recorded our life together in journals and books and continue to do so.

There are so many cats and dogs that are in need of adoption and are just waiting for love and to give it in return.

A cat or dog helps you to focus beyond yourself, and your heart can be lightened and filled with a quiet joy through this committed relationship. If you take a kitten or puppy or a grown cat or dog from the humane society, you are probably saving their lives. And it is said that pet owners are less likely to commit suicide than people without animals and they are more likely to recover from serious illness. Dogs and cats are happy along with you and more important they seem able to grieve with you when you grieve. They need you, and like you, they need to feel needed. You never need to feel lonely with a cat or dog on your lap or by your side or by your feet.

Never turn an animal out that you have adopted or give them away to just anyone without knowing they will be loved and given excellent care. The animals too have deep emotions and to be given away can be traumatic or they can be mistreated. Norma, a woman I know and I have written about rescues cats and keeps them until they are adopted. Often the time is extensive. Once adopted with her approval, she insists and requires the word of the human who has adopted a cat that if they in anyway do not want the animal any longer, the cat must be given back to her. She is like an angel to these dear cats. She also personally has the cat neutered or spayed before giving him to his new owner, and she pays for this as well as a checkup.

Having a cat or dog companion does require you to be a responsible owner and to take charge of the responsibilities involved in order to insure your companion's happiness and health and safety. As a new year begins be sure to keep all dog and cat licenses and vaccination up to date. Remember to check pets for fleas and ticks regularly. As I have written elsewhere it is important to comb your companion regularly and they grow to love this. When I got out Rochester's comb and brush he was always delighted and got up on the table to wait for his grooming to begin. It is important too to brush your companion's teeth for like humans they too can get gum disease.

Travelling with an animal companion you must be sure of safety tips and you can read about these or check with your veterinarian or contact the HSUS.

Toys are a necessity for our companions too. They are not a luxury but a necessity, for our friends need mental and physical exercise. When an animal is not bored it is a great way of preventing behavioral problems. Remember however, your cat or dog cannot judge safety for himself. He needs your help in selecting toys that are safe as well as fun. Rochester's ultimate toy was the soft plastic ring I would remove from each milk or orange juice container. I would toss them on the floor and the fun would begin. He now has a pile of them in all colors on his feeding table. He had several other favorites too but the soft rings were his favorite throughout his life.

Always, always make sure your cat or dog is wearing a collar with an identification tag in case your animal should get outside by mistake without you and get lost.

Some think it not necessary an indoor cat or a dog should wear a collar or tag but it is extremely important. Not only in everyday life if someone should open the door by mistake, often a visitor, but too, for emergency purposes like fires. I think of 911 and all the dear animals whom some left behind and who may not have been found due to lack of identification, or who may have been lost forever on the streets.

The Still Small Voice

Within my heart I often grieve—
For there are many who believe,
That all God's creatures who are dumb—
To pain and cruelty—must be numb!

They do not know that in the glance
Of speechless animal—there by chance—
If time is taken—soul of the wise
Can understand and recognize—
A discourse splendid and from God—
In silent eyes of those who trod
And share this earth with human creatures—
And that dear dumb ones are His teachers.

If these words that are here penned
One simply cannot comprehend—
Then condescend to please befriend—
And to His Creatures love extend.

Two souls will then know still discourse—
From animal to human—with God as source.

Dedicated to   JGK
all God's Creatures   July 5, 1991
                                       New Hampshire

To be totally safe, always keep cats inside and walk your dog on a leash. Never leave your dog alone in a yard if you are not home. Never! Twice in the past week and a half there were stories on the news of two dogs stolen from their yards who had been left there alone when their masters went out. Each was stolen and abused to such degrees that I will not or can not report it in complete detail because I have been in tears over the incidents many times and without warning after seeing the dogs. In one instance two teenagers taped one dog's legs together and dragged the dear dog behind a car for miles. If that alone tells you the importance of keeping your animal safe and guarded then it is written with good purpose. The other dog's eyes were poked out after extensive beating. These were only some of the torture they endured. They are now back with their owners but under continuous veterinary care. Joseph Conrad has written: *"The belief in a supernatural source of evil is not necessary, men alone are quite capable of every wickedness."* One animal administrator on television called the perpetrators *"monsters"* and I find that not even strong enough a term. Three Labrador puppies this past week were also horribly tortured and mutilated after being stolen from their owner and only one survived, and he too is mutilated for life. Could you ever risk allowing this to happen? I can never rip what I saw and heard from my mind and heart. What is done to defenseless animals is so horrendous that new laws have to be made, for many criminals escape punishment totally. Dr. Louis J. Camuti, well known and beloved cat doctor who treated animals for over sixty years and authored *All My Patients Are under the Bed*, states:

Never believe that animals suffer less than humans. Pain is the same for them that it is for us. Even worse, because they cannot help themselves.

Our daughter Janna recently moved from Rhode Island to New Jersey and, loving animals, she took a part-time job of pet sitting. She was taken to lunch by the kind woman in charge and they spent much time together so the woman knew that Janna could be trusted. Having three dogs of her own also added to Janna's competence and love for animals. She works now for a group named Paws Awhile Pet Sitting Inc. in Pitman, New Jersey (pawsawhile@comcast.net) and each staff member strives to provide your pets with the highest level of service and loving care. The group exists so pet-lovers do not have to leave their animal companions in strange untrusted surroundings. Friends, neighbors and relatives often serve in a pinch, but some think it is a tedious imposition. And so that is why the staff and Janna make home visits to pets left alone all day where they get love and attention, their usual food and schedule and exercise, experience no exposure to illnesses of other animals and do not have to have the trauma of being transported to a kennel. Janna stays to visit and play with the animals and also brings her four year old Rebecca.

Turn to the local Humane Society to adopt a companion, for this week also on the local news it was reported how fifty dogs, all ages and sizes, were found confined in pens too small for them and stacked on top of each other in a building that had no light. They were occasionally fed and given water, but only the barest necessities, and all were undernourished. The pens were never cleaned and they were living in their own excrement and that of their companions. The majority of the dogs had never been out of those pens. Most all were very ill and all needed extensive help. Once discovered they were removed to the Humane Society in Concord, NH. Each night we are given a medical report about them and we can see they have been bathed and are being cared for medically, and the workers hold them and love them and are bringing them back to life. Slowly as they become completely recovered they will be permitted to be adopted by loving people. It is not something I will ever be able to forget, that men can be so cruel to dear defenseless animals. Thomas Edison wrote: "*Until we stop harming all living beings, we are still savages*"—and St. Francis of Assisi (1181-1220) said, "*Not to hurt our humble brethren is our first duty to them, but to stop there is not enough. We have a higher mission—to be of service to them wherever they require it.*"

If you love animals or want to learn more in their regard and wish an inspirational guide, you may be interested in reading my book *Compassion for all Creatures* published by Blue Dolphin Publishing. Rochester is on the cover, his precious face and beautiful eyes gazing out at each person.

It is always smart to have your companion spayed or neutered though it is at times a difficult thing to do. But it is a kindness. For the past eight months I have bought only one kind of postage stamp for my letters, that of the United States Postal Service Spay/Neuter stamp to help raise awareness. They depict the faces of a dear dog and sweet cat. When my postmistress knew what these stamps meant to me and that I seemed to be so centered in on them she warned me that they would soon not be issuing them any longer. I felt sad about that for they surely do cause awareness. She wanted to know if I wanted extra sheets before they suddenly were not available. I came back the next day and bought all she had—all $70.00 worth, and am thankful I did. I will be sad when my supply is all gone but I have some time to go before that occurs.

All year every year is *Be Kind to Animals National Pet Week* but the specific week set aside for that is May 2nd in 2004.

Never during hot weather leave any animal in a parked car even for a few minutes for it can be fatal. And be sure to provide for your animal companion's future should something happen to you if you should adopt an animal. If you have a human companion they may be the answer, but not if they do not like your animal companion. You can contact the HSUS for help.

My Rochester enjoyed spending long periods in front of our sliding glass doors watching the birds at the feeders and scampering wildlife. I have written so many poems about this in my books. It was a pastime he loved. This is a wonderful entertainment for your indoor cat. Often the birds, squirrels and chipmunks came right up to the windows eye to eye with Rochester. Even the raccoons! Consider a bird feeder!

May I remind you too to remember the animal less fortunate than your own if you should decide to adopt one. Donate to your favorite animal charity, please.

As I indicated earlier always prepare for disasters for in this era following 9/11 we cannot know what awaits. Make sure you have a plan for your animal companion in the event of any disaster such as flood, tornado, hurricane or fires. If a disaster is impending that you have been given warning about always keep your animal companion and your cat's or small dog's carrier in the same room with you so you can swiftly put them into the carrier if need be. Keep a larger dog's leash right there with you. Having lived safely through an enormous ice storm here in the woods for eight days without electricity or water, Rochester was always in the bedroom at night as he usually was but too, with his carrier in case we had to leave the cottage suddenly. Many trees fell near us and heavy branches on our roof and covering our entrance and porch. His carrier was near in the day and he with me at all times.

Perhaps you may feel I have written too extensively on the subject of animal companions. But you see, I have known and continue to know the utter joy of Rochester's love and companionship in all areas of my life, and I believe that not only in times of normal living are our animals treasures, but when we are sad, depressed or grieving they are Angels of Mercy. I have had Rochester stay with me continuously on my lap when he knew I truly needed him in sad periods in my life. His capacity for love and ministering to me was far beyond that of a human's, for he was constant, giving up his normal activities to remain upon me, his little paws on my hands. It was preciously surreal. I have written a poem describing his ministering to me in this way that has appeared in previous books, but that I would like to share again.

HEALER

Often when I am sad,
    concerned or ill—
He'll clasp both paws around my hands
    with a will
To make me right.
And soon will come light.

He'll never leave my lap—
    nor ever nap.

Long hours shall pass
  he'll hold me fast—
For he is there to heal—
  and it is precious and surreal.

He is God's Angel, in disguise—
  —a joy forever—my divine surprise.

For Rochester   JGK
with love and gratitude   August 28, 1996

Perhaps open your heart to an animal companion and let your life be touched and changed forever for good. Remember, an animal companion is forever.

Rochester—my being of light, God's angel

A Case for Solace

Let your tears come. Let them water your soul.
—Unknown

FOR YEARS AFTER MARRIAGE, as I have related in a previous book, *The Enchantment of Writing*, I always did some bit of personal writing daily while rearing my six children. But that could not be first in my life and was put on hold except for journal writing. I had to wait until the mid eighties to seriously pursue my dream of writing books.

While a young mother, however, I turned to sewing instead and made my five daughters' clothes and also clothes for their dolls. I spent endless enjoyable hours doing this. Many of the dolls' clothes were special matching outfits made from the left over material from my daughters' clothing. I sewed other things for my son but not clothing. I made him more fun things like personalized duffle bags and other boy related items.

Even our three Cairn terriers, Lizzie, Muffin and Crackers, had sweet little white lined drawstring bags made from tan material and covered with pictures of little dogs that looked just like them. I stored their combs and brushes and other items in them then too, and embroidered their names on them. They hung on hooks in our bathroom.

Their bags were used by other family animals long after our three little ones went to Heaven, and Rochester was one who had his personal grooming items stored in one of these drawstring bags. When our little animal companions saw us get these bags down they would become excited knowing they would be combed and brushed.

I also embroidered extensively, mainly heirloom samplers and multiple ones for each of my children. Samplers too for all family members and for friends far and wide. I was touched and honored in a special way for my embroidered samplers that I have shared about in *Enchantment*. Crocheting too became an interest and in less than one year I had created in my zeal eight crocheted afghans for gifts after I had relearned to crochet following long years of absence from it. Knitting I had been taught in childhood and I have always done that at times throughout the years. A sweet quilt was made too for my third daughter Barbara that I sewed while pregnant and expecting her. It covered her in a hand crafted pine cradle after birth and is still in her possession.

One item I created on my sewing machine is the one I wish to mention now for I feel it may have some worth in times of sadness, though the original idea was not with that intent. I called this item a *"get well pillow case"* and each of my children had one. The pillow cases were only permitted to be used when the child was sick in bed. The cases proved to be delightful and often took the child's mind off of his/her sickness. I chose unusual patterns for each pillow case, bright and cheerful. George had colorful racing cars, Barbara an array of many sizes of polka dots and the others were equally as cheery. They were so successful and desirable for our children I began to make them as gifts for other children. It was a sweet gift to give or send to a sick child.

On Christmas Eve our six children also had special pillow cases for that one magical night. I chose colorful Christmas designs in images appealing to children. Each child had a different case. I believe some have been passed down.

Not the get-well pillow cases or the Christmas Eve cases could ever be used except for those occasions indicated. That is what made them so unique and special.

All of these ideas and creations of the past I share now to perhaps inspire you to also be creative. But I want to center in on the idea of a pillow case. Often in deep sadness we become more childlike, and most definitely we need comforting. It does not have to be done by another for frequently there is not another who is sensitive to you at this time. We may have to rely on ourselves to ease our sorrow or to help us be quiet and at peace. It is at this point I would like to suggest a special pillowcase to be used only in those saddest moments when you need comforting and there is no one but yourself to offer it.

If you do sew and you feel up to doing this, go to a store that sells material as part of the entire project. Getting our of the house as a portion of the grief process and going somewhere that would bring help to your soul, could be a goal for a day when you are feeling better. Those days come and go and then return. For me, as I wrote in my previous book "*Corridors*," it was going to a book store having spent seventeen straight days at home following my deep loss. It was there I selected books on grieving and a new journal that would help me to survive, while writing my own book on grief. And then leaving the bookstore I returned to our cottage and the quiet and solitude.

Once at the store of your choice select fabric that truly appeals to you, be it floral, whimsical, childlike, animals, geometrical or with lovely scenes. You will know the right design when you see it. Buy enough to make one pillow case that is uniquely for you. As you sew pray over it and ask God to comfort you through its use. It is not unlike the purpose of a prayer shawl, except it will be for your weary head and tear filled eyes and damp cheeks. Perhaps it will draw you to sleep and you will awaken on it refreshed and with your sadness momentarily directed to new thoughts. But if you are having difficulty again and wish solitary consolation return to your pillow with your special case upon it. Perhaps keep the case or the entire pillow with it on out of sight. It is only for times of despairing when you need to rest in its softness and you need its blessings that you have already prayed into it. It is not for continuous use.

If you have no sewing machine or do not sew even by hand, then on your special outing to the store simply buy yourself a pillowcase that appeals to you. Perhaps one will speak to your inner child.

Once you own your own new case and realize its comforting qualities like a child with its own special blanket, you may want to make one or buy one for someone else who is sad or grieving. It should not be like yours. Through prayer you will be guided, and then pray over the case before wrapping it. Perhaps write a lovely note of explanation to attach to it even if you are delivering it in person and not mailing it. Often when we are grieving we are forgetful, and the recipient of the pillow case may forget its true meaning of healing and solace once it is opened or after you have left their presence if a note is not with it.

Often we are looking for something non-intrusive and gentle to do for another who is sad, and this is a comforting gift that will touch another's heart. It can also be mailed so easily in a larger brown envelope or left gift wrapped in someone's mailbox or at their door if you feel they are not as yet up to receiving visitors. But remember to write your note.

I promise you the pillow cases are meaningful. Some time after one of our children finished college and left home for another state to work some distance away, in a period of anxiety they called and asked if their pillow case still existed. I put it in the mail the next day and we have never discussed it since. It was then at that point I realized it was "*a case of solace*" and was being needed, appreciated, and used in a different way for a different time in life. It just touched my soul. Perhaps you too can comfort yourself and another as well. It will give you quiet joy to do so. Perhaps you can even create a "*Pillow Case Ministry.*"

A Thin Veil

Loved ones enter our lives
like deer
slipping in and out
of the woods.

They touch our earthly presence
and as we stop
to look at them
they disappear as quietly
as they came.

—Unknown

Monday August 11, 2003

*I*T IS VERY EARLY IN THE MORNING and though I am awake I am completely still with my eyes closed. I am sitting up partially against my pillow, and my white bathrobe with pale pink flowers is the only covering over my legs in this warm weather. On top of the bathrobe Rochester slumbers emanating his glorious heat and electric-like currents through my robe to my legs. He has been there all night from the moment I went to bed. It is so reassuring and comforting often bringing me to tears, because he chooses to remain so very close to me night and day. I know his little white paws are extended towards me, and though not visible I hold them together in my right hand as I have done all through the years.

Suddenly with no warning, in the midst of this silence and peacefulness, Rochester is before me. He is sitting on my legs and very close to me just looking into my eyes. He has done this so many times in our own life together. I ache to embrace him and pull him closer to me, but I am afraid he will disappear. His presence is gentle as he is, yet powerfully present. Though he has presented himself while my eyes are closed, I open them slowly. His figure remains, appearing completely as in life He is the same size and his fur looks soft and comforting to touch. His gaze of love leaves me motionless as he holds me with his eyes. For an instant he releases me and turns only his head slowly to the right. Then resuming his original position while his eyes stare into mine and into our one soul, he disappears. The heat remains and increases on my legs. The entire vision in reflecting back, perhaps lasted at least three minutes or more. I was able to capture him completely to cherish anew and forever in my heart. What wondrous gifts he gives to me to assure me he is ever here. There are no earthly words to express my love and gratitude. He reads my soul. He lives there as well as in Heaven.

It is written by John Milton that:

Millions of spiritual creatures walk the earth
Unseen, both when we wake, and when we sleep.

But sometimes we are given the incredible blessing of having a beloved one break through the veil.

> *Only a thin veil hangs between*
> *The pathways where we are —*
> *And God keeps watch 'tween thee and me,*
> *This is my prayer.*

—Julia A. Baker

MEDITATION FIFTY-SIX

Sorrowing and Grieving

I can learn to live creatively with a bruised or broken heart.
A broken heart is a heart made larger and more open than before.
—Alla Renee Bozarth, Ph.D., *A Journey Through Grief*

*I*N MY LATEST BOOK published this year 2003 *Beside the Still Waters— Creative Meditations from the Woods,* one of the meditations is titled "Prayer of Sorrowing and Grieving." I begin this meditation by saying:

I have been putting off writing this meditation for many weeks. My husband feels I am capable of writing an entire book on grief, but I know I am not able to do that as yet. In fact this meditation will probably be the shortest in this book for I am afraid to venture too deeply into the subject at this time. Perhaps I will return to it later.

Two and a half weeks after this book of meditations was accepted by Blue Dolphin for publication in February 2002, my beloved little Rochester died suddenly March 8th and went to Heaven. Overwhelmed by grief I did the only thing I knew could keep me sane. I began to write another book March 10th. It was a book on grief, a book I believed only a short time before that I was not capable of writing. I wrote it in journal form, day by day, to help myself stay alive each day and to help others, and to honor Rochester. It is a book for anyone that is grieving, be it for animal companion or human, for there is no difference. This book on grieving is now out in the world as of the end of 2003 and is titled *In Corridors of Eternal Time—A Passage Through Grief,* as I have mentioned elsewhere in these pages.

I wrote many things in that particular meditation in that previous book *Beside* that apply still to life in the present. I mention that God is in the unexpected, for since June 1999 (and it was June 2, 2001 as I wrote) I have had two major happenings in my life that were unexpected. I share how I am totally healed of one but that it has been a slower process for the incident that occurred first. Each had fallen in a different year, but in succession, and too close together.

One thing I wrote is most appropriate in the present for the third happening, that of Rochester's entrance into Heaven, came not long after. I can again quote from my previous book *Beside* and say:

> *I am still emotionally fragile and vulnerable enough from the first that I cannot say honestly that I am glad they happened and that they made me stronger. I know that would be the correct and valiant message to write or speak to help others, but it would not be my truth at this moment. Maybe that is displeasing to God when I write that. Although I have great faith perhaps He is expecting much more from me in these matters. Because I was affected so deeply by them I am not the same in this area of my life as I am in all the strong areas.*

Though I was in emotional pain from these two events that brought grief, I can say now, as helpless as I felt and so terribly sad, nothing can compare to the physical loss of Rochester. Nothing! Sixteen months later as I write now after his passing, it continually seems to be in the present. But I prayed it would always be so, that I might live on the brink of two worlds with Rochester, and my prayers have been answered.

And so I have been acquainted with grief in its various forms such as physical separation, humiliation, and death, as have countless others in this world. It is written by author Jamie Sams that

> *Humiliation is the one event in human life that becomes unforgettable. The loss of human dignity at the hands of another can be forgiven, but it is rarely, if ever, forgotten.*

Yet when I thought I was writing about grief in *Beside*, I actually was only standing in its vestibule. I had not entered into its entirety and utter depth until Rochester entered the after-life.

Pain of separation in this life from those we love while all are still alive can also cause a form of grief. I have experienced this numerous times and once for an extended period. As I write this now several in our family are going through extensive mourning over a permanent separation. Two in our inner family circle have been extremely close since they were little children. After marriage the elder moved to a New England state to accept a fine position. The younger of the two with spouse and one child moved to the same state so they could all be together and eventually the elder married. The four of them and their growing families of small children, six in all, were involved in so many activities together for their children and also attended the same church. They could spontaneously drop in on each other almost daily and enjoyed a loving way of life together. When the spouse of the younger took a new position in a state out of New England many hours away it was devastating, for life lived now can never ever be the same as it was those eight years spent together in the New England state. It truly has been a terrible time of grieving. Those involved can barely speak of it without tears, for now they will only visit each other instead of living life together. Hearts are truly broken. The younger of the two left for the new state this morning after a visit with us and her sister and family here in New Hampshire. For several months before this separation took place and it was known it would have to occur, the grieving had already begun. It has been a sad, sad time.

We all suffer at some time or many times. If we can teach ourselves something through our suffering then we begin to live again in the midst of it and in our on-going grief. We can help others in the same way for in reaching out to another we also help ourselves to be lifted up and experience moments of grace in our passage of grief.

If you can find an interest you enjoy (aside from writing in your journal) turn to that and try to be active in it. I wrote a new book following my first recent experience of unexpected sorrow in 1999 and this helped me tremendously. It was a happy book written about our life here lived in the beauty of the woods by a lake. Rochester helped me write that happy book that grew thick with many pages as he did all my books and we titled it *Beneath The Stars And Trees—There is a place*.

I began writing yet another book after the second experience a year and five months later. I titled it *Beside the Still Waters—Creative Meditations from the Woods*. And that helped to bring me healing.

Nothing in my life can compare to the physical loss of Rochester and so again I did the only thing I knew could in some way assuage my helplessness, and also help others in grief. I wrote *Corridors* to honor Rochester and to help me survive, and also to reach out to others in pain through this book and the written word.

Please try to write too in your sorrow and grief. Use a journal that appeals to you and confide. Pour yourself out. Write poetry as well. Draw and sketch in your journal. Be creative. And perhaps do it all in the memory of your loved one and dedicate it to the one for whom you grieve. When you complete it begin another. And another. Always write.

I believe that even in the midst of tragedy and grieving and pain, we must not neglect those we have lost. We need to pray in positive and loving ways and thoughts, and talk to our beloved ones. We need to stay in touch whether it be in praying formally for them or informally, or through conversation as though they are right here with us. For they are!

We give them a gift of a surge of love when we pray for them and too, we can ask them to pray for us. In your grieving if you are open and aware you will soon sense the presence of your loved one and you will live life in a new dimension. Rochester and I live each moment in that dimension that's open to all who seek it.

ANOTHER DIMENSION

> Grieving is another dimension—
> We live in sorrow and apprehension.
> For life is not as it was before
> We feel depleted—and implore
> For normalcy and all we had—
> Not endless days of being sad.
>
> We learn through anguish and the pain—
> Yet never shall be as we were again.

August 6, 2003   JGK

The Grassy Green Field

The Lord is my shepherd I shall not want.
He maketh me to lie down in green pastures.
He restoreth my soul.

—Psalm 23

W E ARE SITTING HERE WATCHING A FIELD HOCKEY GAME being played between Kingswood High and Plymouth State University on the grounds of Kingswood in Wolfeboro, New Hampshire. Before me is a beautiful rambling green field with trees of all heights bordering the edges, and a nearby mountain in full view. A lovely large farm house and enclosed yards sit on the far edges of the field closer to the mountain. Across the main street we have just travelled to arrive here is huge Lake Winnepesaukee. People are running and walking all around the green field, and a football practice is going on in the neighboring green field while others run the track around both these fields. It is all so unlike where I went to high school in the city of Philadelphia or where Bob attended high school in a suburb, the same Jenkintown High School our children attended.

Our fifteen-year-old granddaughter Maxine is goalie for Kingswood and is dressed in a huge green and yellow outfit (my grade school's school colors in Philadelphia) with leg pads and helmet. She is doing such an excellent job keeping the ball out of the wire pen. I am not an athlete nor am I knowledgeable about sports, but this is lovely to watch in this beautiful natural setting with the soft winds blowing and the glorious scenery.

My thinking turns to that little red ball in the soft green grass. When we are depressed or sorrowing we can be lying on a field of thick green velvet grass with a baby blue sky above filled with soft puffy white clouds as it is this day, the sun warm on our skin, and yet our minds are filled with activity like that of a crazed red ball rolling from thought to thought, memory to memory, and scattering sadness all through our brain until tears roll from our eyes and down our cheeks and into our ears. We are awash in grief again.

What we need is a symbolic hockey stick to bat that red ball into the far trees. We need to lie and allow our minds to rest, to meditate, and to pray in peace under the heavens, whether it is on a grassy green hockey field in Wolfeboro, New Hampshire or in your own back yard hundreds of miles from New Hampshire. In what ever form it can be available to you we need that *"grassy field."* I certainly do.

And if you have no grassy yard or it is winter when you read this and the snow and cold weather are surrounding you, then I offer a loving and gentle alternative. In your sacred space wherever that may be in your home or apartment that you have created for yourself, sit silently in your special chair. Close your eyes and pray and slowly envision a lovely grassy green field. Capture every detail of it and see the blue sky, white clouds and surrounding trees. Now pick up that hockey stick there and hit that annoying red ball into those distant trees. In imagination lie down on the soft grass and feel the breezes wash over you. Allow your mind to rest under the heavens.

MEDITATION FIFTY-EIGHT

Blessings on the Wind

Prayer Flags are something like prayer circles in that multiple people
praying for someone can make a difference in that person's life.
—Christopher Comins

As I write I am watching my own Prayer Flags blow in the breeze. The set of five is attached to a heavy cord and the ends tied to two strong tree trunks by the lake. It is very comforting to me to observe them daily. Often I go down and touch them and spend time saying prayers. They have survived the strong winds and electrical storms of New Hampshire's summer and still look new and radiant in color on the warm sunny days. It is said they last from three to five years when displayed outdoors depending upon weather, exposure to the sun, and the moisture content in the air. My flags withstand everything well, it would seem. They have been outdoors since May and it is now September. They are supposed to break down in time and when torn or faded they are normally burned. I am told by my friend Chris that they fall apart and need to be replaced and this is a good thing. It makes the prayers more relevant, and keeps them more a part of an active faith, than, for example, like a religious book that is read and put away not be read again.

The Tibetan concept is different, believing in the concept of impermanence, everything eventually dies or changes. I believe the flags were of interest to our Protestant grown children and other family members that visited continuously throughout the summer, and I would give out little bits of information about them at every opportunity.

230

One source I have read indicates that Prayer Flags are traditionally used in Tibet to enliven the spirit of a place, to make spirits happy, and to attract good spirits to favor the people and protect them. The flags blow in the wind, sending prayers to the heavens.

Hung in our gardens, our own Prayer Flags can enrich special ceremonies such as welcoming a new baby, a wedding; and too they can bless a new home or garden and offer thanks. On my set of *Creating Sacred Gardens Knowledge Cards* by Elizabeth Murray, it also indicates that through the hanging of Prayer Flags we can seek comfort and healing for someone ill, or a safe journey and blessings for a loved one who has passed on.

Opposite my set of Prayer Flags and across the green grassy yard sits a bench at the base of the tall trees that are at the edge of our wooded hills. The bench invites one to pause and sit, and I do, and it invites contemplation. I particularly chose that section of trees by the lake to hang my gift of Prayer Flags so as to be opposite from this bench. I do not always have time to sit there but it is a constant and was made by Bob. Having a bench gives encouragement to pause and to take notice to things of nature. Though my wonderful prayer chair on the raised platform by the lake is my holy place for years, I feel now this new area with the flags is of God also. I cannot see the flags from my prayer chair platform so the bench is nice for anyone. A bench has enough room for another person and I have often shared ours with a *"grandogger"* that visits.

My Prayer Flags were a surprise gift from my friend Chris whom I have known *"in spirit"* for many years through Blue Dolphin Publishing and who is Rochester's cherished friend also. His own yard and surroundings in California have many, many Prayer Flags displayed, and too they are hung close to his home. I have seen pictures and the flags look inspiring and beautiful. The flags sent to me are in English which is very rare so far. Because I cannot read or understand Tibetan these were appropriate. Two of the ones sent are Christian prayers I am familiar with: *The Prayer of St. Francis of Assisi* and the *Serenity Prayer*. The others are *Prayer for Loving Kindness*, *Namaste*, *Wind Horse*, and the last that begins *"Breathing in I feel gratitude"* and ends with "OM."

One of the differences in Prayer Flags put up by my friend (beside the ones I have) is that many have 50–100 prayers each, all fluttering in the wind putting out prayers. Having that many as he does can be like being in a church with hundreds of people praying. It builds up a powerful holy vibration that many people can feel and being around it a lot takes some adjustment. When he put up the new flags it was like adding a few thousand prayers going out continuously.

I believe my friend has the largest collection in the county and probably he has inspired many others to put them up at their houses. In extreme contrast to this I can say I have never seen any Prayer Flags displayed in New Hampshire, Maine, or Massachusetts. Perhaps they are there but not that I have been privileged to see.

I am told that the equivalent on a Christian perspective would be to have a life size statue of Jesus, possibly with Him blessing children, then hundreds of images of Saints, Jesus, Mary, and thousands of prayers and psalms.

Learning all of this information has been a blessing to me. We often see a symbol or sign from another religion and wonder about its spiritual significance. Some though are not curious about other faiths.

I have been told also that the various bright colors are nice, and providing many of the colors of a rainbow. For Tibetans the colors also have added meaning. The blue stands for space or in Christianity the Holy Spirit, the green stands for air, or incense used in the Church, the white stands for water and can be parallel to the water in the chapel, also it is tied to Archangel Gabriel. The red stands for fire, the altar candles or others in the Church, and is tied to Archangel Michael. The yellow represents earth, or flowers in the Church.

The Tibetan word for Prayer Flag is "*Lung ta*" meaning "*wind horse.*" When wind blows (by expressing the quality and nature of mind) the sacred Prayer Flag flaps in the breeze.

The prayers on each flag are carried out to all beings as a blessing. Seeing the flags also has a practical benefit of reminding people to be mindful as they go about their business. Now when I see my Prayer Flags either motionless or flying in the breeze, I am reminded of the call to pray for the welfare of all beings everywhere and especially my family and friends and all God's creatures, to work to bring about healing and happiness in the world around me, and written last but truly first, in deep love for my beloved Rochester. They were significantly given to me on the estimated date of Rochester's birth, April

15th. He was born in 1986. Yes, Prayer Flags express Loving-Kindness to all beings.

Mine truly mean so much to me, the brilliant splashes of color and prayer being lifted to God from the side of our lake. Perhaps you will consider displaying a set at your home. I am grateful to have come to know about them in this new and sacred passage in my life from my Tibetan Buddhist friend.

> *Prayer Flags flying, prayer wheels spinning, prayer circles build up a vibration, a presence that blesses everyone that comes in their presence. If a person prays or meditates they build up a blessing presence in the spot they pray or meditate. The more prayers, the more meditation, the more the presence in built up.*
>
> —Christopher Comins

My friend has also expressed, and I agree, that having *In God We Trust* on our coins helps build up a presence. Having people praying in churches, mosques, temples or in nature builds up a presence. Therefore the more ways we can help build up that presence the better for all.

I know my Rochester is aware of the flags and he knows his friend sent them. His spirit sees them from his favorite spot at the front sliding glass doors or from my desk upstairs in our writing room. Rochester too receives the prayers and blessings sent on the winds to Heaven.

In Spring of this year 2003, we witnessed on the news a gathering at Mt. Everest. One hundred seventy-five people gathered at 16,000 feet at a memorial, and colorful Prayer Flags were everywhere blowing in the wind. It was a celebration for Sir Edmund Hillary and his sherpa Tensing Norgay marking the 50 year anniversary of their climb. Their base camp was at 17,500 feet and Prayer Flags too were fluttering in the winds where everyone began the climb.

Tibetan Buddhists for centuries have planted these flags outside their homes and places of spiritual practice for the wind to carry the beneficent vibrations across the countryside. Prayer Flags are said to bring happiness, long life and prosperity to the flag planter and those in the vicinity. Displayed with respect as mine are, these Prayer Flags impart a feeling of harmony and bring to mind precious teachings and goodness for all.

❖ Purchasing Prayer Flags benefits the Tibetan Refugees who make them as cottage industries businesses. If you wish more information concerning Prayer Flags you may visit the following websites
http//www.fourgates.com/flags.asp
http//wwwprayerflags.com

"Blessings on the wind"
My prayer flags by the lake

The Man in Black

Even the death of friends will inspire us as much as their lives....
Their memories will be encrusted over with sublime and pleasing thoughts,
as monuments of other men are overgrown with moss;
for our friends have no place in the graveyard.
—Henry David Thoreau

September 16, 2003

*T*HIS BOOK WOULD NOT BE COMPLETE without paying tribute to a man that has given me much solace in my solitude. Years ago having gone through a conversion experience and the birth of my sixth child my heart was touched daily by the music of this man. It was certainly not my first *turning to God anew* but in the nine month wait for my baby to be born I read the entire Bible beginning to end. Having five other children I was extremely anxious that if I did not make it through this sixth birth I would be abandoning my family. I read the Bible to give me strength and to turn to God and put my life in His Hands. The reading and the birth were life changing for I too was born anew.

As I cared for my tiny baby girl Janna, day after day I played a record that blessed me again and again. I do not remember purchasing it or how it got into my home but I needed it. Over and over I played this beautiful album of hymns sung by Johnny Cash. His unusual voice singing these songs of his faith made me cry, but also built my own faith. My other children were in school except for Jessica who attended a half day of kindergarten.

Part of each weekday baby Janna and our three Cairn Terriers, Lizzie, Muffin, and Crackers and I shared life in solitude with Johnny in the background singing. Sometimes I needed the music very loud, sometimes quite softly. It never disturbed the sleeping Janna. When Jessica was with us she grew to accept his music as she played.

Later I bought his other albums enjoying everything he sang over and over. At Christmas we were all blessed by his loving songs on a Christmas album for weeks before Christmas all during Advent.

Our daughter Barbara always has fun teasing me about anything or anyone I love or obsess upon. She has done her share of imitating me talking about Rochester during his lifetime, but always in love. And she does an incredible imitation of an actor she likes, and would often saunter up to me in John Wayne style and say in a voice that sounded like his, "*Hello Pretty Missy.*" But as a teenager she knew how to reach me with a wonderful imitation of Johnny Cash singing one of his well-known songs. She had a right to do this for she had listened to his music endlessly in our home because I enjoy him so. But I believe she enjoys him too. I did not play his music in the van. It held a special honor from the time I became aware of him, his unique voice, and his songs. It could always be heard at home for years.

But I also knew he was a man of God and great faith, a man who loved his wife June and their children. That meant very much to me.

This black-haired man in black that stood tall and sang his songs, appeared on Larry King's show on CNN in November 2002. I was stunned by his appearance for he was ill, yet as handsome as ever. His faith was strong, his humor touched me, and the exchange between Larry and he was inspiring. It meant so much to me! Several months later, in April I believe of 2003, his beloved wife June passed away. Only several weeks ago the program on which he appeared with Larry was repeated and I watched it again. A week or two later on Thursday, September 12th we heard it announced that Johnny too had passed and now was with his June. It struck me deeply and I have tears over his passing often. He brought such faith and goodness to others through his music and his life and his person and especially to me. He will be greatly missed by countless humans who appreciated all that he was, a circle that seems to expand the more it is mentioned. I watched again for the third time when his interview was repeated Sunday, September 14th, and too the next evening on Larry King when family members were on to speak about him and pay tribute. He was so deeply loved.

I have learned Johnny Cash recorded more that 1,500 songs and won Grammys in five different decades. He was one of few to sell fifty million recordings. He won ten Grammy awards in two eras and these were for Country music in 1980 and Rock and Roll in 1992. He was made a National Member of the Arts, an award presented by President Bush in April 2003. He served in the Air force in the Korean War but in later years has suffered with various illnesses.

This fine man who always wore black revealed more of his subtle humor on Larry King when Larry asked Johnny about his black clothes. Johnny smiled and said it was very dark in his closet. I liked that. Johnny Cash was born on February 26, 1932 in Kinsgland, Arkansas and I am blessed *he walked the line*. I am better for having been touched by his music, his life, his witness of love for God and his devotion to his wife and family. One day with Rochester in my arms (for he listened to Johnny too), we shall hopefully have the joy of meeting Johnny in Heaven, for Johnny was our friend.

Finding Solace in Strengthening Actions

I went for walks. I got out in nature even if it meant sitting in the backyard.
Get outside. Look at the trees, the flowers, watch the birds.
Take time to notice the insects too. Try to get near water—
a lake, a stream, a brook. If you can't physically get outdoors
open the window or have someone rent a nature tape for you to watch.
Let nature tell its story to you.

—Melody Beattie
(thoughts following the death of her son)

TEN THOUGHTS FOLLOW to help you when you are experiencing loss, sadness or grief. People react in different ways to the same kind of loss, so try to adopt as many of these as you are able to strengthen you.

1. Avoid stress—especially people and situations that cause this.
2. Eat at regular intervals.
3. Get a good night's sleep.
4. Make time for exercise—perhaps just walking outdoors.
5. Allow for periods of meditation—and of prayer.
6. Try not to worry about the future.
7. When you have feelings of panic or fear take long deep breaths and breathe out slowly.
8. Remember that it is okay to feel sad.

9. Do not make yourself feel cheerful if that is not how you feel.
10. Write in a journal.

I would add too all the opening suggestions by author Melody Beattie that begin this meditation, for they are all the things I turned to here in the woods and have been doing since March 8, 2002, and written about in this book and *Corridors*. Yes, get out in nature!

Please find something to do that brings you solace, then do it. Just reading this list or all the meditations in this book or thinking about it all will not do it until you begin to take action and make yourself do one thing, then another, then another.

It Will Always Be So

Dream visitations stand out from other dreams; they are clearly significant
or meaningful—they are far more vivid, persistent and real
than the usual dream. They seem like real visits because they are real visits.
Deceased loved ones appear as they did in life.

—Joel Martin and Patricia Romanowski,
Love Beyond Life: The Healing Power
of After-Death Communications

October 5, 2003

ON FRIDAY, SEPTEMBER 12TH, 2003 at the end of my prayer hour as I sit silently in the writing room I share with Rochester—with eyes closed I suddenly see Rochester! I have been praying the Rosary for him, a prayer extremely powerful in blessings and in keeping us closely connected. Without warning but with gentleness, his sweet face is before me in a vision in hypnogogic imagery. It is clear, so close, and most handsome. His golden eyes look into mine and then he fades. Thank you sweet Chester. I sit and cry.

Early Sunday morning September 14th I have a dream or a vision. I cannot tell if it has come before I am fully awake or while still lying quietly with eyes closed. Because I ask for him to come to me each night before I sleep I am truly expectant. In this appearance Rochester is lying on the sofa in the living room close to its back. He is lying facing the television and window at the other end of the room. In life he often did this when he was waiting for me to join him on the sofa. Once I sat down he would

240

reposition and lie facing me upon my extended legs down the cushions. This dream or vision is totally as in life as it occurred repeatedly in our years together. He is confirming again—"*it will always be so.*"

Later in the afternoon as I am writing and working on completing this book I suddenly feel a poem happening. I grab another sheet of paper and the words just form and flow out my pencil to the sheet. It is an unusual poem, one I would not deliberately write at all. It ties in with the visions I have been having. I get it all copied down then make another copy. It is meant for this meditation, I believe.

IT WILL ALWAYS BE SO

They say—
Boys don't make passes
At girls who wear glasses—
But everyday
You made passes
      at me.

You did not mind
I wore glasses to read—
You were so kind
For you saw the need—
      and now they' re the key!

When you were in body
I saw you so clearly—
Now through these same glasses
I am seeing you!—Really!
How can that be?

Perhaps they are magic
To keep you with me?
For your dear spirit body
I so often still see.

It will always be so
Glasses or no—

It is a gift you bestow.

In gratitude—   JGK
to dear Rochester!   September 14, 2003

In very early morning of Monday, September 16th I am communicating with Rochester as I lay absolutely still. I ask prayerfully if he can
increase his heat and electricity upon my legs. He increases it gradually
within no more than a minute. Shortly after this increase occurs I have
a vision or dream of Rochester. I am overcome with emotion within as it
occurs. Again as before it is totally as in life, exactly as we are right now
in these moments in bed.

Rochester comes up from my lower legs where he has been lying and
comes so close to me. He lays on the top of my legs leaning against my
tummy and facing the wall to our left. Soon he presses closer to me and
begins to shift. He lays against my tummy pressing a bit more. Slowly he
shifts again to lie back into my right arm like a baby. He has done this
often in his life with me before he passes.

After lying like this in my arm on his back looking up at me for a few
moments or however long it is, he moves out of my right arm still on his
back. He lies down my legs in this same position with his tiny feet close
to and touching my tummy. He is so precious just looking at me the entire
time when in my arm and on his back on my legs. Gradually he
disappears. I have tears and cannot bear to move. He is always with me.

Friday, September 19th, while in prayer during the Holy Hour I keep,
Rochester appears to me again, his sweet face before me in a vision
exactly like last Friday's appearance. Each time I just weep afterwards. I
never take anything for granted. I am so overwhelmed I should receive
such visits, each such a Holy gift. This week there has been four! I have
been praying to be more aware, to be able to be receptive, to learn more.
But always I know each visit is a gift from God and Mary and Rochester.
I pray and pray such visits will occur and believe, and am totally
receptive. I am so grateful for these miracles.

Feast of St. Francis of Assisi

October 4, 2003

Two weeks after the week of September 12th through 19th when I received four visits from Rochester I am blessed with still yet another. Early in the morning of October 4th while still in bed and after feeling the heat on my legs continuously of Rochester's spirit since the night before on the sofa, — the heat seems to diminish slightly. I pray and talk to Rochester and ask him to intensify his heat. Within a couple minutes it begins and becomes very hot and remains that way. I then drift off to sleep and wake a short time later because I dream of Rochester. Each time I do I waken. Dreams of Rochester are not like other dreams I have that I forget or that fade at once. Rochester I never forget nor do they fade beyond my capturing them. I always wake immediately.

In this dream he is as natural as when in body. He is walking across the kitchen floor in the area near his feeding table and the refrigerator and headed toward the bedroom door just beyond. His little tongue has just passed over his upper lip as he did at times after eating. He is totally as in life as are all the dreams and visions I am blessed to receive. It is still yet another visit to me as clear as can be, and all the while his heat is on my legs. Thank you sweet Rochester.

October 11, 2003

Again—early in the morning I have a dream. I am in the living room on the sofa my legs extended down the length of the cushions, and Chester is on my legs. He is there in spirit not in body. We are watching a program on television with John Edward. John is looking out from the television screen directly at me and telling me personal things about Rochester that I have been experiencing. He closes by telling me that Rochester is always with me. It is all as if in reality and life and I wake immediately—Chester's heat enormously on my legs. I immediately record the dream and these words I heard said to me by John.

"Rochester is a teaching soul. Rosary and prayer are so important."

How grateful I am!

While we soon forget most dreams, dream visitations seem to engage our waking attention and are remembered in great detail long after they have happened. Unlike ordinary dreams, direct contact dreams rarely require analysis. Their meaning is nearly literal or at least fairly obvious. Their essential message is generally brief: "I love you."

—from *Love Beyond Life*

Hypnogogic Imagery

In this form of prayer one sits as in meditation and gradually becomes aware of the images that appear on the inner eye. Images arise that are absolutely remarkable and usually extremely clear, as if you were viewing them on a screen. They come and go and often stay and always mystify, that such a phenomenon can occur. I have notebooks filled with prayer times recorded of the details of these images. It is also referred to as "twilight imagery."

—Janice Gray Kolb,
*Beneath the Stars and Trees—
there is a place*

To Think Upon

REPRINTS OF TWO ARTICLES FOLLOW which appeared in the Summer 2003 edition of *Animal Writes*, a publication of PAWS (Protection of Animals in Wakefield Society). The first is by Mark Sardella who is on the Board of Directors of this group in Wakefield, Massachusetts, and who is also our personal friend for many years. His kind words appear on the cover of my book *Beneath the Stars and Trees* and also inside my other two books that followed. Too, he is a columnist for *The Wakefield Daily Item,* in Wakefield, Massachusetts. He is companion and main person and friend to his fine cat Teddy.

The second article is one I was invited to write by Mark to appear in the same edition of *Animal Writes.* May these articles add to the thoughts in the meditation titled *Animals Are Forever.*

May they too bring some insightfulness, new thoughts, concern and solace in your solitude for our animal friends and our relationship to them.

Pet Tips—How to Train Your Cat

It is almost universally agreed that dogs are easier to train than cats are. That's probably true if you're looking for a pet to fetch the newspaper or sit up and beg. For complex reasons of evolution and genetics, dogs are by nature more eager to please than cats are. Cats are eager to please too, but are primarily interested in pleasing themselves.

And this is the key to cat training.

While it's true that many cats can be trained to do dog-like party tricks like "sit" and "roll over," these stunts have no practical use and are probably boring to your cat. The key to successful cat training is to train your cat to do things he wants to do anyway. And what does a cat want to do? Judging by my own cat, the answer is "eat," primarily. And sleep. And sit in the window.

Many cat owners notice that, completely by accident, the cat has learned the English word associated with a thing or activity. For example, to my own cat, the most important word in the English language is "dinner." A distant second would be "window," followed by other words in his vocabulary, like "bird," "bug," "bed, "up," "down" (usually ignored), and "kitty" (in the sense of an outdoor cat, seen through a window). There are more words that I suspect he understands, but those are just a few of the words I'm absolutely sure he knows.

The way to get your cat to learn more words is to talk to your cat. As you're opening a window for your appreciative feline, say the word "window" over and over. Do this consistently, and before long you'll be able to say to your cat, "Do you want the window?" and she will race you to the nearest one.

The same applies to other favorite cat activities, like going to bed, especially if you are hitting the hay too. As your cat joins you on the mattress, ask him if he wants to go to bed. Before long he will know what the word "bed" means.

Whenever my cat spies a bird from the window, I repeat the word "bird." Now, wherever he is in the house, if I ask him where the bird is, he looks toward the nearest window.

Whenever he spots a bug flying around the house, I repeat the word, "bug." If I were to ask him right now to find the bug, his eyes would dart around the room, intently searching the ceiling and the walls for bugs.

I admit that there is nothing remarkable about any of this, and it will come as no surprise to cat owners that their cats pick up on verbal cues for certain things that interest them. What is remarkable is the cat's capacity to learn, as long as you make it in his interest to learn. I've read that cats can learn up to about thirty words. I suspect that they could learn many more than that. (How many synonyms are there for "food?")

Cats are extremely gifted at detecting sequences of events that lead to something that interests them—primarily food and windows. If you make the sound of certain words part of the sequence of events that leads to certain good things, like "dinner," your cat will catch on faster than you think.

Most people probably haven't come close to exhausting their cat's capacity to learn. Teaching your cat to understand certain words can be fun, and not just for you—for your cat too.

For example, if certain activities or areas of our house are off-limits to your cat, by teaching him the word "no" you make it much more fun for your cat to ignore you and eat that plant anyway.

Teddy, companion and friend to Mark Sardella

Paws Article

*I*N RECENT YEARS my compassion for all God's creatures has increased to dimensions I never thought possible. I cannot bear to hear of any cruelty to any creature, no matter how large or how small. Animals and other living species have no voice. They are often tortured and killed mercilessly as if they are incapable of pain. This is so horrendous and I have tried to be their voice through my writing.

Living in the woods amongst nature and on the shore of a lake has changed the way my husband and I view life. Wild little creatures come up onto our porch and peer through our sliding glass doors. We have learned how intelligent these little beings are. We have seen them too outwit us—and been amazed. We have watched the interchange between birds and squirrels and chipmunks all feeding at the same bird feeders at the same moments. We have been surprised and overwhelmed by families of raccoons silently observing us through the glass, patiently waiting to search our faces and responses. We have watched the beautiful herons land in our cove and the families of ducks waddle up our beach to wait for us to feed them, so trustingly. These mallards have become our friends. They actually knock on our sliding glass doors with their beaks to tell us they are there, then waddle down quickly to our front door to await my appearance with some seed and bread. I talk to them and spend time with them and wonder how anyone could ever intentionally hurt them.

Living enfolded in nature in all seasons of the year gives one a new perspective. The earth and trees and God's creatures are part of us, and I would not kill a bug or ant. How we love the wail of the loon in day or night and observe them dive for food into the lake or run across the water preliminary to flight. I have spent hours alone over a two week period talking to and keeping company with a female moose on our property. I took detailed notes and photos so that I might later write about her beauty, characteristics, and habits. Each animal has something to tell us and teach us. I love creatures so much.

Though I have always loved animals, it was my deep personal love for my little cat Rochester that taught me the meaning of *Ahimsa*. This precious little cat I adopted in Rochester, New Hampshire and in deeply loving him and he me, my life was changed. Because of him and through my reading I learned that *Ahimsa* means "harmlessness" or not hurting, and that it is a Sanskrit word for "compassion." Wherever *Ahimsa* is found, there is deep compassion, unselfishness, and service to others, and a refraining from causing pain and suffering to any living creature. It naturally implies non-killing. Actually it means total abstinence from causing any harm or pain whatsoever to any living creature, either by thought, word, or deed. It is LOVE! Universal Love! It is said to be the highest and noblest of traits.

My little Rochester has taught me well in his School of Love. One small marmalade and white cat turned my existence upside down and caused me to reflect on numerous things, which before June 23, 1986 were not foremost in my thinking. I had to be gently shown, in love, and daily educated by a most unusual and precious teacher. We spent the last almost sixteen years of our life together day and night, for ever since Rochester owned me I have spent every day writing. A beautiful golden eyed creature of God lives with me, sleeps with me, and spends the majority of his hours near me or on me—and my life is enriched because of him.

Through his unconditional love and instructions heart to heart, mind to mind, his presence in our lives caused my husband and I to become vegetarians for the animals sake in 1989.

Though Rochester passed away March 8, 2002 I still write about him in the present tense, for his spirit has never left me and his presence and enlightenment is constant and enormous. We have written still yet another book together begun the weekend in March he had to leave, a book on grieving, and it is his book, for he was guiding me and communicating as always—through every word. We had learned to deeply communicate while we shared life, and now too in this new dimension of living. In this book we are extending *"compassion"* to those who grieve for animal or human.

I am devastated by his passing. Each day it is fresh and as if it is in the present moment of it occurring. But he continues to teach me things daily in spirit, my compassionate soulmate, companion, and teacher— and one day we will be together again forever, for I have an unshakable belief that we share Heaven with our beloved animal friends and all creatures.

MEDITATION SIXTY-FOUR

Our Poem-Prayer

These little rituals to us are sacrosanct.
—Jan from *Beside The Still Waters:*
Creative Meditations from the Woods
by Janice Gray Kolb

MANY TIMES IN THE PASt, especially in difficult situations, the child's
prayer, "Now I Lay Me Down To Sleep," did not seem to help. My
thoughts seemed to center on the words, "If I should die before I wake"—
and afforded me no comfort. Later when discussing this with Bob we
decided to write a replacement prayer that would give us some true
comfort and better express what our thoughts were in a nightly conversation with God. Bob surprised me one day with a new prayer, and it was
so perfect for me that I did not want to add any other words to it. It is
consoling to us both and I also whisper it every night for Rochester—
while he was in body and now in spirit hold his little paws as he lies on my
legs and faces me. Too, I bless his forehead, in the name of the Father,
Son and Holy Spirit. I have done this to my angel since he was a kitten
and have continued since he is in spirit. The blessing follows the reading
of the poem.

Sometime later Bob wrote music that is lovely for the prayer and put
it on cassette tape. Each night after the prayer would be verbally prayed
as always, then I would play the gentle musical version of the prayer
before playing my ethereal haunting music of *The Fairy Ring* for Rochester and myself. When Bob wrote the prayer he also presented me with a

251

mediation he had written for it. We gave this and the prayer to each of our children at that time.

Perhaps his words concerning the prayer will bring solace to those reading this book. Though Bob wrote it in the singular I pray it in the plural since it is for the three of us. Often a simple prayer and a child-like acceptance of God's love and care can bring us unfathomable peace and consolation far beyond eloquent "grown up" prayers that fail to soothe our heart and fears and pain.

The poem-prayer set to music appears in the back of my book *Beside the Still Waters*. The meditation about it that follows is written by Bob.

—Jan

A Child's Bedtime Prayer

Now I lay me down to sleep
I pray Thee Lord my soul to keep.
If I should die before I wake
I pray Thee Lord my soul to take.

This prayer deals with only the subject of physical death for the child. It's frightening to a young mind that has no concept of "Heaven" or "the soul." It doesn't address the real concerns a child has and in no way attempts to bring the child closer to God's love. It only gives the Lord instructions on what to do if the unthinkable—death—might occur. It deals only with supplication and ignores other necessary attributes of prayer. A nighttime prayer that better faces the reality of childhood and a child's relationship with a Father image who loves and protects would be vastly better. May I suggest the following simple prayer that has the possibility to comfort a child and bring him/her closer to God.

As I lay down to sleep this night,
Please keep me safe 'til morning light.
Grant me sleep and needed rest
And fill my dreams with happiness.
For Lord I know that with You near,
There's nothing that I have to fear

Guide me where you want to lead,
And be with those I love and need.

Amen

In this prayer the child is addressing his real concerns—safety, unwanted scary dreams, refreshment of stamina and vigor, and an assurance that God is near. Much like crawling in bed with Mommy and Daddy when strange noises are heard or bad dreams occur. It also is concerned with requesting an ongoing presence of God to guide and help with the tough decisions. And finally, it asks God to also be a source of strength to those individuals in family, community or experience whom the child loves and whom the child needs to fulfill and make his/her life happy.

—Robert A. Kolb Jr. ©
September 5, 1996

I Will Not Leave You Comfortless

*More than any other type of ADC (After Death Communication),
full appearances assure us that our deceased loved ones continue to exist.*
—Hello from Heaven by Bill Guggenheim and Judy Guggenheim

November 3, 2003

AT TEN PM I SIT DOWN ON THE SOFA TO WATCH TELEVISION, my legs extended down the length of the sofa as always. I am seated only a few moments and looking straight ahead when suddenly below the television screen the figure of Chester runs across the rug in front of the set. He runs behind the striped chair that sits at the base of the living room stairs. He does not go up the stairs. I sit motionless for almost five minutes with tears, hoping he will return. He does not—but the heat then gets intense on my legs. I tell Bob then, who was sitting in his recliner also facing the television. He is dumb-founded and does not know what to say.

This is one of several times I have clearly seen him in this area. One earlier time (written about in this book) I ran from the kitchen area and chased him up the stairs but he disappeared. I longed to hold him! This time I just sat and thanked God that Rochester is ever present and with us in this small cottage—his home. Such a gift!

The Guggenheims, in their wonderful book *Hello from Heaven*, state, as do other authors, that a number of ADCs occur just as people are falling asleep or waking up. They state that this half awake, half asleep level of awareness is usually referred to as the twilight state or alpha state, and this experience is a fairly common type of after-death communication.

Too, many people report they had been contacted by a decreased loved one while they were sound asleep. Because they did not have any other name for their experience, they usually called it a *"dream,"* but said quickly that it just was not like an ordinary dream. I understand.

In this same week I have two additional appearances of Rochester, and they were *"not like ordinary dreams,"* and a third appearance the following week that definitely was not a dream.

Tuesday, November 4th, 2003

I have an instant dream of Chester immediately before permanently waking. I had been slightly awake earlier. I see Chester sitting on the back of the living room sofa at the windows in the living room. He is looking into the room and not out the window. He slowly turns his head to the left toward the door and then he is gone, he disappears there on the sofa back. It is as in life, he is so real.

Thursday, November 6, 2003

I have an instant vision or dream of Chester shortly before waking. He is on his maple feeding table in the kitchen facing the refrigerator and the bedroom door. He is crouched down comfortably on the table waiting for me and to give him his breakfast. It is totally as he did frequently in life. Oh thank you, dear Rochester.

Such comforting appearances!

Wednesday, November 12, 2003

Soon after I am in bed this night I am sitting there praying the Rosary. In the semi light that is provided by the nightlight in the bathroom across the hall, and the small one in the bedroom, I feel Chester jump lightly onto the bottom of the bed as he often did. I see him come across the lower bed and then he jumps onto me. He disappears. I am fully awake. It is as in real life. I am in tears and so grateful.

This has also been a week of Rochester leaving me pennies to let me know he is ever here. It may sound strange and not believable but when you live in a cottage this small you have little ways of trying to keep some order. I keep my pocketbook in one place on a shelf by the door. In that is a little purse and the only place I have change. It stays there day in and day out. We use Bob's change when we go to the Post Office or corner store which is kept neatly on another shelf. We never throw change on a table or surface or keep in pockets.

Therefore on Sunday, November 2, 2003 when a penny appears on the table next to where I sit on the sofa it is enough for me to take notice and thank Rochester at the same time. It is placed right on the spot where I normally have my coffee cup.

Later this same day I place two books on top of each other on the end of the kitchen table. They are new and have just been ordered by e-mail by a customer on our on-line bookshop. Bob has brought them over from his office for me after receiving the order, to wrap and to include a personal note within the books. I leave the books I have placed on the table for no more than a minute to get the wrapping paper and tape from inside the maple louvered cabinet that is Rochester's feeding table. It is just a few feet away. When I return to the two books I find two shiny pennies lying on top of them. I am here in this cottage alone with only the spirit of Rochester. Bob is over in his office and returned there at once after dropping off the books. The pennies were not on the books when I placed them on the table. Pennies anew from Heaven!

On Tuesday, November 4th I pull the quilt up to cover the bed early in the morning and smooth it. I leave the room and return a few minutes later to get my steno pad I have forgotten, the steno pad I immediately record all wonderful things like this into before I forget them or the dates. (But I never forget such wonders!) As I reach over to get my steno pad on the shelf next to the wall there in the middle of the quilt lies a shiny penny. Even Bob is amazed too at the gifts of these pennies. I keep them

all in my Rosary purse by the bed. They are heavenly too like the Rosary.
I have many more however sent by Rochester, kept safely in another
container. They began to appear shortly after he went to Heaven.

If all this is not wonder enough from a precious Angel companion, on
Tuesday, November 4th we go to Sanford, Maine on errands. The day is
bitter cold and windy and I did not wear a coat, only a sweater. We leave
the large store in which several months ago Rochester led me to the
lovely statue of Mary in a deep carton filled with strange garden gnomes.
Because I am cold I almost run across the parking lot to reach our car. No
one else is around which is strange, though there are many cars. Suddenly
a gust of wind blows something at my feet. That in itself is unusual
because it could have been blown to any other place on this large lot, or
under a car, or up in the air, but it comes to my feet. I pick it up and it is
two bills, a one dollar bill and a five folded together. Just amazing! Money
out of the blue! Money from Heaven! After discussion Bob feels we
cannot find the owner because it has been blowing around outside, and
there is no one out here with us, and we are some distance from the store.
Since it was sent from Heaven to once again say *"I am everywhere you
are,"* once home I send it to a favorite animal group in Massachusetts and
add money to it so that a gift donation can be given to help another
animal. It is sent in Rochester's name.

As I have written elsewhere—each time I go out I pray that Rochester teaches me to be aware of his presence while we are not at home. Over
and over again he has shown me things, sent me gifts and made me aware
that he is ever here no matter where I am. It is like a *School of Awareness*
I am attending under his direction. It is also as always his *School of Love.*

Thank you, dear Rochester, for gifts so incredible this past week! If
only we are aware we will continually receive our loved ones' presence in
ways most loving and amazing.

The very simple little poem that follows written in 1999 when I
needed Rochester's precious presence more than ever through some
difficult times, is relevant anytime, and especially in light of the sweetness of his presence he has given to me as written about in these journal
entries I have shared in this meditation. He truly is forever my Angel and
Shadow and little love—eternally.

My Little One

You have been here through the years—
You have been here through the tears—
You have always made me smile—
You have gone the extra mile.
Through every kind of weather—
We have always been together.
You are my shadow, my little love—
You are my angel from above.

Thank you God—
for my beloved Rochester.

For Rochester   Jan
my angel   September 14, 1999

Wherever you are—he is.
                    —John Edward, December 11, 2003

Afterword

We each have within ourselves what we need for our own journey.
The answers aren't out there, out in the world, but within us.
And we will only hear those answers if we are quiet enough.
                                        —Lionel Fisher from *Celebrating Time Alone*

*F*OR MANY YEARS each time we would come to this cottage in the woods
of New Hampshire on summer vacation with our children I would
read many books while here. But there was one book I read every summer
for many years. I had to read it here in the woods by the lake and never
anywhere else, even though the author had written it by the ocean.
Perhaps many of you have read it also. It is *A Gift from the Sea* by Anne
Morrow Lindbergh. I used to buy and give copies away but no one fully
understood why I found it so inspiring for I was in a different period of my
life than the others. Because of this small inspirational book I went on to
also obtain and read her volumes of personal journals, for like myself she
was a woman , wife, mother, a writer, a journal keeper and one who loved
solitude. She exhorts in her *Gift from the Sea*—"*We must relearn to be
alone. Instead of planting our solitude with dream blossoms, we choke the space
with continuous music, chatter, and companionship to which we do not even
listen. It is simply there to fill the vacuum.*"

This was a wife and a mother of five children who found it necessary
to come apart alone that summer and live by the sea and write down her
thoughts. But too, she needed and kept periods of solitude in her daily
living with her large family just as I did when my children were all at

259

home. Also she had a deep sadness of losing a child, one the world has known about for many years.

I am not lifting her up over hundreds who have authored books in a similar genre or who so tragically lost a loved one. I am simply stating her as an example of one who saw the importance of and allowed for daily periods of solitude into her life though deeply involved in many areas of living. I have read many books on solitude since authored by both women and men that have blessed me tremendously, each seeming to be discovered and meant to be for the particular point in my life I was experiencing at the time I found them, or they found me. When you need them and go to a bookstore they seem to be waiting and light up and draw you to them. Authors who write about solitude tend to be journal keepers, though not always.

> *To everyone else, the death of that being you love for his own sake, for her own sake, is an event that occurs on a certain day. For you, the death only begins that day. It is not an event: it is only the first moment in a process that lives in you, springing up into the present, engulfing your years, decades later, as though it were the first moment again.*
> —Alice Koller from *The Stations of Solitude*

In the mid eighties I discovered a book titled *An Unknown Woman* by Alice Koller. This had a profound affect upon me and again I shared it with others. With only two exceptions—each time I had given it (and there were many) I had heard Him correctly, for each except those two who received the book needed it as I had and wrote or called to say that the book was about her life as well as Alice Koller's. The affect on myself was so deep that in September 1986 I came away to our cottage in New Hampshire from Pennsylvania to make my first retreat with only my dear little kitten Rochester as companion. I had never stayed in the woods alone before and Rochester's presence gave me the courage to do so. The author Alice Koller spent three months on her retreat thirty miles out to sea on Nantucket with only her new puppy Logos in dead of winter many years before. I had only a week here in New Hampshire, but it was this author and book that inspired me to do this for I needed to find strength and answers in a deeply troubling portion of life I have written about previously. I then read *An Unknown Woman* several times as support and waited hopefully for her next book to see what had transpired in her life since her retreat so long before.

Four years later I was able to buy and read here in New Hampshire *The Stations of Solitude*. This was equally as rewarding for me as her first book had been. Not long after my own retreat in our cottage I began to write my book *Higher Ground* from a journal I kept while on that retreat of one week. I mention Alice Koller's inspiration to me in *Higher Ground*. Though I had never written to an author before, I was moved to write to this one and received a very caring and informal reply encouraging me to take time alone, and also answering questions I had posed to her before making my retreat. She gave me the encouragement to go to New Hampshire that week in September 1986. Later after Higher Ground was published I wrote her again in 1993 to thank her and remind her of how she had encouraged me and received a very kind reply.

Sadly she too had the devastation of the death of her beloved German Shepherd Logos and writes of this in her second book near the closing. It is a very long chapter of forty-five pages in a large book. Her grief is so deep it throbs from the pages yet it was written long after his death. I cried through it all when reading it with Rochester on my lap or legs or by my side. I could not imagine how she endured this loss. She writes not to look for consolation, that it is small change in the hands of others. She states, *"What you want is to be again with that being you love, and even you cannot bring it about."* She writes that *"you mourn because you love: there is no other reason. So there is nothing to be healed of. Would you be healed of your loving?"*

She is as I am. I could have written her very passages in regard to Logos for my own Rochester, and I have written similar from the depths of my heart in *Corridors* and this book. She reveals how people want to cure you of mourning and that you must accept his/her death and get on with your life. I too have written about this. She states how Logos was the center of her life for twelve years after leaving Nantucket. His death would normally devastate her but there were circumstances and questions surrounding it that also added to the pain that never ended for her.

Like myself she states, *"My mourning will end only when I end."* All things in her life changed and she mentions many of these that were similar to things I have done and still do. She states too that for six years she did not touch or wear jewelry. In the beginning she fasted as I did except for liquids.

To read this now for the first time since Rochester passed is overwhelming. These two books of hers have been friends and deep support, and her Logos was so alive to me. Though I was horrified at his death and the circumstances, and so utterly saddened by her mourning, I could not fully realize the very depths and pain and torture of it until now rereading it without my Rochester with me in body on my lap or legs. Until I entered into my own despair and mourning there simply could not be the total depth of understanding for hers no matter how enormously it affected me (and it did!) when I read of it in 1990. You never think it will happen to you! As with Martin Scot Kosins for his beloved Maya, and Cleveland Amory for his precious Polar Bear, and myself for my dear little Rochester, the grief and longing and missing is beyond explanation. To even suggest that animal companions are not loved and not mourned with the same intensity or passion or despair of humans, or that they are replaceable because they are not human is atrocious.! The agony is unbearable and their meaning and love they gave and continue to give to our lives is in a very special wrapping of eternal love within our hearts forever until we are again together for all eternity.

It seems I have been writing about solitude ever since I have been writing and keeping journals. From the enforced solitude upon me as a child and teenager to the solitude I needed and made time for in prayer and writing when I was a young mother of six, and right into the present. All of my books I have written have also spoken of it and its importance. Two men I especially looked to for confirmation and wisdom in the 70s and 80s were Henry David Thoreau and Thomas Merton. Thoreau authored Walden and too, other books, and Thomas Merton, a Catholic Monk, wrote many spiritual books, journals and a huge volume of poetry. The book that affected me most deeply after beginning to read him was his early journal written in the Trappestine Monastery of Gethsemani and titled *Sign of Jonas*. Merton entered the novitiate of the Trappestine Order on December 13 (1941). I did not know that until later. I chose December 13, (1978) to enter the Catholic Church and later learned of our same date. He too had been Protestant.

I have a sweet memory given to me by a dear friend I mention often in my books, Francis J. McGeary, an obstetrician. I named him *"Friar Francis"* and he called me *"Trappestine Jan"* because we both received such inspiration from Thomas Merton. While Francis was dying of cancer he asked to read my manuscript of *Higher Ground* in 1990. It affected him so he sent his copy to the Head Abbot at the Trappestine Monastery where Merton had lived because of the many references to the contemplative life and too, Thomas Merton. Also the manuscript blessed my dear friend Francis. Francis received a very moving letter back from the Abbot of that Monastery in Kentucky. It was mainly for me stating his deep appreciation for the still yet unpublished book and that it had blessed him greatly. Francis died at age 90 in July of that same year and this was only one of many spiritual gifts he bestowed on me in the intense five years of our friendship.

Francis passed away with a framed picture of Rochester next to a bouquet of flowers on his bedside table. Rochester had become a sweet special friend to him though they had never met, and he loved this picture of him (see page 250) and kept it next to him until he died. Though pro-life he had never considered animals and was astounded he had ignored them. He wished he could have been a vegetarian and was in awe that I was one. It was too late for him to do this. He was suddenly overcome by the wisdom that the same Lord who had breathed life into his body, breathes it into the animals, and that we are created in the exact way as God's creatures. Truly Rochester brought him joy. He loved hearing about him. Rochester was a ministering Angel to Francis.

Thoreau writes in Walden—*"I love to be alone, I never found the companion that was so companionable as solitude."* Thomas Merton expressed this joy of solitude well when he writes in his journal, *Sign of Jonas,* *"Once God has called you to solitude, everything you touch leads you further into solitude. Everything that affects you builds you into a hermit—"*

Our Lord had long ago begun His hermit-building within me. Thoreau also turned and lived in the woods and stated *"I went to the woods because I wish to live deliberately, to front only the essential facts of life."* Alice Koller, like myself, was moved by Thoreau and understood the private business he went to transact at Walden.

I have tried to express in the writing of this book the importance of solitude not only in times of sadness and grieving but just in the living of any life. It is in solitude we find the strengths to go on in our sadness and that we learn truths in the stillness that we would not have received or observed in the rush of life amongst others. But we need solitude at all times not only in grieving and sadness. We have to come to realize that it is all right to be alone and even to want to be alone. Sometimes we think we are only somebody when we are with someone else or with many. Some are afraid to be alone even for a very short period. But you will never truly know yourself and your journey until you allow yourself time alone. Some make a retreat each year alone which is good but certainly not sufficient. I know it to be insufficient for I did this for several years in the late 70s after my Dad's death. Though each was a spiritual retreat of silence and contemplation with occasional words from a speaker in a lovely large Retreat House outside Philadelphia, and though I retained the long weekend of retreat within myself for long after, these few days were not at all sufficient for myself until the next retreat the next year. I still maintained my own daily silence and solitude as a constant.

Some have time daily alone in the privacy of their homes, and some choose to live in a quiet place of solitude as we have here in the woods. I need solitude as I do air and water, but solitude permeated with Rochester's spirit.

It is this solitude that I have been led on my journey in my passage through grief. It is in this solitude that I have learned enormous secrets and truths that are there for all to discover if only they are willing to experience the *Solace of Solitude.* So many many have been on this journey for some time.

Do not let others discourage you or make you feel uncomfortable for wanting solitude in your life. By making this choice to allow solitude into your life you will open yourself up to truth and beauty and consolation even if you are grieving. I know this to be true. But the world in general does not understand the importance and need to be alone. If you tell someone you prefer to be alone, or need to be alone, or this is the particular hour you keep for yourself, you are thought to be strange. You feel the need at times to apologize for it, and yet being alone is one of the most important periods in one's life.

Added to the solitude that too you are being shown your walk through this corridor, and that you are learning to live this new life, then you truly may not be understood. Especially by those closest to you. Remember, it simply does not matter! Just keep praying, meditating, and "travelling" through the *Corridors of Eternal Time*.

Now it is time to speak of the mysteries I was shown following Rochester's entering Heaven. As I have written in *Corridors* and now in this book, Rochester's spirit became evident to me shortly after he physically left. I also carry within myself his "*Anima*," the incredible gift and miracle I had been given moments after his passing in the Veterinarian's office, and that I cherish every moment of my life with a love beyond words, —also recorded in *Corridors*—and shared in depth.

I knew that from March 8th on I would live always as if Rochester was ever with me in spirit just as he was in life. I knew without a doubt it was a truth. And this truth began to be shown to me in many ways as you have been reading about in these pages. They were shown to me by Rochester alone. I had no outside helps in those earlier six months, it was just Rochester and myself as it was when we spent our days in our writing room alone as we wrote our books. His contacts began shortly after he passed and as recorded in *Corridors*. They have never stopped! I had no one to discuss these mysteries with except Bob who was kind about them but could not accept them. My friend Chris in California did believe me because he has experienced far more mystical things than have I, the most precious of all to me being his experience of witnessing Rochester in his early moments of passing into eternal life! But basically it was just Rochester and myself interchanging here in our little green cottage in ways recorded in *Corridors* and in these pages. I wrote everything down and prayed his contacts would never cease. They never have. They increase.

Perhaps these have happened because of my carrying his *Anima*, but perhaps too they are pure gift like his Anima is. Perhaps our love and need for each other after his passing has caused this glorious connection. He has told me in his communications, the same type we had in the years before he passed and written about in *Journal of Love* that they will never cease. I live in pure gratefulness for this enormous bond and connection that shall exist until we are together in Heaven—and then continue for all eternity.

I will share with you now some facts that can lead you through your passage, or at least help you if you are willing to be open and trust. I repeat

Antoinne deSaint Exupery's quotation that appears in this Introduction and *Corridors*, for you will discover its truth as you travel this corridor. *It Is Such A Secret Place—the land of tears.*

In Quietness and Confidence

I walk by the rippling lake
And beneath the tall green trees—
Head back I gaze at stars
And feel the prevailing breeze.

I watch a butterfly take sudden flight
A chipmunk smiling at me
from the door of his hole—
And I am given light
For my depleted, saddened soul.

If I do not minister to myself
In solitude and silence—
I miss the wealth
In each present moment.
I am tense
And live on the edge.
But in quietness and confidence
I shall wait—
And meditate—
And find God and myself anew.

Jan
September 7, 2003

Final Thoughts
ADCs

Tears are often the telescope through which we see far into Heaven.
                                                              —Henry Ward Beecher

*I*T IS IMPORTANT TO KNOW that an ADC or After-Death Communication is a spiritual experience that occurs when someone is contacted directly and spontaneously by a deceased family member or friend. This definition appears in the Guggenheims's book I have mentioned numerous times throughout this book. I would also add the contacts can come from a beloved animal. All my contacts from Rochester have been and are ADCs. I am contacted directly and spontaneously by Rochester.

As the Guggenheims and others state an ADC has no intermediary or third party such as psychic or medium, or hypnotist. The deceased contacts the living person directly one on one.

In this same book it is stated an ADC is a spontaneous event because the deceased loved one initiates the contact by choosing when, where, and how he or she will communicate with the living person.

The Guggenheims tell us that because many religions and other sources specifically warn against summoning "spirits" they excluded from their research all experiences that included any rituals or devices. All that is recorded in their book are spontaneous contacts as I receive from Rochester, and as do many other Christians who too receive such contacts from their loved ones. Those too of all religions receive such

267

contacts. All of the contacts that can occur that are written about in these chapters of their book I have experienced from Rochester and this overwhelms me! I would suggest the Guggenheim's book to you for these are occurrences that no one has summoned. They are loved ones from beyond reaching out to contact their loved ones here. It can happen to anyone if they do not shut down the possibility and desire it and await it and then do not deny it. Yes, these contacts arrive as surprises but I believe you should desire them and not shut the door between you and a loved one, either out of disbelief or fear. There is nothing to fear.

Each one of my contacts I cherish and record. Bob is a skeptic and backs off and closes himself off to the contacts from Rochester though he is so happy for me. But he is like that in other areas of life including how he approaches his personal faith. But he believes me, has been present for happenings he cannot explain, and has typed this book and *Corridors*. We have long discussions about Rochester's contacts and our personal faith. I believe it is only a matter of time that a personal contact will come to him so strongly he will understand the sacredness and joy of such a gift and he will no longer smile and tease me. We are so one in most matters of our faith and yet for many years we simply were quite different. To me these contacts are a living extension of my Christian faith. Obviously if I did not believe them I would not have written this book. It is difficult to stand alone for a truth you believe in with all your heart. But Rochester stands with me. He taught me and he desires to be with me, and I am so grateful. I feel certain there are many reading who too have experienced ADC's but perhaps are hesitant to admit it or have no one with whom to share such an extraordinary gift. May my sharings help you now.

All through this Journal I have included significant quotations for myself and hopefully to readers at the beginnings of each journal entry (or meditation) or in the contents or closing of them. Hopefully many of these have suggested to you other sources that have been of great help to me and to others, and now may be of help to you also aside from the traditional Christian quotations and scripture I have recorded.

In early June of 2002 author and animal communicator Sonya Fitzpatrick began her new program *The Pet Psychic* on the Animal Planet channel each Monday evening. I had also mentioned her book in the closing of my own book *Journal of Love—Spiritual Communication with Animals Through Journal Writing*. Her book is titled *What the Animals Tell*

Me. On her hour TV program, fifteen minutes is set aside for her to communicate with beloved pets in spirit who have crossed over. Their owners are there with her and bring pictures of their dear animals. It is such a moving segment. Many have been mourning their animals for years. Often too a human in spirit brings the animal through to its grieving owner. Sonya is tender, loving and kind in this segment on grieving as she is in all her communications shown with animals and owners throughout the programs and I cry all through them. When this program was aired it was such a blessing in my grief. I began to watch it faithfully. The books on grieving I bought ten days after Rochester passed and Martin Scot Kosins's book *Maya's First Rose,* and Sonya's program were my spiritual helps along with daily prayer in those months that followed.

Then came my conversation with our two extended family members that re-gave me the knowledge first presented to me by our mutual friend. Through this knowledge I slowly gained incredible new comfort and knowledge of my own by viewing John Edward on his program of several years *Crossing Over.* He is also the author of a number of fine books, a husband, new father, and affectionate owner and companion of two little dogs. His program had been on several years before I knew of it and too, I have seen him given great esteem and interviewed several times by Larry King on CNN. I would not write of all this if I did not trust him.

I add too James VanPraagh who also had a program on television but recently it was cancelled, and it is sad because he helps many. I learned of him shortly after learning of John. Too, he is author of numerous books and one is specifically on grief. Hopefully he will return to television as well. He too was remarkable as Larry King's guest on CNN. When both James and John were on Larry King's program they took calls from viewers and were able to connect with the callers' loved ones in spirit. James is a caring man with great gifts. I had bought and owned the book he wrote on grief before Rochester passed. I selected it due to an earlier period in my life I have already written about elsewhere, but then could not bring myself to read of grief of any kind and put it away. I did not remember it again and that I owned it until some months after Rochester went to Heaven. The book then prepared me for learning about James's gifts that he uses to help others, his television program, and his other books.

While I was attending this *"School of Love"* that Rochester was leading me through, Bob learned of several other books he thought I might be interested in while ordering another book on-line for me. He ordered them as a surprise and I am thankful for they did help and teach and bless significantly. These books were co-authored and written by authors Joel Martin and Patricia Romanowski about a fine and sensitive man named George Anderson who helps so many who have lost loved ones. The books are titled *We Don't Die* and *We Are Not Forgotten*. I consumed them, and reread. George Anderson had been on television for eight years with Joel Martin helping others. Through reading these two books I learned George had written two books also. The one I found first in Walden Books became a constant companion along with *Maya's First Rose*. I read it numerous times and learned through the writings of this very sensitive man that he was indeed truly gifted and kind, gentle, and completely shy. This book is so underlined, and I weep at these many passages that forever touch my soul and bring me spiritual strength. It is titled *Walking in the Garden of Souls*. All of these books I have mentioned by and about these men had been on the New York Times Best Sellers List. Each man, John, James and George, has their own website that you can investigate, as does Sonya Fitzpatrick.

All three of these men love animals and make heavenly connections with them giving owners so much consolation. All three have a Catholic background. George Anderson has a great devotion to St. Philomena and he shares about this in his writings. I am so grateful to these three men whose only desire is to use their God given gifts to help those who grieve. A statement in *Walking in the Garden of Souls* I have written in my journals and reread again and again in tears, for it gives me enormous peace and strength. Too, it is my total belief and it is what I have been experiencing since Rochester passed but had not seen it written before. George writes:

> *I have been told many times by the souls in the hereafter that when we experience the loss of a loved one, part of the profound change that comes over us is our link to a world we have never experienced, much less thought about. But the link to our loved ones can never be broken, not even in physical death, and it connects us to a world we now feel and can be affected by.*

May this console others who read also. George states so many things that help me. He goes on to write—

The gifts of perception that we receive from the hereafter are not always conscious—we may not know or even feel that they are happening, but our loved ones assure us that the gifts come as they are needed.

He concludes these thoughts by telling his readers that these gifts are sent to us not only at the time of our loss and thereafter, but sometimes they are sent as a way of preparing us to deal with grief for an imminent death of a loved one.

Too, throughout his *Walking in the Garden of Souls* he mentions his and our beloved animals and one statement is so especially consoling.

I have been told by the hereafter that pets are the closest thing to the Infinite Light on earth since they love without condition and forgive without question. Could you think of a finer friend?

He always refers to God as *The Infinite Light.*

One last book I will mention that has informed me greatly and confirmed again and again the experiences I have been having since March 2002. I do not need the confirmation but to know it is there in this book and all books I have mentioned here in my own book is a consoling factor.

This title is *Love Beyond Life—The Healing Power of After-Death Communications* by Joel Martin and Patricia Romanowski, the man and woman who have written three books about George Anderson. George, as I mentioned earlier had been on television with Joel Martin for eight years also. *Love Beyond Life* covers real-life stories and offers hope and healing and compelling evidence that love can survive death. It is based on years of research.

All the books I have mentioned are written by those who have worked in this field for many years and have helped thousands in their grieving. All stress emphatically however, that you do *not* need them, that *you alone* are quite capable of connecting with your loved ones on a regular basis by yourself. I can attest to this, for the only help I have ever received is from Rochester and through prayer—especially the Rosary. To understand and learn, I prayed always and allowed myself to be led to books and television viewing that could inspire and confirm my own experiences. But as I have written, I did not doubt. My experiences are so precious and real I could never doubt. I can never be shaken about them even if ridiculed.

There are two other books I have read that are written by those like myself who let themselves be shown by their loved ones who passed that they truly are always with them. They did not work in this field, but now they are trying to help others learn what they have discovered. One lost her Mother and one lost a teenage son. Like myself they needed this connection but were in awe and gratefulness when it began to occur shortly after their loved ones passed, and only increases as does my connection with Rochester. I am trying to help others through the writing of my books. Later perhaps there will be other ways to reach out.

I feel going to a bookstore or on-line bookstores is part of your passage, just as I stated this about finding books on grieving in *Corridors*. And I still read these latter books too for I grieve.

Many feel they cannot talk of after-death communications. As I have stated frequently in the quotation I need: "*It Is Such A Secret Place—the land of tears.*" Mostly they fear they will be disbelieved or ridiculed if they share the communications they receive. If you can be scolded for even having tears in grief as I was, how much more will you be ridiculed if you share this precious knowledge about ADCs!

Perhaps, as I have learned, we must accept that people who do not believe in ADCs may have profound reasons for thinking as they do and so we must respect their beliefs. On the other hand they may just be fearful and so seem to direct their arguments at you when actually it is really at the uncertainty and fear your experience may inspire. You will be given discernment, I feel. It is easier for me to write about the communications I receive in my two books than it is to share them with family or friends. In this book form it will be hopefully read at some distance from me and in their own homes at their own pace. In quietness and confidence perhaps their hearts will be open to the message. It is not a message you can ever force on anyone and it is likely it will be religiously condemned by some. If they are meant to hear, God will prepare their hearts. Obviously He prepared mine.

The loved one on the other side can or may announce his visit through various means I have written about in this book as Rochester does. The contacts can be prolonged or fleeting, happen once, several times or daily. It is generally believed, and as I have experienced, most contacts occur spontaneously. We do know though that through prayer and meditation, and simply refusing to disbelieve, we who live in body can facilitate if not initiate them. As you have read in my meditations, many of Rochester's contacts have been when I was in prayer or meditation or in a relaxed state. That too is when Rochester has kissed me. I feel electricity from him. When we are active or busy we may miss contacts regularly. John Edward has stated numerous times: *"Quiet the mind — the signs of our loved ones are all around us."*

I found various polls interesting but one in particular stated that in a survey released in 1987, Roman Catholic Priest Father Andrew Greeley, also author and sociologist discovered that 42 percent of Americans reported visits from the deceased. This correlates exactly with findings from the International Social Survey Program of 1991.

ADCs (or After Death Communications) include meeting the loved one in a visit or dream, sensing the presence of the loved one, feeling a touch, hearing a voice, seeing the one in spirit, or smelling a fragrance. Too, messages can be received in symbolic ways, unusual appearances of birds and animals (I have written about this in particular in *Corridors*— and again in this book) and other unusual occurrences that you will know in your heart is your loved one. Too, there can be combinations of the above. Some occur immediately after death, within weeks, or go on for years, or until you yourself join your loved one in Heaven. Rochester comes to me in all these varied ways. Rochester was sent by God to help me and share life in 1986. I believe He has allowed Rochester to continue to be with me to teach and console, and that I might write these blessings down to help others who grieve. This blessing is for all. Death is the beginning of the next chapter in the journey.

And so I continue along my *corridor* and pray that what I have written down for you may help you also in your *passage* through it now or when the time arrives. In every vision appearance Rochester has made since March 8th, 2002 he has been in places he enjoys in this cottage. It is the place he lived in body and still loves and here he takes care of me in spirit. Each Sunday here at home we continue to have a private little spiritual service for him using our own original prayers and meditations as well as attending Mass.

Everything that I wrote about in *In Corridors of Eternal Time* in regard to the life we lived and that I continue to live with Rochester in spirit still remains the same. It is as if he *just passed*. It is as I hoped it would be and prayed for with all my heart.

All the dear remembrances shall always remain that I wrote of in *Corridors*. His flowered tin containing his ashes still accompanies me all about the cottage. Wherever I am it is with me. It does not sit on a shelf. It is part of my life. I wear and always shall wear Rochester's red collar upon my left arm. I never remove it. And each evening after completing my day of writing I kneel down next to the bed in our writing room beside his fluffy wildlife quilt he loved to lie in the center of as I wrote, and I say prayers for us and talk to him about many things. Each Friday at 5 PM I still keep our Holy Hour, the Hour within which Rochester entered Heaven. The Hour is always extended for I am lost in prayer and another world with him. To honor him his water dish is always filled on his small maple table and several pieces of Iams are on a plate, a different plate of his each day. Iams was his "treat" not his basic food. Pennies arrive regularly for me from Heaven, and upon my arrival home from anywhere I still go to the bedroom where I know he has run ahead in spirit to wait and greet me on the side of the bed even though he has also been with me on any outing. *Wherever I am—he is!* These are just a few of my never ending Holy Connections with him. There are so many more. Always keep Holy Connections with your loved one. Your loved ones are with you.

And as I complete these "Final Thoughts" I am at last going to listen to Rochester's and my precious music of *The Fairy Ring* by Mike Rowland, music we listened to together before sleep every night since 1989. It was ours. I never listened again after March 8, 2002. It is mystical and ethereal music and I have not yet been able to have those strains wash over me. I wrote that I at last would listen in Corridors. But I could not play it. Now a year later and another book it is time to listen with Rochester.

My grief is as fresh and overwhelming today as it was March 8, 2002 as I prayed it always would be. We are on the brink of two worlds together and this is how it shall be until I too pass. As I wrote in *Corridors*, "*Our grief itself becomes the passage way or opening that connects us forevermore to our loved ones. Therefore it becomes Holy for it is a divine connection or link, never shut off. We live it continually and it is absorbed into souls, into our hearts, and it is a necessary part of living. That is my grieving.*" We are never what we were before.

I have been given "*The Gift of Tears*" that I prayed for and this is a gift divine. My tears flow every day for Rochester. I pray now as I did upon completion of writing *Corridors* that I may always have deep understanding for others in their grief, and try to help them even if from afar, yet never interfere. This book *Solace* and our book *Corridors* are Rochester's and my gifts to you, and we pray they will fill you with love and consolation in your grieving and living. We lived out our love for our entire lives together before March 8, 2002, and in the days since, and will in all the days we have left before we are together in Heaven. And until then I continue always to hear his "*Heartbeat*" as written about in *Corridors*. It is a divine mystery—one that only I am able to hear. How well he takes care of me in spirit.

ROCHESTER LIVES!

I close my eyes
And he arrives—
Close to my face
This treasured place.
And I in awe
Hold his dear paw.

His intervention
From Holy dimension—
He tenderly gives—
Affirms he lives!

For
dear Rochester

Jan
December 7, 2003

Ask,
and it will be given you;
search,
and you will find;
knock,
and the door
will be opened for you.
For everyone
who asks receives,
and everyone
who searches finds,
and for everyone
who knocks,
the door will be opened.

—Luke 11:9-10

A Time For God

Robert A. Kolb Jr.

Janice Kolb along with her husband Bob are the parents of six grown children and have nineteen grandchildren. Their life has revolved around raising a loving family with religious values. In addition to raising their family, Janice developed a letter writing and audio tape ministry that gives encouragement and spiritual support to those who need it all over the United States.

Other inspirational works published by Janice Kolb include: *Journal of Love, Compassion for All Creatures, Higher Ground, The Enchantment of Writing, Beneath the Stars and Trees . . . there is a place, Beside the Still Waters, In Corridors of Eternal Time* and *The Pine Cone Journal.* In a cooperative effort, Janice wrote the book, *Whispered Notes,* with her husband Bob.

Jan Kolb can be contacted via e-mail at: jan@janicegraykolb.com or by mail: P.O. Box 5, East Wakefield, NH 03830

Also by Janice Gray Kolb

Journal of Love
Spiritual Communication with Animals Through Journal Writing

ISBN: 1-57733-046-3, 180 pp., 30 illus., 6x9, $14.95

"Animal whisperer" Janice Kolb shares her heart-lifting journey of discovery as she learns to communicate with her beloved feline companion, Rochester—first by using her intuition and then by writing a journal of their "conversations."

"*Once again the delightful and insightful Jan Kolb has provided all of us who truly love animals with another warm and wonderful book about how we may enter into deeper communication with our beloved pets. Journal of Love is destined to become a classic in the field of transpecies communication.*"
—Brad Steiger and Sherry Hansen Steiger, authors of *Animal Miracles*

Compassion for All Creatures
An Inspirational Guide for Healing the Ostrich Syndrome

ISBN: 1-57733-008-0, 264 pp., 47 illus., 6x9, $12.95

A very personal book of experiences, confessions, and deep thoughts praising all God's creatures through photos, poems and meditations. This book lends an impassioned voice for examining animal rights from Mother Nature's point of view.

"*Jan Kolb has written a very special book that will surprise you in many ways. Learning compassion and reverence by way of the animal kingdom makes perfect sense. She ponders deep questions and important issues which inspire her passion for all of life. Whether or not you join her crusade for the animal kingdom, you will end up thinking, and awareness leads to change.*"
—Terry Lynn Taylor, author of *Messengers of Light*

The Enchantment of Writing
Spiritual Healing and Delight
Through the Written Word
ISBN: 1-57733-073-0, 312 pp., 48 illus., 6x9, $17.95

Janice Kolb shares events from her life that illustrate how to train yourself to write daily. Her encouragement and guidance for writing lead naturally to self-discovery. By preserving your thoughts and experiences, you discover new sources of guidance and insight.

"There are angels cheering for us when we lift up our pens, because they know we want to do it. In this torrential moment we have decided to change the energy of the world. We are going to write down what we think. Right or wrong doesn't matter. We are standing up and saying who we are."
—Natalie Goldberg from *Wild Mind*

Higher Ground
ISBN: 1-57733-071-4, 176 pp., 16 illus., 5.75 x 8.75 hardcover, $14.95

Written freely, and from the heart, *Higher Ground* is a small treasure reserved for those who retreat into the silence and who wish to renew their purpose for living. It chronicles the experiences and thoughts of a woman on retreat in the woods of New Hampshire as she deals with personal fears and family problems and shares her faith.

From the book: *Like Thoreau—I went to the woods to be alone. Always this had been a dream—to stay by myself in our cottage in New Hampshire. Now that time had come. Depression and sadness had been settling in on me for too many months due to personal and family concerns. Each day's existence had become a hardship. My eyes filled with tears at unexpected moments. Though never intended, there were often times when I would sit for a minute to try to get myself together only to find later I had been there immobile for an extended period. Everything mattered intensely yet nothing mattered at all. The smallest chore was too big. Merely trying to begin anything was such an effort that I frequently just gave up completely....*

Beneath the Stars & Trees ... there is a place
A Woodland Retreat

ISBN: 1-57733-106-0, 372 pp., 47 illus., 6x9, $19.95

Beneath the Stars & Trees will help you withdraw from life's distractions and retreat to a place where you can see clearly the multitude of complex factors that make up your life. Share in thoughts and experiences which can open your mind to a world of peace and new possibilities for your life.

"*Join Janice Kolb in a sometimes quirky, always perky, jaunt through lake-in-the-woods living, full of shapeshifting and kitty-cat angels, touching journal entries and frolicking poems, prayer chairs and little gnome tea parties—plus a spiritual encounter with a moose you're sure to remember forever.*" —Michael Burnham, writer/journalist

"*Jan's Woodland Retreat is a place teeming with animal and human life, and yet peaceful and serene. It is a perfect place to meditate, reflect, and renew your spirit. Beneath the stars and trees, there truly is a special place, and Jan's book will transport you there, as often as you wish.*" —Mark Sardella, columnist, *The Wakefield Daily Item*

Beside the Still Waters
Creative Meditations from the Woods

ISBN: 1-57733-122-2, 276 pp., 11 illus., 6x9, $16.95

Beside the Still Waters is a personal view of prayer. Jan suggests a variety of ways to be in constant contact with God. These meditations can transform your prayer life into a source of personal fulfillment, power and strength. Many of these prayers may be familiar; others may be new to you. Being open to all that you read, you may discover new pathways to God and loving consolation. Though written from a Christian perspective, these prayers can be adapted to other traditions.

In Corridors of Eternal Time
A Passage Through Grief: A Journal

ISBN: 1-57733-135-4, 272 pp., 38 illus., 6x9,
paperback, $16.95

As readers of Jan Kolb's previous books know well, the author has had a deeply loving and sacred relationship with her cat, Rochester. He spent his entire life with her as companion, encourager, precious friend, and Angel. With his sudden illness and death, Jan's life was plunged into grief, and she began this book immediately to honor Rochester and help herself and others experiencing grief.

The book is a passage through grief, written in journal form. It is for human grief also, as there is no difference in grief—we all experience it when we lose someone we love. It explores dreams, visions, walking, memory loss, depression, the consolation of cremation, examples of ways humans have grieved for humans, journal writing, ways to help ourselves, and through it all, the passage through days and nights of mourning the physical absence of a beloved companion.

Many do not anticipate that our loved ones' spirits never leave us, even though they have gone to Heaven and await us there. Many do not want to have a continual presence of a loved one who has passed, but many do. For those who are open to this prayerfully, it truly happens, as Jan attests in her experience of the blessing and comfort of Rochester's continuing spiritual presence. This book can bring comfort to those who love deeply and desire this incredible bond.

"In Corridors of Eternal Time is a remarkable book, not just because the author takes us through the various stages of her grief at the death of her pet, but because, after death, her pet cat repeatedly and in continuously new ways let her know that he is still conscious and still cares for her the same as when he was alive. We are left wondering if there are similar ways in which our own deceased pets may also be attempting to communicate with us."

—Christopher Comins

"Many of us are blessed by a deep love for animals. Jan Kolb is blessed by a talent for giving voice to this deep love. Through Jan, we connect to our deepest, loveliest feelings. Her gift is a natural gift, and we are truly the better for it." —Martin Scot Kosins, author, *Maya's First Rose*

A Guide to the Dolphin Divination Cards

One hundred and two oracular readings inspired by the Dolphins: A guide for the use and personal interpretation of the Dolphin Divination Cards
Nancy Clemens
ISBN: 1-57733-017-X, 384 pp., 6x9, paper, $18.00
Each reading is designed with a short preface for quick, easy reference, followed by a longer teaching and explanation. Woven through the readings are friendly counsel, a universal spiritual understanding, and an environmental message.

Dolphin Divination Cards
Nancy Clemens
ISBN: 0-931892-79-1, 108 circular cards, $13.00, boxed
Words of counsel and affirmation on round cards that fit comfortably in your hand

Wish for the World
A Daily Meditation for Personal & Planetary Peace
Keren Clark Posey with Ethan & Dyson Posey
ISBN: 1-57733-132-X, 384 pp., 5.5 x 6.25, paper, $15.95

A wish for each day of the year, covering such areas of concern as the environment, the earth's creatures, war, disease and famine. Each wish is accompanied by an inspirational quotation.

Summer with the Leprechauns
A True Story
Tanis Helliwell
ISBN: 1-57733-001-3, 208 pp., 5.5 x 8.5, paper, $13.00
During a summer spent in Ireland, Tanis Helliwell was befriended by a Leprechaun. She recounts the instructions from the Leprechaun on how humans can interact with elemental beings, as well as revealing the fascinating relationship that developed.

Mary's Message to the World
As sent by Mary, the Mother of Jesus
Annie Kirkwood
ISBN 0-931892-66-X, 204 pp., 5.5 x 8.5, $12.95

"The message and specific prophecies given in Mary's Message to the World *should be read by people of all faiths. I have added Annie Kirkwood's book to my 'top five' recommended book list!"*
—Gordon-Michael Scallion,
author of "Earth Changes Report,"

Mother Mary, in a series of "talks" given between 1987 and 1991, predicts earth changes that will disrupt every individual on the planet. She urges all peoples, regardless of culture or beliefs, to open their minds and hearts to God. Her eloquent discussions on life, energy, truth and prayer—and a special message to families—reveal a most compassionate and universal Mother.

"Must reading for every individual on the planet."
—Pyramid Books and the New Age Collection

Also available on:
CD—7-CD set, ISBN: 1-57733-169-9, $49.95
Audio Tape—Five 90-min. tapes, ISBN: 0-931892-57-0, $49.95

Messages to Our Family
From the Brotherhood, Mother Mary & Jesus
Annie & Byron Kirkwood
ISBN: 0-931892-81-3, 432 pp., 6x9, paper, $24.95

Originally conveyed over five years to Annie and Byron for their weekly family gatherings, these powerful and beautiful teachings convey life-changing spiritual lessons. This profound book contains many helpful tools for releasing abuse, resentment, and anger—and for healing earthly wounds to the soul.

"Families everywhere will be blessed and awakened to their potential by this wonderful book of messages, which is destined to become one of the greatest works of our era." —Jean Foster, The God-Mind Connection

Printed in the United States
30418LVS00003B/157-180

9 781577 331537